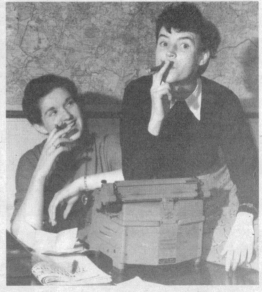

Where Memories Go

Where Memories Go

WHY DEMENTIA CHANGES EVERYTHING

SALLY MAGNUSSON

www.tworoadsbooks.com

First published in Great Britain in 2014 by Two Roads
An imprint of John Murray Press
An Hachette UK company

First published in paperback in 2015

1

Copyright © Sally Magnusson 2014

The right of Sally Magnusson to be identified as the Author of the Work has been asserted by her in accordance with the Copyright, Designs and Patents Act 1988.

All rights reserved. No part of this publication may be reproduced, stored in a retrieval system, or transmitted, in any form or by any means without the prior written permission of the publisher, nor be otherwise circulated in any form of binding or cover other than that in which it is published and without a similar condition being imposed on the subsequent purchaser.

A CIP catalogue record for this title is available from the British Library

ISBN 978 1 444 75181 9
Ebook ISBN 978 1 444 75180 2

Printed and bound by CPI Group (UK) Ltd, Croydon, CR0 4YY

Hodder & Stoughton policy is to use papers that are natural, renewable and recyclable products and made from wood grown in sustainable forests. The logging and manufacturing processes are expected to conform to the environmental regulations of the country of origin.

Hodder & Stoughton Ltd
338 Euston Road
London NW1 3BH

www.hodder.co.uk

For Anna Lisa, Calum, Ellie, Jamie, Louis,
Magnus, Robbie, Rossie and Siggy.
To replenish your own memories.

To a steigh brae, a stubborn back
Addressin' daily;
An' up the rude, unbieldy track
O' life, gang gaily.

Robert Louis Stevenson,
'The Counterblast', 1886

Contents

Preface

This is a book about the life of my mother, the writer and raconteur Mamie Baird Magnusson, and the way dementia changed it for her and for everyone who loved her.

It is also a book about dementia itself, and how society regards the most fragile of its citizens, and how urgently this needs to change.

Mamie was never famous in the way her husband Magnus became, when he found himself in the living rooms of the land for twenty-five years as the stern interrogator on the BBC quiz game *Mastermind*. She came not from saga-steeped Reykjavík and a douce Edinburgh villa, as he did, but from the poor tenements of a small industrial town on the edge of Glasgow, where she developed the keen eye and light, humorous writing style that would make her what the great *Daily Express* editor Arthur Christiansen was to describe as 'a very fine journalist indeed'.

She loved words and taught her children to cherish them, too. Then, little by little, she lost them. What follows are my words for my mother, words to recover a life forgotten.

I have agonised over publishing so personal a story. But then I meet someone else's family, and someone else's, and another, and another, each one struggling to balance a great love with the overwhelming demands of looking after a person with dementia, at home or elsewhere. And I read yet another account of gross institutional neglect in a world that has woken up too slowly to the implications of longevity and the brain diseases to which it is rendering more and more of us vulnerable. And I think then that our story matters. Not because it is ours, but because it could be anybody's.

'All this ought to be written down,' says Chekhov's Irina in *The Three Sisters*. We can't all be professors, doctors or policy-makers, but there are other ways of advancing the understanding of dementia. Writing and talking about our experiences is the best way to undermine the stigma surrounding this condition and enable it to be seen as perhaps the greatest social, medical, economic, scientific, philosophical and ethical challenge of our times.

I began documenting the progression of my mother's illness in early 2009, although I had kept jottings before that. For her past life I was able to mine a rich seam of recordings from nearly twenty years earlier. I made these not because I sensed that my mother might one day lose those memories, but rather because I knew that in the natural scheme of things I would one day lose her. It was my own memory I mistrusted, always a flimsier instrument than hers and more like that of my father, who, when I approached him with the microphone to solicit his own reminiscences, backed away hastily, protesting that he could remember nothing about anything. My mother, typically, flew for the kettle at once and was rattling off stories while I was still wrestling with the cassette record button. These anecdotes form the basis of the account of her life here.

The writing began as an attempt to keep hold of my mother as her personality changed shape. I'm a reporter. I wanted a record of the fun, the wit, the banter, the normal, the joyously happy times as well as the not so good. I found myself, quite naturally, talking to her as I wrote.

Later, as the enormity of the social phenomenon in which we were caught up began to dawn – one I discovered we were sharing with more than a third of the UK population who have a close friend or relative with dementia – I wrote with the thought that other invisible lives might be nudged into the light through the telling of this one story and the questions it made me ask.

To be clear, it was never my intention to attempt a comprehensive critique of social policy, which varies too widely across the UK anyway and is being modified all the time, nor to take political sides. But living closely with dementia for more than a decade has changed me, just as in a different way it changed my mother. It has made me think deeply about what it means to be, first, a human being and, second, a community, and the kinds of societal change we need to strive for if we are genuinely to call ourselves civilised. In that sense I found the memoir evolving into a *credo*.

It is as faithful an account as I could make it. The names of those who appear inadvertently, without having had the chance to be consulted, have been altered. Some of the investigation of the broader issues was done at a later point than it appears in the narrative (indeed a few of the inquiry reports and interviews post-date my mother's death in April 2012), but the questions that stimulated the journalism occurred as described.

I may be kidding myself to think that my mother herself, inveterate storyteller as she was, would have approved of this venture, but I do have one piece of evidence. One evening she noticed me scribbling on a piece of paper and asked what I was writing.

'I'm noting down what you just said.'

She laughed. 'Oh, was it interesting?'

'Very. Actually, I'm thinking of writing a book about you. How would you feel about that?'

'I'd be honoured,' she beamed.

'Listen, Mum. If I were to write about our conversations,' I said carefully, conscious all at once of framing a question that mattered, 'and about, you know, the things you find hard and the things we all do to help you, would it feel invasive?'

I wish now that she had asked me what I meant by 'invasive', but instead she batted straight back with a smile.

'No, I'd be absolutely thrilled.'

'You'd trust me?'

'Of course. Yes.'

We carried on nibbling our chocolate biscuits and sipping our tea, with a feeling on my part of having settled something. Far though this exchange was in reality from any meaningful concept of consent, I felt as if I had received a kind of blessing to carry on reporting the biggest story of my life.

But I have to acknowledge a cost here. In writing so personally I am sharing a mother – and a father – who belong equally to my sisters and brother. Every relationship with a parent in any family is different and uniquely nuanced: my siblings, Margaret, Anna (alias Topsy) and Jon Magnusson, have been staggeringly generous in allowing me to write in a way that mainly reflects mine. Our mother's twin sister, Anna Baird, has been equally gracious in permitting me to share her own part in the story, in the hope that it might help others.

But that doesn't mean it is anything other than painful for any of them. I am offering up to the gaze and comment of strangers an experience exquisitely precious to us all. Saying thank you does not begin to express what I owe them.

1

Let me count the ways

Elizabeth Barrett Browning, Sonnet 43

'Things I Love About You', I write, thinking about you in the sturdy old family house three miles along the road where I have just tucked you into bed. It is dark outside. A half-hearted line of snow has settled along the bottom of the window.

On the wall in front of my desk it is summertime. There is a photo of you in your most vibrantly pink jacket and lipstick, arm flung around my father's shoulder with the eye-dancing smile you have not lost. It was taken on your fiftieth wedding anniversary. The rest of us are clustered around you both in the June sunshine – four children, nine grandchildren, your twin sister Anna – all grinning madly, as well we might. We were hardly able to believe our luck that day that Magnus was alive at all.

I look across at the picture and think about you now, four and a half years on from that golden afternoon, not always sure who this 'Magnus' refers to but still indisput-ably the girl with the merry smile he fell for across a clattering newspaper office all those decades ago. I think, too, of the fun you and I had earlier this evening when I bundled you into the car on a whim and off on a wintry adventure; of your continuing capacity for wonder, your infectious joy in the moment.

And I start to count the ways I love you.

Memories go, as you know better than anyone, and there are some I badly want to hold fast. In the jargon in which, thanks to you, I have lately become proficient, I have to find ways of ensuring that the axons in my brain grow fresh synapses and new proteins are produced in the cytoplasm of a neuron so that certain scenes involving you will be embedded in my long-term memory, where with any luck they will stay for a while.

What I mean is that I want to remember you. I want to remember everything about you.

I tap late into the night, eager to round up your slippery self before it slides into yet another shape. It's as if I have to catch you now, as if by the time I see you again tomorrow it may all have changed, as indeed there is every chance it will. If I can only pin you by the bullet point, secure you with headings, trap you in words, corral you within a list, then perhaps I can hold you beside me here for ever, the mother who clapped her hands to see the snow at night, who has lost so much of her self but not yet, not yet, the thrill of being alive.

So I write my list. And somehow it happens that I find myself talking to you.

Things I love about you

Your delight in the mad whirl of snow. Remember, Mum, the way it skipped off the windscreen on our way home this evening? I suppose you'll have forgotten by now, but I remember. The snow rushing towards us in the beam of the headlights, making it feel more of a blizzard than it really was. You were pink-faced with exhilaration. 'What a great journey,' you kept saying.

Your unquenchable enthusiasm for sliding down banisters.

'That's how I'd like to go down these stairs,' you murmured the other day, eyeing the one outside your bedroom with alarming intent.

'You're eighty-three, Mum,' I said. 'You broke your hip four weeks ago.'

You looked at it longingly all the same. I like to imagine that same gleam in your eye just before you vaulted a dustbin on Buchanan Street on the way to your first interview with the *Sunday Post*.

'For goodness sake, Mamie,' your mother had sighed when you landed, 'try and act like a lady.'

Those husky harmonies layering every song you have ever sung. And the way, when everything else is slipping away, every skill, every talent, you still want to sing. Last Sunday we stood swaying with our arms around each other in the middle of my kitchen, crooning an old Ink Spots number. Your fifteen-year-old grandson Magnus muttered to his friend Jason: 'You may have noticed we have a mad family.' Jason doesn't know the half of it. But song brings you alive. Your ear for harmony is as keen as ever.

The way you peer into the mirror, push your fingers through your hair and sculpt it forward into a wave. Strong hair, white with a few fugitive threads of black; hair that has always scorned a curler. I've been watching you do this all my life.

Your eyes. Brown, and still shining more often than I dared hope when I first realised the journey we were on. The old glee sparkles on. You respond to banter and teasing with such a whoosh of merriment that it feels as if you're back.

Your wit. It keeps surprising us. Even in your foggiest moments it flashes through just often enough to remind us how sharp you were, how dry, how you used to make audiences cry with laughter.

'It's as well I've got two ears,' you murmured a few nights ago during our routine bedtime combat with your polo-neck. 'Perhaps you could leave me the other one.'

The way you stroke my hair when I'm kneeling to take your socks off. You do it almost apologetically, as if to say, 'You shouldn't be doing this.' But you've no idea how to do it yourself. Not the faintest idea how to start. The tenderness more than makes up for your having lately introduced me to my sister with the words, 'Now, do you two know each other?'

Things I miss about you

The way you would offer stories of your life to the most casual stranger on a bus, train or aeroplane and extract theirs in an instant.

The stories themselves. Your childhood. Your war. Those adventures on the newspaper beat you never tired of recounting. Like the time you got your fur glove stuck in the doorbell of the house near Balmoral being prepared for Princess Elizabeth and Prince Philip's honeymoon: a Post Office engineer was summoned to mend the interminably clanging bell while you talked the housekeeper into a world-exclusive tour of the house. The first trip to Iceland with your new husband, when you were served raw shark and sank under the weight of cream in the pastries. Your incompetent attempts to bake a cake or sew on a button. Your spontaneous serenading of the Queen at a posh banquet you graced with my father, which led to the whole staid Edinburgh table joining in to bellow 'Will ye no come back again?' to an astonished monarch.

So many stories. You still try to tell them. But now they wander far and wide in search of a lost punchline.

The sight of you striding along the road with those long legs, exulting in the wind on your face.

Your knack of arriving unannounced exactly when I need you.

'I thought you sounded a bit desperate on the phone last night, so here I am,' you once explained blithely after materialising unexpectedly on my doorstep like Mary Poppins, though I lived hundreds of miles away in the south-east of England at the time. You promptly rounded up four children under six and sent me to bed.

You were thrilled, of course, when a fifth pregnancy enticed me back to Scotland. For years you had been plying me with For Sale notices from the property pages of the *Glasgow Herald*. I would find them tucked into letters with a scribbled note: 'Just in case.' In the end one torn cutting advertising a house in the next village popped through the post and that was that. I think I had an inkling, even then, that by returning to live within a five-minute drive of my childhood home I was putting down a marker for a distant future when our roles might be reversed. But at the time I was the one who needed you, the all-singing, wisecracking, up-for-anything grandma on the other side of the hill.

The words I miss most: 'You look tired. Let me do that.'

Things I observe with dread

Empty eyes.

Grim mouth.

Vacant expression.

Stony face. In a memoir of his novelist wife, Iris Murdoch, John Bayley calls this the 'lion face', a look of leonine impassivity. It makes me think of the stone lion that a previous owner with a taste for the grandiose left on your garden patio. He lies there, custodian of the pansy pots, eyes dead. Truth to tell, he gives me the shivers – and so do you when you look like that.

Aggressive sniping at the twin sister whose mind has remained lively while yours has not. This is the worst thing, the very worst thing, of all.

*

If dementia care were a country, it would be the world's eighteenth largest economy: somewhere between Turkey and Indonesia, they reckon. As a company measured by annual revenue, it would be the world's largest. Dementia is one of the biggest healthcare challenges on the planet.

There are thought to be 44 million people with it across the world – the ones we know about anyway – with an extra 7.7 million cases predicted every year. There are up to 850,000 in the UK and around 5 million in the US. Nor is it just a disease of the West. More than half of those with dementia are in developing countries, a number expected to rise to 71% by 2050, with the fastest growth projected in China, India, South Asia and the Western Pacific. Although there are hopes – and even a little evidence – that healthier, more active ageing might delay the condition enough to mitigate the most apocalyptic predictions, the numbers are likely to remain alarming. The World Health Organisation estimates one new case every four seconds and thinks the global figure is likely to double every twenty years, reaching 135 million by 2050.

So this is a disease that respects neither geography, ethnicity, class nor gender. You, my darling mother, are unique in all sorts of ways, but not in succumbing to this disease. Not by a long way.

The cost of care is astronomical. Looking after people with the various symptoms of dementia, whether caused by Alzheimer's or one of the other forms, is already costing 1% of global GDP – that's around £400 billion a year. In the UK the figure is over £23 billion, more than the cost of care for stroke, heart disease and cancer combined. All those bills are poised to rise to dizzying levels in years to come.

Most of us will be touched by dementia in one way or another, either as relatives, friends or the one in three over the age of sixty-five who will eventually die with it ourselves. Those not immediately affected will be contributing to the health and social care bills, so nobody escapes. More than any other modern ailment we really are all in this together.

Dementia is not a form of natural ageing. Having watched a pair of twins approach old age together, I can see this as well as anyone. As you, my mother, succumb to a vicious brain affliction that hijacks memory, personality and functional capacity, I observe your non-identical twin slowing down gradually while retaining a sure ability to name half the British cabinet, beat the family at crosswords and spot a bank statement error from five paces. Dementia might be increasingly common, but it is not 'normal'.

On the other hand, dementia is certainly age-related. The longer we live, the higher our chance of contracting it, which is why the ageing of the world's population (with 22% predicted to be over sixty by 2050) is leading to such a rise in numbers.

Some people develop symptoms as early as their thirties or forties, but the vast majority of people with dementia are old. And being old, some are treated as if they are barely human, *de facto* as expendable as the children of the nineteenth-century poor. At least Oliver Twist had the advantage of looking cute under the grime. Our society likes cute. We coo over pandas and agonise over seals but are too busy running away from our own mortality to confront the fate of the elderly, who don't by and large have the advantage of being very cute at all.

Early one morning I woke to a radio interview with the National Health Service ombudsman for England, Ann Abraham, on Radio 4. *Today*'s normally dispassionate inquisitor John Humphrys was struggling to keep his voice under control as he questioned her about a report showing that hospitals in England were processing elderly people without care, dignity or respect. He suggested that the case-studies of patients routinely denied enough food or water, or left in beds reeking of faeces, must surely beggar belief.

'Sadly,' Abraham replied drily, 'it doesn't beggar belief.'

That autumn the Care Quality Commission in England found that more than half the hospitals it visited unannounced were failing to offer basic care to elderly patients. Lack of money was not the main problem, the inspectors said, but lack of imagination and empathy.

The following year the same regulator disclosed that almost half of all care homes and treatment centres were failing to protect elderly and disabled people. The report described staff refusing to take residents to the toilet, shouting at them and failing to respond to call bells. It made chilling reading. I imagined you as the one being yelled at, you who would hardly know how to locate a call bell, never mind ring it.

Not that we should forget the good practice, the people

who dedicate lives of unheralded service to caring properly, the hospitals trying to do better and the majority of care homes where staff *can* be bothered to take residents to the toilet. But well into the second decade of the twenty-first century there is an under-the-radar culture of poor practice in a system never designed for the longevity we have created for ourselves and painfully slow to adapt to the explosion in dementia numbers.

Dearest mother, as I watch your own sparky intellect flounder and your very identity dissolve before my eyes, I am beginning to conclude that dementia holds a dagger to the heart of Western morality. It confronts us with profound philosophical as well as scientific questions about what it means to be human. It challenges our social complacency and our financial priorities. It compels us to ask whether we have any right to call ourselves a civilised society at all.

*

Things I want never to forget about you even, as Shakespeare would say, to the edge of doom (or at least until the day I have trouble remembering my own children's names, too)

Your voice. Low and slightly throaty. Often on the edge of laughter. Accent and idioms emphatically west of Scotland, but without the glottal stop.

In a recording I made of your memories back in 1990 there's a part where you say, 'We were poor but we learned to talk properly. My father came from Ayrshire stock and he taught us some good Scots words. He always said, "Use them. It's fine to call your stomach a *wain*. But if you're speaking English, don't say *walkin'* when it should be *walking*."'

You never do.

I can still read the transcripts of those reminiscences to hear you talking the way you used to: fluent and funny, every narrative peppered with direct speech, syntax irreproachable, grammar perfect. It's hard to think of a happier complement to a husband who believed splitting an infinitive to be a capital offence.

Your laugh. The way you hurl your head back and show off a row of fine teeth, all your own and still more or less even, although one of the front two has edged slightly over its partner. You used to be more proud of those teeth, brushed with soot during the war and kept ever after when all around were losing theirs, than just about anything else – with the possible exception of hailing from the Royal Burgh of Rutherglen and having a granny from the Isle of Mull whose cow once swam all the way home.

Your smile. Dazzling, people say, which is a bit of a cliché, but yours does have an almost tangible radiance. It reminds my sister Topsy of an image from Gerard Manley Hopkins: 'It will flame out, like shining from shook foil.' She calls it your nuclear smile.

If I forget everything else, let me not forget this.

2

Of isles the fairest

Dugald MacPhail, *An t'Eilean Muileach* ('The Isle of Mull')

Tobermory has a flamboyant air in the sunshine. Colourful buildings elbow each other jauntily along the main street. The bay, sheltered by a flank of Calve Island, shimmers placidly below us. It is the summer of 1999 and you and I are thinking about cows.

The story of the heroic cow that saved the ancestral croft was passed from your grandmother, the doughty Annie McKechnie, to your father, and from him to you and you to me. I don't know which of us delighted in it more.

Annie McKechnie had grown up on the Isle of Mull. On his Scottish tour in 1773 a wet, out-of-humour Dr Johnson dismissed Mull as 'this gloom of desolation', although on a sunnier day it must even then have laid claim to being the loveliest of the Hebridean islands. However, he was on surer ground when he grumbled about the ubiquitous penury. When Annie was born there in 1850, during the cataclysmic social upheaval of the later Highland Clearances, penury was still what distinguished the island.

Her father James had a rented croft in Ardmore, a few miles north of Tobermory, where he eked a chancy living from cattle and crops. After he died, so the story goes, the family struggled on with little except one cow to provide milk and butter and, if they were lucky, a youngster that could be sold at market. The cow was the crofter's lifeline, but that also made it vulnerable. Landowners looking for ways to force indigent tenants off the land to make way for sheep found that confiscating the cow often did the trick.

'The day came when it was our family's turn to lose their cow,' you had told me years earlier, a light in your eye as you rehearsed the old story in the kitchen before my whirring cassette recorder, as my baby daughter dozed beside us in her carry-cot.

'It was taken from them, along with other cows from neighbouring crofts, and put on an island off Tobermory known as Calve Island, which I thought for ages had got its name from this custom but am told is a much earlier Norse word. Anyway, lo and behold, to their amazement, that cow turned up again at the croft. Somehow it had managed to swim right across the Sound of Mull again and walk back to the family croft. It was thought to be a tremendous thing, that a cow should help the family resist eviction by swimming home.'

I have always liked the way this story opened a tiny window on our family history in the Hebrides. It has the ring of myth about it for sure, even your own 'lo and behold' lending it the insubstantiality of an old yarn, but you thought it might be true. Thousands of people were forcibly removed from their living during the Highland Clearances, as the huge estates across the highlands and islands of Scotland turned to sheep farming and new forms of land management. The Clearances on Mull were at their height in the 1850s and 1860s. The family legend seemed to fit.

From the moment I heard the story I wanted to follow it up.

In the months before our trip to Mull I chased genealogical leads, pursued archivists, fired off obscure questions to weary librarians and pored over musty records. I soon had names and places and a historical context in which to set the misty heritage Annie had bequeathed us. I knew exactly why she had grown up on a remote island but spent the rest of her life in a town in Scotland's industrial belt. I understood at last something of the legacy that left your family poor but proud, and your father blazing with conviction that economic systems needed to be organised in a more egalitarian way. I couldn't wait to tell you what I had found.

But something was wrong. You ought to have been thrilled, but you weren't engaging with my research. Given how often you had regaled me with the exploits of the homesick cow, I was puzzled and even a little hurt to find you so detached. I found myself grappling with a sensation I couldn't identify, an obscure sense that something about you was not as it should be.

Everyone notices the onset of dementia in a loved one differently: the discovery of house keys in the oven, perhaps, the repeated disappearance of spectacles, a meeting missed, an easy word lost. Common in ageing, normal in all sorts of stressed lives, it is only in hindsight that these incidents acquire a more sinister meaning. I don't recall any house key incidents, and you had been faithfully losing your glasses since the day you acquired your first pair in your early fifties, so nothing new there. What I was starting to notice was a mislaying not of spectacles but of curiosity. Here was a subtle withdrawing of interest and insecurity with detail I had not registered before.

'Mmm,' you said of the 1851 census return that I placed before you.

'Look,' I persevered, 'I've found your great-grandparents.'

There was Annie McEachern, her surname not yet anglicised to McKechnie, appearing as a five-month-old baby in a croft in Ardmore with her father James, mother Christina, three-year-old sister Mary and uncle Allan, James's older brother. I was dizzy with excitement.

'That's interesting,' you said politely, sounding as if it wasn't really.

This was baffling.

However I did persuade you to join me on an excursion to see the place for ourselves. You said, 'Would we not be better with a trip to Tenerife?' and I said, 'That's not the point, Mum, we're not going for the sunbathing – surely you'd like to see where our people lived and worked?' and you said, 'Oh, all right.' So we set out by car from Glasgow on a sun-drenched August day, taking nine-year-old Anna Lisa along too. I liked the romance of three generations of women going in search of ancestors who were famous for nothing and built nothing that was not either knocked down or left to decay among the sheep bones. You, so strangely unenthused by the details of the story, responded at once to the adventure. You sang us along Loch Lomond and up the winding road to Oban, vivacious as ever.

On the ferry, between mouthfuls of Caledonian MacBrayne lasagne, you taught us Dugald MacPhail's paean to the island, translated from the Gaelic:

> The Isle of Mull is of the isles the fairest,
> Of ocean's gems 'tis the first and rarest;
> Green grassy island of sparkling fountains,
> Of waving woods and high tow'ring mountains.

We sang the melody, you harmonised. This was more like it. You, sparky and engaged and raring for whatever lay ahead.

Nothing, surely, was amiss at all.

*

So here we are, the three of us, peering earnestly across Tobermory's unfurrowed bay to the knobbly contours of Calve Island, as if we half expect to spot a distant cow

lumbering down those grassy slopes into the sea and striking off for home.

My great discovery has been that our kinsfolk really did
own such a beast. Poring through the records I had turned
up an application for poor relief in February 1858 by Allan
McEachern, Annie's unmarried uncle and by then head of
his late brother's family. 'Allan McEachern Ardmore refused
on the ground that he is able bodied and has a cow,' the
clerk had recorded neatly.

Suppose this were indeed *the* cow, we are musing now.
How did she carry it off? How well can these animals swim?
Do they have a homing instinct? Is it credible that she could
have been sequestrated by the landowner and then returned
on her own to the croft? She would either have had to cross
the narrow tidal channel that separates the southern half of
Calve Island from Mull itself and then plod for miles up the
headland to Ardmore – would a cow walk that far? – or else
tackle the open sea of the Sound of Mull further up in what
I can't help feeling would be an improbable feat of bovine
athleticism.

We agree that we are all lamentably ill-informed about
cows and must look into it.

Next day we drive around the north of Mull, through
valleys strewn with the derelict remains of crofters'
cottages. Historians never tire of arguing about the
reasons for the Clearances and the depopulation of the
highlands, but there is nothing academic about these
bleak, fern-infested ruins. Knowing that some of them

belonged to our own kin makes more acute the sense of loss and stunted opportunity that lingers in the bereft glens. You, though, are more taken with the higgledy-piggledy arrangement of the houses, tucked with little apparent order into the lee of the hill.

'My mother always said the highlanders were a bit *hithery*,' you murmur, using a Scots word for untidy, before offering for good measure the words of a song that suddenly pops into your head:

> *Where else would ye*
> *Expect to see*
> *The end of a bed where a gate should be?*

We are making our way to Ardmore, at the most northerly point of the island, where your great-grandparents James McEachern from Baliacradh and Christina McLean from Sorne set up home together in the late 1840s and farmed cattle on ten acres of rented land until James's early death.

Ahead of us we catch glimpses of a blue slash of sea. The great mound of the Ardnamurchan peninsula is nosing across the far side and away in the distance crouches the violet shadow of what might be the Isle of Rum. It's a gorgeous afternoon. A golden light is playing across the hills and, as we climb out of the car where the road gives out, I catch the whistle of a curlew above us. No wonder your grandmother used to cry for this childhood island of hers. You too, for all your lack of interest in the genealogical detail,

are moved by the thought of wandering among the ruins of
the place she wept for as an old lady in Rutherglen when she
was singing you the songs of the isles in Gaelic.

It is baking hot and we have been driving and walking
around the island for hours already. Once out of the car you
are keen to get started again, although I dare say this may
be a ploy to get it over with quicker: you were always astonishingly good at suppressing your own desires and going
along with things. The problem is that for years the ruined
remains of the Ardmore settlement have been swallowed by
forest. Local people say they can be found among the trees,
as long as you know where to look. In proposing this excursion I have rather played down the fact that I don't have a
clue where to look.

I watch in awe as you stride off in the heat down the
Forestry Commission track between dark, featureless lines
of Sitka spruce. Coming up for seventy-four in October,
you are in white trousers and a shocking pink T-shirt under
which I happen to know you are wearing neither bra nor
knickers. You took them off earlier on the white sands of
Calgary Bay after an impromptu swim in your underwear.
To Anna Lisa's whooping admiration, you plunged into the
whip-cold Atlantic breakers faster than she did, carrying it
off with the same daredevil insouciance that had launched
you down your grandchildren's waterslide in the garden a
couple of weeks before.

You are brimming with the outdoor vitality with which
you have always glowed in our memories. 'I see her digging

potatoes in the vegetable patch,' Topsy says, 'wearing tiny pale blue shorts and a bandana round her head, pushing her hair back from her forehead.'

We all remember you like that as children. We remember you leaning on your spade and letting fly in your best Texas twang the Bing Crosby song that starts:

> Oh, give me land, lots of land under starry skies above,
> Don't fence me in.

As you march into the Ardmore forest to look for your ancestors this August afternoon, how ridiculous to think you could ever be fenced in; how unimaginable the idea that deep in the part of your brain they call the entorhinal cortex the posts had already been firmly hammered in.

As it turns out, our search for the place where Annie McEachern spent her childhood is fruitless.

'What are you expecting to find down there?' you call, as I lower myself gingerly into yet another clump of waist-high ferns, looking for signs of former habitation. 'Photos on the mantelpiece?'

We must be in the wrong place. I will have to come back another time if I am to find the remains of the township from which the McEacherns were eventually evicted. But there is one more place I am anxious to see before we stop. I know you would prefer a bath and a cup of tea but you acquiesce with a tolerant sigh.

The three of us drive back to town and then up the same sharp hill that thirteen-year-old Annie McEachern walked down on her way to the pier and a new life in Glasgow. As we go, I explain that the McEacherns had been among the last of the Ardmore tenants to be evicted in 1863: when sheep inherited the estate, Annie's mother Christina and her uncle Allan, by then both registered paupers, moved with the children into one of the slums at the top of Tobermory's Back Brae, an area already teeming with the destitute from other cleared townships across the island. There the adults were put to outside labour, while young Annie and her two sisters joined the queue for the daily steamer to the Clydeside ports in search of work.

'It's no wonder my father said so little about his family,' you say sadly, looking around. '*Pauper* is a stark word. Both he and my mother were very proud. Poverty was something they were ashamed of.'

Again, though, there is nothing to be seen. All that remains of Annie's last home up the Back Brae is the gully where the blackhouses used to stand.

Christina was still living there when an official toiled up the hill in March 1881 to take the census. He marked her down as 'outdoor worker'. She died in January 1897 at the age of eighty-three of what her death certificate describes as 'acute bronchitis and senile decay'.

'Acute bronchitis and senile decay,' you chuckle. 'That's me.'

You are joking, of course. Or at least I think you are. Your chest might be prone to infections, but nothing could be harder to imagine on this balmy day on Mull than senility. You with your girlish vigour and the stamina of an ox.

Senile decay?

*

But something happened on Mull, something that makes me look back on that brief excursion as both a glorious high-point of normality – you still the daring, sharp-witted, loquacious companion of old – and also the shadowy beginning of something new. Most of our time on the island was idyllic, full of walks and songs, steaming bags of chips, sunny moods and easy conversation. But there was one incident that I now place beside the peculiar absence of curiosity as marking the beginning of the journey we have been on ever since.

I was in bed in the room I was sharing with Anna Lisa in the guest-house, reading, when there was a knock at the door.

You were standing there wearing nothing but a short pyjama jacket and, thank goodness, a pair of knickers. You were laughing. You explained that you had got out of bed in your room up the stairs to go to the toilet along the corridor. Your bedroom door had slammed shut behind you, with the key inside. I snorted with laughter, too, and hustled you inside. Anna Lisa woke up and grinned sleepily at another of Grandma's famous scrapes, destined no doubt for the family annals along with falling out of a punt into the River Cherwell, tumbling down a Glasgow manhole and half drowning during the vigorous self-cleaning cycle of an automatic French toilet. Yet something felt odd about this latest escapade. Why were you not wearing your pyjama trousers in a strange house where you might meet the owners or another guest on your way?

You joined us in our room for the rest of the night and I thought little of it at the time beyond a twinge of . . . well, what? Alarm is too strong. Unease maybe. Disquiet. The feeling tumbles away from me when I try to pin it down. There was just something about the blank look you gave me when I interrogated you about the absence of half your pyjamas that is now horribly familiar.

Of course, as beginnings go this one is illusory. I probably only remember it because I was keeping a diary at the time with the thought of writing the story of our Mull forebears one day. There must have been dozens of other telltale signs before, if I had only registered them. Even at this distance I find myself scanning back through the years preceding the trip to see if I can somehow, as it were, catch you out.

You stopped writing. When did that happen? The skill and the will just seemed to ebb away. It's not that you started to write badly, as others have when the disease has begun to interfere with the brain connections responsible for language; you just let it lapse. Textual analysis of Iris Murdoch's novels has revealed that her last one, *Jackson's Dilemma*, which she finished not long before being diagnosed with Alzheimer's, has a simplified syntax and impoverished vocabulary. A similar study suggests that the famously muddled and meandering plots of crime writer Agatha Christie's later novels also show signs of encroaching dementia. But in your case there was nothing at all to analyse latterly, if anyone had cared to try.

Yet all my life you had been dashing off something on the typewriter: freelance articles, ruminative columns, ideas for speeches, whole chapters of books you were content to see published under my father's name, a couple of your own, the church magazine, screeds of letters to your far-flung brood. When one of your children died at the age of eleven, it was words that saved you; some days you barely put your pen down on the book you were working at, compulsively writing on and on to deaden the pain. Words were the air you breathed. Words, from the age of seventeen, were what you did.

I recently uncovered three sheets of scribbled notes that look like the plan for an introduction to a memoir about your life as a journalist. It begins: 'Hadn't noticed how much fun I had, how many millions of words I wrote about thousands of different subjects. It's put me in the notion to write a book.'

You had jotted down all the areas you might cover, page

after page of them, including mysterious ones like 'night life of a policeman (love lorn), the strange sights seen by a chiropodist (slices of bacon), telephone girls (Button B)'. Such a lot you were going to write about, in the light, anecdotal style you had made your own, but it never happened. From time to time you would lament your difficulty in 'getting round to things'. You blamed your inactivity on being lazy and out of practice. I can't think why none of us thought it remarkable that your productivity had dried up so completely.

What probably made it less obvious was that you retained your sparkling interest in words themselves – in their meaning, their sound, their spelling, punning potential, beauty or plainness – an interest that even now continues to flash. Perhaps that is what fooled us all into thinking for a long time that you would still be able to put those words together on paper if only you felt like it. Perhaps you thought so too.

So there are many possible beginnings to your story. My siblings have their own. Margaret remembers an early stab of unease at the cinema, when the movie *Gladiator* turned out to be more violent than she had expected and you failed to register the mood, remaining slightly too cheerful throughout.

Jon recalls the day two huge gangsta types came and sat opposite you both on the London tube and how, entranced, you offered them a beaming recitation of a line from an old movie: 'Well, button my boots and freeze my face – dat man don't b'long no human race', delivered in an impeccable southern drawl. Showing off to strangers was nothing unusual, but your failure to grasp the social nuance here (not to mention the gaping social pitfall) does make my brother wonder. ('Fortunately the men just looked faintly bemused,' he says, 'otherwise they might possibly have killed me.')

Our father, too, must have quietly carried his own moment of sudden apprehension. I remember his slight irritation one night after you dropped your notes in the middle of a speech and he had to scrabble around helping to pick them up. Was it something like that for him?

The real beginning will forever remain a mystery, your mystery, a secret locked within some long-expired neuron in your brain. In its absence I must chisel something from my own perceptions, a marker, no more, but one from which I can start shaping the experience that was to change your life, and mine. And here I return to the first fleeting sense of disquiet on the night you locked yourself out of a hotel bedroom all those years ago. This is my beginning. I place it here, on a small Scottish island among the ances-tors who gave you life and, for all anyone knows, an increased genetic risk of a lingering kind of death.

*

It is to be a long time before I make it back to Mull. By then the area around Ardmore Point will have been cleared of trees, allowing access to the buried township at last. Tying up the loose ends of our family legend, I will learn then that highlanders have been swimming their cattle to island grazings for centuries, that drovers used to walk their beasts for days on end, and that the channel between Calve Island and Mull is so narrow at one point that our plucky cow, though perfectly capable of the swim, could practically have skipped across it at low tide.

I will fantasise then about dashing home to tell you. I will imagine you throwing back your head to say with a laugh, 'Not so daft after all, my old granny.'

But by then, years on from our Hebridean adventure in the last summer of the old millennium, there will be no point in even mentioning it. By that time you will not have the slightest clue what I am on about.

3

Where memories go

Neurobiologist Frank Gunn-Moore

St Andrews University. In the light of the laboratory microscope the nerve cells and the threads running between them look like a tangle of Christmas lights. Each cell glows like a golden crystal; each trails a number of airy strands that connect to other globules of gold. These are healthy, newly formed neurons, grown in a Petri dish and lacking only the electric charge delivered by a human heart-beat to make them hum with life and decay.

Each of us has 100 billion of these neurons in our brain, and each of them can have up to 100,000 thread-like connections. We need only multiply 100 billion by 100,000, remembering how many untold millions of chemical processes are also occurring inside just one of those cells, to get an inkling of why the brain is far and away the most complex entity we know of in the universe.

I gave up science at school much too early, as I point out weakly to Dr Frank Gunn-Moore, the university's professor of molecular neurobiology, who spends his life figuring out what is going on inside neurons and is trying to explain it to me. If I am to understand what had begun happening to you the summer we went to Mull I really must get to grips with these neurons. Because here, right here where these golden shapes are on the point of talking to one another, is where memory resides.

In a living brain each of these neurons would be carrying an electrical signal to other neurons, and on these signals depend all our memories, thoughts and feelings. The point where the signals make contact is known as the 'synapse', from the Greek *sunapsis*, a joining together. When a charge reaches a synapse, it triggers the release of tiny bursts of chemicals called neurotransmitters, which travel across the synapse carrying the signals to other cells. It is these synapses that are affected in Alzheimer's.

Describing what goes on in the brain is almost impossible without metaphors, something those who named its parts also recognised. The wrinkly grey outer layer is known as the cerebral 'cortex' from the Latin word for bark, because it looks like a wet tree-trunk. Some of the strands branching out from the neurons are called 'dendrites', from the Greek *dendron* for tree: the dendrites bring information to the cell, while their opposite number, 'axons', take it away.

Alzheimer's disease uproots the forest. It disrupts both the way electrical charges travel within cells and the activity of the neurotransmitters. That makes it a double whammy, causing havoc not only to the nerve cells themselves, which gradually die, but also to their connections to one another.

After a while it looks under the microscope as if an earthquake has ruptured a complex road system or someone has taken a hammer and pliers to my pretty Christmas lights. Cells are missing; strands hang loose or have disappeared altogether. And with the breaking of the nerve connections, the precious frontal lobe and limbic areas of the brain that are responsible for consciousness, emotion and memory, for so much of what makes us the people we are, are irreparably damaged.

'When you're a baby you've got many more neurons than you'll ever need,' says Gunn-Moore. 'So, because the brain is fantastic at programming itself, if a baby makes a movement or something else that works well for the body, chemicals will be produced at these synapses to make the connection more sticky, so that it will stay. We think that physically the contact points get bigger. That's what we think may be a long-term memory.

'Your brain is also very plastic and can rewire itself through adulthood. That plasticity depends on your short-term memory. Physically what that means is that these are probably smaller, less strong connections, so they can break and come apart and reform on a different point. They're smaller synapses. We could be wrong, but that's what we currently think is the difference.'

I have sought this leading neurobiologist out to help me imagine what might have been going on inside your own head that summer, when vagueness over detail was starting to blunt your usually sharp grasp of facts and you were forgetting to put on your pyjamas. From what Frank Gunn-Moore says, as the short-term memory on which the plasticity of the brain depends became compromised, your lights were slowly, ever so slowly, beginning to go out.

'What tends to happen in Alzheimer's disease is that you lose the short-term memory – the small, shorter synapses seem to be the ones being affected first – and in later stages the longer-term memory goes as well. All the connections you're seeing there start to go.'

He watches as I peer through the microscope, unable to tear my eyes away from those cells of light and the glittering fragility of their golden threads.

'You ask me what memory is,' he says to my bent head. 'Well, it can be defined in many ways, but for me that's it there. Right there. You're looking at the place where memories go.'

4

The light fantastic
John Milton, 'L'Allegro'

It is a shock to hear the words out loud. We are here for another reason altogether. This is not supposed to be about you.

'I see your mother has dementia too,' the matron has said, drawing me to one side while you are busy talking to someone else. I catch my breath.

'Well, yes, we have begun to realise that,' I say defensively. 'Is it so very obvious?'

'Yes,' she says bluntly. I feel vaguely ashamed, as if she had pointed out a hole in my tights that I had imagined more or less out of sight. 'The signs,' she adds, 'are all there.'

She is right, of course. The signs *are* there. This is 2004 and there is about you now the indefinable aura of a personality in retreat and a mind wobbling slightly on its anchorage. Yet beside my poor, confused Aunt Harriet you are so vital and whole that it seems a nonsense to define you both with the same stomach-churning word.

You and I have brought your older sister to visit this comfortably appointed care home on the outskirts of Glasgow with a view to placing her on the waiting list. It has a dementia unit upstairs. Life with Harriet at home is becoming challenging.

Earlier we had all sat down in the matron's office to talk. You were charming and relaxed, tucking into tea and biscuits, talking nineteen to the dozen. I was aware, though, that you kept taking us off the subject. I found myself leaping in when you paused for breath, trying to divert your attention back. It had been a while, I realised, since I had watched you operating in a brisk social situation of this kind and it was making me uncomfortable. You were consistently missing the point of what we were there for, which was to explain what we felt Harriet needed and to satisfy ourselves that she would be happy and cared for here. Instead you were offering cheery anecdotes that raced off at a tangent and never quite returned.

Still, it is one thing to be aware of this, and another to hear it confirmed by the voice of officialdom, devoid of euphemism.

'Have you had your mother tested?' the matron continues inexorably.

I shake my head. Is one relative with dementia not enough for now?

*

Next morning I take Harriet on a short walk. Despite the clouds sagging with rain she ventures out gamely along the country road that runs past your house.

She had been living with you for a couple of years by then. Yet, as the matron so quickly spotted, you were curiously disengaged from her plight. It was your other sister Anna, your twin, a fixture of your home from the moment she had moved in to help with your babies forty years ago, who had lobbied to bring her to join the household. It was she who realised that Harriet could no longer live on her own in the Yorkshire town where she had settled as a post-war bride.

My father had acquiesced to this further expansion of the sisterhood with the affability with which he always opened his home. His own refuge was his study, the place to which he had ever retreated from the domestic demands of family life with a *sang-froid* that few modern fathers would get away with. He was the brooding, benevolent presence at the heart of the home, reading and typing and pacing and smoking while the household magically ran itself around him. As long as the study remained a secure retreat and the occasional meal announced itself, he seemed content that the house, long emptied of children, should fill up with sisters-in-law.

But his benign detachment and your growing disengagement meant it was Anna who bore the weight of caring for Harriet. You were still first in line to sing a song with her or reminisce over old mishaps at her job with the City Bakeries, but in the practical aspects of her welfare in which you would once have seized the lead you were taking only the most cursory interest. Anna was struggling on her own.

Out walking with Harriet I try to imagine you turning into this. Fawn scarf dangling near the ground at a 90-degree angle, she is bent so far over that you could eat your tea off her back. She looks like a question mark. As she shuffles past clumps of ragged daffodils, head bowed, eyes fixed on the ground, I have a sudden vision of her doing the charleston, her Hogmanay party piece for as long as I can remember. She is spinning around and singing at the top of her voice, legs flying, hair bouncing. You are accompanying her on the mouth organ, hand cupped over one end, letting it rip. Born performers, both of you.

Now all that vitality is gone, everything diminished except the colour of my aunt's hair. It is tucked into a fawn beret set at a rakish angle over one ear. The escaping wisps are still like spun gold.

By the time we turn back I am literally holding her up, left arm still linked in hers, right hand reaching under her head to support her other arm.

'Look,' I say when we are safely inside. 'We've only just escaped the rain.'

'Yes,' she murmurs, looking out of the window. 'And where are we?'

No, my mother, never this. Not dementia. Not for you. Not like this. I cannot imagine it. I simply cannot imagine it.

*

Harriet and Archie, Anna and Mamie. The first two were born just sixteen months apart – almost like twins, your mother used to say. The real twins came along seven years later.

Harriet was born in January 1918 in West Yorkshire. Your mother Sarah's own mother, Harriet Ramsden, had come from Dewsbury and you never discovered how she met your maternal grandfather, John Fulton Greig, a dark-moustachioed music compositor at the Glasgow printworks of Aird and Coghill. Sarah gave birth to Harriet during a visit to her Aunt Charlotte's in Dewsbury, just three or four miles along the road from the town of Mirfield to which, in a quirk of fate, Harriet would return nearly thirty years later as a bride.

Archie, Anna and you were born in Rutherglen, the town where John Fulton Greig moved his family to escape the fetid fumes of Glasgow and where your paternal grandmother, Annie McKechnie from Mull, had put down new roots of her own in the 1880s. You were proud – passionately, volubly, uncritically and, I admit it, infectiously proud – of belonging to Rutherglen. Just as you considered self-evident the innate superiority of Scotland to everywhere else on the planet and were quick to rehearse its achievements in inventing macadamised roads, tyres, the telephone, television, raincoats, steam engines, the bicycle, penicillin, golf and Loch Lomond, you were equally convinced of your singular good fortune in having been born in Glasgow's plucky little next-door neighbour.

Glasgow had grown at breakneck speed during the Industrial Revolution, as the destitute poured in from the highlands and Ireland in search of work. Annie McKechnie was among them. After leaving Mull as a thirteen-year-old she found a position in the city as a domestic servant and in 1877 married a joiner by the name of Archibald Baird, who hailed from Ayrshire. The couple lived at a succession of addresses in and around the Gorbals district of Glasgow, a city so shockingly unhealthy at the time that its pioneering Medical Officer of Health, Dr James Burn Russell, described it as 'semi-asphyxiated'. It was safer to fall asleep under a tree in central Africa, he observed, than under a lamp-post in Glasgow's swarming Briggait.

Russell also noted that one in every five children born in the disease-ridden tenements never saw the end of its first year. Annie's family was a case in point: they lost two infant sons to tuberculosis in quick succession. Like the Greig family they decamped as soon as they could in search of cleaner air. With their two surviving boys, one of whom was already an invalid, they moved to the town on Glasgow's south-east boundary.

As industrialisation crept eastwards Rutherglen had accumulated plenty of packed tenements and noxious chimneys of its own, the latter immortalised in the local tongue-twister, 'Lang may Ru'glen's wee roon red lums reek briskly'. But along with shipbuilding, paper manufacture and later chemical production, it still boasted working farms, a smattering of fields and streams and, on the edge of town, the windy slopes of Cathkin Braes. To achieve a move to countrified Rutherglen, as Dr James Burn Russell's own family had during his childhood, was to savour the exhilaration of escape.

In the case of the Bairds, however, the TB moved with them. Archie the elder died at the age of forty of what was officially called *phthisis pulmonalis*, and their ailing youngest son, a second Archie, succumbed at seventeen. Annie Baird was spared only one son, John, your father, who was left with a fetish for fresh air and the habit of marching his own children on long Sunday walks to Cathkin's breezy braes, where you first learned to stretch your long legs and stride like a man.

Your pride in Rutherglen was chiefly focused on its not being Glasgow. Rutherglen was cleaner, greener, older, had bigger pavements, more historic visitors (the medieval patriot William Wallace once attended a meeting of the Scottish parliament there, you assured us) and boasted immaculate royal credentials, having been granted its burgh charter by King Robert the Bruce in 1323 in which reference is made to an earlier one from King David I in 1126. That I can still remember these dates without checking is a testament to your powers of indoctrination and, doubtless, some sticky childhood synapses.

As you so frequently reminded us, Rutherglen had been the main commercial centre on the lower Clyde for centuries before Glasgow, the upstart village next door, grew to become the second city of the Empire and started to push it around. Glasgow tried so often to annex Rutherglen under one Boundaries Bill or another that the Lord Provost eventually marched off to the House of Lords to protest. He waved King Robert's charter under the noses of their lordships to such powerful effect that a telegram later arrived at the town hall from London declaring 'Independence maintained'. The bell was rung in the old steeple and folk danced in the streets, a scene you described in such vivid detail that I thought you must have been one of them. I now discover it happened in 1912.

By the time local authority reorganisation in 1975 eventually swallowed this burgh into Glasgow, we had already moved away, but your indignation at the takeover simmered from a distance. Whenever I tell people, for ease of explanation, that I come from Glasgow, I still feel a twitch of treachery and the heat of your instant correction: 'You most certainly don't, my girl. You're from Rutherglen.'

Annie McKechnie, the Widow Baird as she was known, sailed along the broad pavements of Main Street with her hair piled high and a dark hat perched imperiously on top. Although she had to take in washing to make ends meet, she insisted on the best cut at the butcher's and held her head so regally that people called her the Duchess. She had a formidable temper, inherited by her son, who more than once felt the crack of her umbrella across his back when he failed to be home on the precise tick of the mantelpiece clock.

When John moved his shy bride into the house in 1917, Sarah lived in terror of Annie McKechnie's sharp tongue and insatiable criticisms, although it was said that in the end your mother's sweet nature softened her. One day they went together to buy linoleum for the kitchen floor and the shop assistant tried to encourage your grandmother to buy one with a pattern of flowers.

'We don't need any more flowers in our home while my lovely daughter-in-law is in it,' she declared in her deceptively soft highland lilt. Sarah nearly fainted away at the compliment.

John Baird had met Sarah Greig at Rutherglen's Alexander Chair Works, where he worked as a wood machinist and she was a French polisher. Once upon a time Sarah had believed she would grow up to be a princess. Her father John Fulton Greig, the typesetter who composed Scots verse and hymns in his spare time, was the only man in the street who went to work in a bowler hat rather than a cap. This could only mean she was destined for a palace. Young Sarah clung to that conviction until the day she found herself polishing wood on her knees in a noisy chair factory.

The couple were still living with John's mother in Regent Street when Harriet and Archie were born. By the time you and Anna arrived on 24 October 1925 the family had escaped your grandmother's iron rule for a room and kitchen in Rutherglen's East Main Street. You were taken to visit her in Regent Street every weekend until she died. Many decades later you could still describe in detail the big black-leaded kitchen range, the itchy prickle of the horse-hair sofa under your bare legs and the tin mugs she kept on the mantelpiece over the hearth, one for you and one for Anna.

Anna was born first, large and pink, and it was to blank amazement and general consternation that you followed twenty minutes later. As you were fond of recounting, your mother had no idea she was expecting twins and your father was initially dismayed. It had taken him months to save up the two-guinea fee for a single delivery.

'Will there be anything extra for the second birth?' he asked the midwife nervously as she washed her hands at the kitchen sink.

She cast a withering glance at the wizened, half-starved specimen swaddled in half a shawl and pronounced that for this one ten shillings would do.

You were given the name Mary, after one of your mother's many sisters. In a nod to your father's Hebridean roots the middle name Ian was added, the Gaelic version of his own name, John. You were proud of that Ian, not least because you always wished you had been born a boy, since they patently had more fun and opportunities in life. Your sister was christened Annie McKechnie, although a character less like her fearsome namesake would be hard to imagine. Soon Annie became Anna and Mary became Mamie, and the strong healthy one grew up to be shy and retiring, while the emaciated afterthought revealed herself to be confident and forward, a born leader who has lately taken it very badly, as you well know, to find the natural order of things reversed.

The next family home was in one of the first council houses in Rutherglen, a brand new first-floor tenement flat with a living room, bedroom, inside bathroom and kitchenette, although even there it was a squash, especially after your mother's younger sister Betty moved in. Harriet slept at one end of the narrow bed, you and Anna at the bottom, your mother and aunt in another single bed in the same room, while your father and Archie took the living room.

'I've still got memories,' you said in the days when you did, 'of the horror of sleeping with someone's foot up my nose.'

Early on, Harriet appointed herself your and Anna's guardian, chasing off any child rash enough to venture near the pram with fiery threats. She had fight and cheek in her that used to madden your father, but he was proud of her hair, golden red like his own.

The family was poor, although your mother performed such magic in making food, coal and clothing last that you never quite felt you were, and your father had such a passion for education that no sacrifice was too great to keep first Archie and then you at school beyond the statutory age of fourteen. Anna took no pleasure in studying and followed Harriet to the City Bakeries. At school she had been humiliated by teachers who terrified her and, on one cruel occasion, compared an English essay of hers publicly to yours. A teacher strapped you once for leaning over to help her with a sum, one of seven times that you were belted on the hand at school. None of your children was surprised to learn that most of your encounters with the strap were for talking.

Harriet thrived behind the counter. Although in her enthusiasm she dropped so many cakes and squashed so many pies that there was sometimes next to nothing left in her wage packet, she could count fast, carry a tray on the flat of her hand and speak well. Her 'May I be of service, please?' was a model of its kind. Eventually she graduated to manageress of one of the biggest baker's shops in Glasgow, the famous Ca'D'Oro near Central Station, and wore a black dress.

At weekends she would bring home a fern cake, a Swiss tart with apple and powdered sugar, a square fruit cake called the Fly Cemetery (your father's favourite), a couple of the cherry-topped German biscuits that later underwent a pointed name-change to Empire biscuits and a fancy Eiffel Tower.

During the Depression your father was put on half-time at the chair factory. Unable to bring in enough to keep the family, he took the post of assistant janitor at Rutherglen Academy, where the pay was meagre but the rent subsidised. In 1935 he was promoted to janitor of a new school, Bankhead Primary, and four years later you all moved into another council house close by. This one was an upstairs flat in Milrig Road with a small, shared garden and a burn pottering along the bottom.

It was there you were living as you prepared to leave school in 1943. Harriet and Anna were rising in the bakery ranks and Archie was away at war, having left an architectural apprenticeship and a budding football career in Aberdeen to join the medical corps. The trade you were hoping to join would have intrigued your grandfather, the versifying printer. You had been thinking about it since the day Mr Cowper, the English teacher at Rutherglen Academy, had marched into the classroom with a pile of exercise books in his arms and lifted one off the top.

'Now settle down back there,' he began. 'All of you, sit up and listen to this.'

James Cowper was your inspiration. A writer himself, he was one of those unassuming English teachers who quietly furnished the minds of working-class youngsters and gave them the confidence to seize opportunities denied to their parents. It was he who first encouraged your writing. He fed a growing appreciation of tone and irony by introducing you to stylists like the early nineteenth-century essayist Charles Lamb.

At first nobody knew whose exercise book he had picked up from the top of the pile, but you quickly realised it was yours. It was an essay about wartime queues, modelled on Lamb's witty treatment of everyday subjects in *Essays of Elia* but shot through with Glasgow dialect. You had hit on a seam of writing you were to make your own.

Mr Cowper kept reading until he got to a point where you had reached, as you put it, 'a sort of crescendo in my description'. Gratifyingly, the audience was chuckling. Then he stopped. He had still not mentioned the name of the author. With a flick of the wrist he tossed the jotter in the air.

'That, ladies and gentlemen, is writing,' he told the class. 'For that, I'll forgive her anything. When I come into the room and find her tap-dancing on top of my desk, when I see her hurtling down the school banisters, I'll look the other way, because *this girl can write*.'

This was the moment you realised what you wanted to do in life. You had always known that university was beyond your father's means, but now you saw the way ahead. You wanted to write for a living and you wanted to make people laugh. It didn't take much longer to decide there was only one kind of job that fitted the bill.

It was this decision that began to steer you in the direction of a young man from a very different world. He was currently in short trousers at Edinburgh Academy, running the birdwatching club and inviting what his Icelandic mother insisted on calling his school 'chumps' home for tea. He was younger than you and much posher, but one day he too would realise – also in a kind of epiphany – that more than anything in the world he wanted to be a journalist.

The coordinates, one might say, were set.

*

Less than a year after our chat with the matron my father stood up in an old country church to give a funeral address.

'It is my privilege today,' he began, 'to say a few words about our dear Harriet. Happy Harry, as I always called her.'

Harriet had not lasted long in the care home. Bereft of the familiar, confused, unhappy and tormented by nameless fears, she declined with appalling speed. Well, the rest of us were appalled. I am not sure you noticed. Anna saw her every day, her son John drove up from Mirfield and we nieces popped in when we could, but you rarely initiated a visit. Already you had begun to drift.

My father reminded those who had gathered for her funeral of the match that had drawn Harriet back to the Yorkshire of her birth.

The war had ended in Britain, but the men of the 14th Army were still locked in battle with the Japanese. Harriet had a letter in her pocket from a young tank driver by the name of Frank Garforth, asking her to marry him as soon as the war in Burma ended. They had been corresponding for four years, ever since Harriet arranged tea and musical entertainment for a unit of soldiers in a Rutherglen barracks waiting to be shipped abroad. She wore a blue dress to match her eyes and sang 'In My Sweet Little Alice Blue Gown'.

She married Frank, moved into one of Mirfield's new prefabricated houses for returned ex-servicemen, adopted a baby son, cooked endearingly slapdash meals and later became a formidable dinner lady at the local school.

My father concluded: 'If there are two words which sum up Harriet in our hearts, they are "sweetness" and "laughter". She loved fun. Music – any music – would have her on her feet, dancing with wild abandon. She was the very epitome of Milton's "L'Allegro", bringing with her

> Jest and youthful jollity,
> Quips and cranks, and wanton wiles,
> Nods, and becks, and wreathed smiles.
> . . .
> Sport that wrinkled care derides,
> And laughter holding both its sides.
> Come, and trip it as ye go,
> On the light fantastic toe.'

The last time I saw Harriet she was wholly in the grip of wrinkled care. Slumped in an armchair in the care home, she sat twisting her hands feverishly on her lap. Other old ladies wandered past. One, with a plastic handbag dangling over her arm, declared she was looking for her bag. She thanked me for pointing out its whereabouts and then asked if I had by any chance spotted her handbag.

Harriet was oblivious to everything. She sat rocking backwards and forwards in the chair. 'Help me,' she said, over and over. Her cheeks were wet with tears. 'Please help me. Please, please help me.'

A few days later she had fallen and was in hospital. A few days after that she was dead. They found food in her mouth from an old meal, unswallowed.

The owner of the home came to her funeral. The staff, too, seemed kind. But the memory of Harriet's inconsolable 'Help me, help me', and the twisting of her hands, the deep and desperate aloneness of her – that I cannot erase.

When your time comes, I said to myself with a kind of fierce elation, we will keep you at home. Whatever it takes, whatever it costs, we will not let you go.

I had no idea. None of us had any idea.

5

I have lost myself

Auguste Deter to Alois Alzheimer, 1901

April 1906, Munich. Dr Alois Alzheimer is staring into the microscope, his large head bent in the attitude with which students in his laboratory have become familiar. His pince-nez dangles by his side on a long string and as usual a stump of cigar lies abandoned on the table beside him. He is notorious for leaving these stumps around the lab, sometimes as many as twenty a day.

Already tending to the corpulent at forty-two, with a greying moustache and thinning hair, he is peering keenly at a thinly sliced piece of brain tissue that just a few days previously had housed the living being of a German housewife by the name of Auguste Deter.

I have become curious about this man whose name has infiltrated my family. If I am to understand what happened to Harriet and what may one day become of you, I need to know what Alois Alzheimer saw that day in the microscope.

By 1906 Alzheimer was already one of Europe's leading neurologists, celebrated for his classical descriptions of arteriosclerosis of the brain and known particularly for his fastidious insistence on charting his patients' symptoms during life and then attempting to correlate them with changes in the brain after death. Auguste D., as he called her in his notes, had been brought for treatment in November 1901 to the mental asylum in Frankfurt am Main, where Alzheimer was in charge of admissions.

Frankfurt's grandly designed Municipal Institution of the Mentally Ill and Epileptics was a more innovative place than its local nickname, Palace of the Mad, suggested. It had attracted the young Dr Alzheimer because it was founded not only on the principle that psychiatry should be based on scientific investigation of the brain, with post-mortem autopsies of patients a common procedure, but also that mentally ill patients should be treated humanely. Working closely there with the great neuropathologist Franz Nissl, Alzheimer set out to use microscopic analysis to understand the physical bases of diseases of the mind, in order that once understood they might be treated. It was pioneering work: this kind of correlation had been done in other areas of medicine, but not in psychiatry.

When her husband Karl brought Auguste Deter to the neo-Gothic pile for examination, he described her as having been a happy, healthy, even-tempered *hausfrau* until she had unaccountably begun to change in her late forties. In personality she had become jealous and resentful, quick to fly into a rage when she couldn't find things, prone to wild accusations that he was having an affair or trying in some other way to trick her. He had found her hairbrush in the oven, his pipe secreted in the laundry pile. She had become lost on her way back home from the butcher's shop. She made mistakes when preparing food and then stopped cooking altogether, could no longer dress herself and seemed to have forgotten the names of the simplest household objects. Her sleep was disturbed and she had started waking up in the night and screaming so loud that the neighbours became alarmed. She would pace the apartment for hours, dragging the bed-clothes and small pieces of furniture behind her. Her husband was at his wit's end. He could look after her at home no longer.

When Alzheimer interviewed Auguste herself, he noted that she spoke clearly and articulated well but often stopped in the middle of a sentence, or even a word. She said 'milk-jug' when she meant 'cup'. In reading she pronounced words in a meaningless fashion, and when he asked her to write her name she stopped after the word for 'Mrs', *Frau*. At one point, in obvious frustration at her inability to write down what had been said to her as she was asked, she tried to explain what it felt like.

'*Ich habe mich sozusagen verloren,*' she said. ('I have, so to speak, lost myself.')

Later, while she was chewing pork for lunch, he asked what she was eating. 'Spinach,' she replied confidently.

Alzheimer admitted her to the asylum and kept up with the case over the next four and a half years. After he left the Frankfurt institution in 1903, to work in Heidelberg at first and then to take over the big anatomical laboratory attached to the Royal Psychiatric Clinic in Munich, he continued to read the medical notes from Frankfurt, following Auguste's decline with keen medical interest. A photograph shows her in a loose, high-necked hospital gown looking troubled, her dark hair limp and straggly, hands clasped over her chest. She has a faraway expression on her face. She looks, just as she said, lost.

As her condition worsened, she began to hallucinate. She frequently shouted out nonsense for hours on end. Sometimes she would greet her doctors like old friends, but at other times was in a state of intense fear and vigorously resisted all attempts to examine or wash her. Catch her another day and she was quite apathetic. Alzheimer was intrigued, puzzled as to what could have gone wrong to produce such an effect on her brain. She died on 8 April 1906 at the age of fifty-five, curled in a foetal position in bed and unaware of her surroundings.

Within days Alzheimer was holding Auguste's brain in his hands, sent post-haste from the medical director at Frankfurt. He immediately wondered at its size: it was at least a third smaller than normal, and it looked shrivelled.

It was then that he looked through the microscope at sections of the brain tissue and observed the astounding features of the disease that would shortly be named after him. First, he noticed that numerous neurons, the nerve cells themselves, had totally disappeared. Then he realised there was something odd going on inside the remaining cells, where single fibres had become thick, like rope, and in some cells had accumulated to form dense bundles. Alzheimer reckoned that between a quarter and a third of the cells in Auguste's brain had been overwhelmed by these bundles of fibres. He also noticed another abnormality: over the entire cerebral cortex could be seen deposits of an unidentified substance in the form of what had already been described by the Austrian neurologist Emil Redlich as 'plaques'. Under the microscope they looked like dense black blobs.

It was a close friend of his, the eminent psychiatrist Emil Kraepelin, who first drew attention to Alzheimer's discovery in a paper published in 1910; he may have been at least partly motivated by a desire to deliver one in the eye to his great rival Sigmund Freud in Vienna, who was proposing different explanations for psychiatric problems. In this paper Kraepelin dubbed the disease *Alzheimers Krankheit* – the disease that most commonly produces the symptoms we know as dementia.

Alois Alzheimer's three key discoveries remain valid to this day as a description of what happens to the brain of a person suffering from Alzheimer's disease: the massive loss of brain cells; the jumble of neurofibrillary tangles now understood to consist primarily of a protein called tau; and the accumulation of what are these days known as amyloid plaques.

Much though I want to understand what is going on inside your own head, I find all this painful to think about. I try to place your features on Auguste Deter's and find I cannot. My will balks at sending my imagination there. There are places it is not wise to go too soon.

Alzheimer never had the chance to find out how his own neurons might have stood up in old age. He contracted an infection in 1912 that left him severely weakened. The heavy burden of psychiatric cases thrown up by the First World War sapped his strength further, although he did manage to publish an article on the effects of war on the psyche. He died in December 1915 at the age of fifty-one, and was buried in Frankfurt.

In his obituary his friend Franz Nissl emphasised that Alzheimer had not just been a brilliant scientist but a kind doctor, who did not regard mentally ill people as inferior (contrary to the prevailing belief that would reach its most horrific expression in the extermination policies of Nazi Germany), but treated his patients with enormous compassion. And indeed, although Alzheimer was never able to do much to alleviate their symptoms, he always ensured that his frail patients were well supervised and adequately nourished.

In this, as much as in his scientific observations, there is still much to learn from Alois Alzheimer.

6

A token flick

Mamie Magnusson

Why did I never ask him? Why did I never talk to my father about what was happening to you?

He accepted an invitation once, around the time when the change in you was becoming palpable, to present a public service video about Alzheimer's disease.

'Interesting?' I asked.

'Very,' he said.

Neither of us brought up your name. Neither of us was ready to be as blunt as the plain-speaking matron at Harriet's care home. Now I can't imagine why. I think we each hoped the other might not have noticed. Or perhaps we were too busy trying not to notice ourselves, believing that the longer we went without acknowledging it, the longer life would remain more or less normal. A conspiracy of willed ignorance.

In any case, it was easier than in most households for everyone to adjust around you. I doubt if my father even realised how little you were contributing to the running of yours. With Anna keeping house, you could slip into doing nothing on the domestic front with ease.

Anna had been part of the *ménage* for decades. As my father's career as a print journalist morphed into the life of a roving television presenter, making first archaeology programmes and then the quiz show *Mastermind*, she had given up her job as a hotel manageress and moved in to help you at home. While you nursed us through illness, helped with homework, soothed us past emotional crises, comforted us, disciplined us and made us laugh, it was Anna who changed the beds, cleaned the carpets, planted the spring bulbs, polished our shoes and had vats of thick soup waiting for us when we got home from school. She sang us Italian pop songs from records she had picked up on her summer holidays on the Adriatic, from where she returned bronzed and laden with gifts.

You liked to imagine yourself as Mary in the biblical story of Martha and Mary, the two sisters visited by Jesus. You would have sat pouring perfume on his feet, no problem, while Anna was cooking the dinner. You would have been telling him a limerick even as she scooted around the pair of you with a carpet sweeper.

I found an old letter the other day, in which you describe a frantic burst of house cleaning before Anna got back from one of her holidays. Her imminent return always threw you into feverish activity, invariably accompanied by guilt and ardent pledges of reform.

I've been doing housework like mad today. I even washed out the fireplace and dusted every inch of

> *the lounge, including all the ornaments on the*
> *mantelpiece. I also dusted every bit of Topsy's*
> *room and all the books to make the air clearer next*
> *time she comes home. I gave a token flick of the*
> *duster in your and Margaret's room, just for love's*
> *sake, if you know what I mean. Now I'm*
> *exhausted. It makes me realise how hard Anna*
> *works all the time. I must give her more help.*

You frequently made resolutions of this kind, but rarely to noticeable effect. You simply could not make yourself care how the house looked, while Anna did. But it was she who gave you the freedom not to care. To her you owed the luxury of being able to turn a day's housework into an opportunity for emotional connection with your departed children, the luxury of feeling exhausted after doing what most housewives of the time would have regarded as not very much at all. We loved you for it, of course. Having inherited varying degrees of domestic insouciance ourselves, your three daughters empathised deeply with the spirit of those duster-flicks and only came to appreciate much later the real hard work with cloths, vacuum cleaners, mops and brushes that Anna put in behind it all.

So this is how it always was. This is why it took us longer than it might have in a more conventional home to begin to register, through those early years of the new millennium, how very, *very* little you were doing and how far you had withdrawn from household decisions of any kind and anything practical whatsoever.

*

In the early summer of 1943 you were preparing to leave school without the faintest idea of how to fulfil your dream of becoming a journalist. A friend's mother had arranged an interview with the *Glasgow Herald*, but it came to nothing and you were feeling dispirited.

However, one of the papers your father took was the couthie *Sunday Post*, published in Dundee. In it you read an article arguing against proposals to raise the school leaving age to fifteen, there being no point in giving extra education to children who were going to be plumbers and bricklayers. This, as you said, 'made me mad'. Right away you fired off a reply, page after scathing page, arguing that education was valuable for its own sake and that youngsters would make better bricklayers if they had more of it. A heavily subbed version appeared the following Sunday. And that letter started everything.

The *Sunday Post*, 23 May 1943

I have completed almost thirteen years at school. I have got a good knowledge of maths. I know enough French to be eager to learn more.

I have learned Latin, which has gone a long way towards perfecting my understanding of my own

language; science, which has unfolded for me a few of
the mysteries of nature and modern progress; history,
which has acquainted me with wrong decisions and
foolish blunders of the past to be avoided in future.

I have learned sufficient of all these subjects to
be able to participate in an intelligent conversation,
which is surely an advantage in an age when
discussions never wander far from Bob Hope and
Dorothy Lamour!

But education has something greater to offer,
something vital to the whole life of future generations.
For in it lies the recognition of the value of education.

Mamie I. Baird, Rutherglen Academy

As it transpired, your Latin teacher lived in the same street in Burnside as the Glasgow editor of the *Sunday Post*, James Borthwick. They were standing at the tram-stop on the Monday morning, chatting while they waited.

'By the way, Mrs Emsley,' said he, 'did you see there was a letter in my paper yesterday by somebody from your school?'

'Yes, indeed. I know that girl well.'

'It was very good.'

'Actually she wants to be a journalist,' said Mrs Emsley, 'but she's been having difficulty getting in.'

The very next day a letter arrived from James Borthwick asking you to come and see him. This you did, dressed in your school blazer and grey ankle socks and leaping over a dustbin in Buchanan Street on the way; your mother was black affronted. You told Mr Borthwick you liked to make people laugh. He said that was just the kind of writing he was looking for and asked to see a sample. You sent him the essay that Mr Cowper had so admired, reworked in what you hoped was a more journalistic style. The piece was about the women whose war-effort was standing in queues for food and it roared to an ironic Churchillian climax that was rather sophisticated for a seventeen-year-old school-girl:

> Who can doubt our might, our valour, while a
> horde of brave souls, after three years of war, can
> thrust behind them their many cares and woes and
> muster up enough strength to fight for a Swiss roll?

The *Sunday Post* printed it under the magnificent headline 'Keep Your Elbow Oot o' My Ribs' and offered you a job at a pound a week.

There, and on its sister paper the *Weekly News*, you did a variety of jobs: plenty of straight reportage, a column written in the guise of a letter from dim Private Archie to his sweetheart Gladys (whom you swiftly demobbed in favour of Wee Wilma, an accident-prone shop-girl based on Harriet) and fictional stories of a banality so staggering that long afterwards you could quote wires from the head office by heart. 'Suggest Miss Baird writes piece about mother going for picnic with children. As they are sitting down to the picnic, they see a bull coming across the field. Denouement.'

Your powers of inspiration were also tested by the requirement to write a limerick every week. Perhaps it was the sheer, sweat-inducing effort of composition that entrenched those verses in your memory, but you remember many of them still, even now. Especially this one:

> *A fellow who lived out in Yoker,*
> *Hit his wife as she slept with a poker.*
> *When charged with assault,*
> *He said, 'S' no' my fault,*
> *I thought that wee bang would have woke her.'*

In later years you could always raise a laugh by inserting this verse into a talk. Memories go, but to this day the Yoker man remains, bringing the illusion of fluency when you crave it and a way of evoking laughter when you struggle for the right thing to say. I could recite it in my sleep.

You were grateful for the training on the *Sunday Post* but well aware of the limitations. In May 1947 you sought out Mr Borthwick to explain that you were being poached by the *Scottish Daily Express*. You apologised for leaving but said you had to experience a different kind of journalism.

'Look, lass,' he said. 'Far be it from me to stop you. I knew this would happen. You're good and – don't quote me – it's the good ones that go if they've got any sense at all.'

He led you to his ancient roll-top desk and from one of the pigeon-holes produced a wad of telegraph wires that head office had sent to James Cameron, the renowned foreign correspondent who was by then forging his career in Fleet Street.

'James Cameron went through exactly the same as you,' he said. 'The man could really write. He came here full of enthusiasm and bright ideas, and he got sickened at having to write a lot of nonsense week after week. Each time these ridiculous ideas came down from Dundee on the wire, Jimmy would groan and have to be persuaded by me to do them.'

He held up the roll of telegrams and flipped his finger through them. 'I kept these wires so I can show the management if I ever hear them boasting about the famous James Cameron having started work here. "Look at these," I'll tell them. "That's why James Cameron left."'

The *Daily Express* was a different proposition. In those days it managed both an unparalleled popular touch and a lightly worn air of cultivation, making an art of getting everything into a story accurately, entertainingly and without an unnecessary word: you once counted forty-eight stories on the front page. Lord Beaverbrook had set up the Glasgow operation with its own printing press in 1928, at a time when the parent paper was the most widely read newspaper in the world. It was brash and confident, with a swagger that famously encouraged the driver ferrying a reporter and photographer through the factory gates during an industrial dispute to announce loftily: 'This is the *Scottish Daily Express* and we're moving in.'

You did every kind of reporting there, from murder leads, disaster spreads and royal exclusives to three paragraphs on the discovery of a deadly Colorado beetle in a sack of potatoes at the docks, for which you won the paper's £5 prize for the best-written story of the month (you likened the insect's colouring to the old black and gold strip of your brother Archie's Aberdeen Football Club). You would never have claimed to be a great writer, but you were a good one. You had found a style – sharp-eyed, light-hearted, economical and readable – that suited the times and especially the growing female readership of newspapers.

In time you came to the attention of head office and were invited to London to take over the great Eve Perrick's column for a week. You wrote it as the *ingénue* supposedly bedazzled by the big city and were promptly offered a permanent job in Fleet Street with a salary increase from 12 to 17 guineas a week. You agreed to stay, but only for a short time.

Two months later the legendary Arthur Christiansen summoned you to his office to try and persuade you to stay longer. One of the finest editors of his generation, he was already a renowned figure in Fleet Street. Plump, with a high forehead and crinkly brilliantined hair, he would march around the editorial floor, missing nothing. He admired your work. I notice that among your newspaper cuttings is a copy of a letter sent by Christiansen to the Glasgow office in May 1956, with one sentence proudly underlined by my father: 'Mamie Baird is, of course, a very fine journalist indeed.' This was the man who wanted you in Fleet Street.

'I like it here,' you told him. 'I love it in fact, and if I stayed much longer, maybe I wouldn't go back. But Scotland is where I want to spend my life, and my mother and twin sister are there.'

'Bring them down, then,' urged Christiansen grandly. 'We'll buy you a house. You can name your salary.'

He leaned back in his chair and pushed up his gold spectacles. 'This is exactly what happened to me, you know. I was in the north of England and they wanted me to come to London and they persuaded me – just as I'm trying to do with you.'

In the end you thanked him warmly and returned to the reporter's beat back home.

It is just as well you did, because this story requires you to be in the Edinburgh office of the *Scottish Daily Express* in the late summer of 1953, when an exotic figure not long up from university will follow you to lunch.

At the moment Magnus is still immersed in Anglo-Saxon poetry and Jesus College cricket. He has never ceased to rejoice in his good fortune at being in Oxford. When he first arrived to sit the exam for a scholarship in English, he had wandered past a little church where bell-ringers were practising. He could see the shadow of the bells moving across one of the windows in the tower and stood watching it for a long time.

'I want to be in this place,' he had thought.

He loves it as much as he knew he would. He has entered extravagantly into the sartorial spirit by investing in a pair of yellow pigskin gloves, a silver-headed cane and an umbrella. He writes sport reports for the university magazine *Isis*. When not punting on the river and trying out hopefully for the rugby team, he is composing earnest plays. He has even become engaged to a fellow student who, as his mother back in Edinburgh is thrilled to have learned, is a princess of the royal house of Norway.

Fortunately for those of us with a vested interest in the pair of you getting together, he is already reviewing this decision.

*

How much did my father know? I have no idea. But he must have noticed that you were changing.

No more hammering out a column on the typewriter or helping him to research his latest book. No more hopping on a plane to visit grandchildren or whizzing round the garden on your once prized sit-on lawnmower. No more babysitting, not after the time you toppled backwards into a flowerpot in my garden and had to be rescued by one of the children you were supposed to be looking after. No more, in fact, of so much that we all used to take for granted, as we did your laid-back, easy-going personality, so different from Anna's more anxious disposition and my father's volatile temperament with his testy bursts of impatience and periodic Nordic glooms.

Laid-back? By this time you were protesting that your life was overcrowded – hectically, stressfully busy – when the plumber and the window-cleaner called in the same week.

Well, everyone slows down, don't they, even a seventy-something as blithe of heart as you? In older age the world contracts, doesn't it? So my siblings and I assured each other at first.

But with the tragically diminished figure of your older sister so recently before us, we could soon see that ageing alone did not explain the way you kept missing the big picture while becoming vastly over-exercised by the small, fussing over unimportant details while disengaging from crucial ones. You used to be so relaxed about minutiae. Losing a child had confirmed to you the relative unimportance of almost everything except having and loving each other; nothing, you used to believe, was worth fighting over. Now we would hear you arguing noisily with Anna over her use of the vacuum cleaner outside my father's study, unable to grasp that the squawk of bickering sisters was more likely to disturb his concentration than the steady buzz of the hoover. This intolerance of Anna's presence near him was an ominous development.

While never referring directly to what were clearly the symptoms of early dementia, my father did find a word for how you seemed at these times. 'Distraite,' he called it. In this he chose, as usual, well. It is from the Latin *distrahere*, to pull apart. In the episodes of distraction we were observing, in the cloud of vagueness that had begun to settle around you, it uncannily captures the loss of crucial connections in your brain.

It felt to us at the time like a slippage of moorings. I imagined you as a small boat bobbing away inexorably towards the grey mist.

7

De mentis

Philippe Pinel

ementia. I hate the name. At least Alzheimer's disease arrives on the tongue with solid, Germanic probity; it may be a mouthful, but it has the air of a sober, respectable ailment that can show its face in company. Dementia is different. It is feckless and French. It hisses and seethes. It conjures up madness, asylums, insanity, lunacy, something inchoate and uncontainable and dangerous.

A Paris doctor called Philippe Pinel, celebrated as the great liberator of the mentally ill in revolutionary France, holds the dubious honour of having invented the word *démence*. He coined it in 1797 from the Latin *de mentis*, meaning 'out of one's mind', which as a matter of fact is not all that *précis* a description of the subtle mental changes over the years which dementia brings, since people with the symptoms are manifestly not out of their minds at all for a lot of the time; if anything, they feel increasingly trapped within them.

Still, Pinel has landed us with the word, and we do need a label to cover this family of diseases. Technically dementia itself is a syndrome, not a disease. It is caused by a number of illnesses in which there is progressive decline in multiple areas of function, including memory, reasoning, communication skills and the ability to carry out daily activities. Many people will not have the form that Alois Alzheimer was first to identify, but rather vascular dementia, the second most common type, caused by impaired circulation of blood around the brain; or Lewy body disease which affects more than 100,000 people in the UK; or fronto-temporal dementia covering a number of more rare conditions. They all result in structural and chemical changes leading to the death of brain tissue. Some people will have different kinds of affliction going on at once.

However, even if we might have hoped for a kinder word from him, I do have a soft spot for Philippe Pinel. Haunted by the way a mentally ill friend had been treated, he went to work at a private sanatorium for the treatment of insanity in Paris. There he began to formulate a more humane psychological approach to the custody and care of psychiatric patients. In August 1793 he was appointed 'physician of the infirmaries' at Bicêtre Hospital where, along with the governor Jean-Baptiste Pussin, he developed a strictly non-violent method of managing mental patients and did away with bleeding, purging and blistering in favour of the novel approach of talking to the patient, often several times a day, and taking careful notes.

Legend has it that at Bicêtre Pinel also single-handedly liberated 200 mentally ill men from their iron shackles. It was probably Pussin who actually freed the men, but Pinel certainly removed the chains from patients at his next institution, the Hospice de la Salpêtrière, where he became chief physician in 1795. In his *Memoir on Madness*, still regarded as a fundamental text of modern psychiatry, he makes the case for the careful psychological study of individuals over time and calls for more humanitarian asylum practices.

If this man wants to call what you have *dementia*, I am prepared to forgive him.

*

All the same, names matter here – and mostly because they contribute to stigma, a chilling word itself: literally a mark of disgrace made by a pointed stick. The stigma around dementia is what keeps people isolated, reluctant to admit to symptoms and terrified of being branded. Everywhere in the world names have an effect.

In Punjabi, Hindi and Urdu the emotionally loaded word for insanity or madness, *paagal*, is used, encouraging people to see dementia as bad karma and a curse on the family, rather than a disorder with a pathology like any other illness.

Until recently Japanese terminology also clashed with medical reality. The original word for dementia, *chiho*, comes from *chi*, foolishness, and *ho*, dumb or disorientated. At the end of 2004 the government announced it was officially changing the word to *ninchisho*, which means 'disease of cognition'. Media and academic groups followed. Within seven or eight years the new word had become accepted across Japan.

Even in those European languages where Pinel's definition has at least established the concept of a medical condition (French *démence*, Spanish *demencia*, German *Demenz*, Romanian *demenţă*, Swedish *demens*, Italian *demenza* and so on), the connotations provoke unease. The Icelanders, for instance, one of the most linguistically self-aware of nations, reserve *demens* for doctors and have developed the kinder *heilabilun* (literally, 'brain ailment') for more popular use, with the avowed intention of preserving the dignity of those who have it.

In English there has been a tendency to stumble around not knowing quite what to say. *Alzheimer's* is accurate enough in some instances, but not others; *dementia* is terribly hard to love. Admittedly Pinel's word has been formally embraced by a growing number of people who were diagnosed with the illness early and have decided they do want to be called a 'person with dementia'. This is now the accepted terminology. On the other hand they recoil strongly from the adjective 'demented', which may not be entirely logical but goes to show how messy language can be when operating in such delicate social territory.

I still reckon we need a less emotive word than Pinel's hissy French one. Perhaps we too should invent a new name. A national vote would at least get everyone talking. As happened with cancer, it is talking that kills stigma in the end.

But as long as the word remains *dementia*, I really do have to say it without wincing. So here goes.

Dementia. The tag I avoided for years out of cowardice, because I could not bring myself to associate it with you.

Dementia. The word that will only be redeemed if people like me use it and people like you, my radiant, light-hearted mother, lead lives that defy its stigma for as long as you, and they, possibly can.

8

Men do not limp

The Saga of Gunnlaug Ormstunga

We are sitting in a bleak waiting room outside the intensive care ward. Margaret, Jon and I have hurtled across Glasgow from the airport. You and Topsy followed the ambulance and were here before us. The five of us look at each other. My siblings' faces are grey as putty; yours is flushed. But in another sense your face is transformed. Gone is the distrait manner. Your eyes are glittering with the light of battle. You have become our mother again, in charge and rallying us, as you did all those years ago when Siggy lay, terribly injured, on another intensive care bed in this same hospital.

'Come on, everyone, your dad's going to be all right,' you are saying. 'Let's will the best. Let's act as if we believe it.'

It is May 2004. I last saw my father two days earlier when I popped in to say goodbye before leaving on a filming trip to London. Later that day he was due to go into hospital for tests on his bowel, which was causing enough discomfort for him to have, first, admitted it and, second, consulted a doctor, both of which went strongly against the grain. He liked to model himself on the medieval Icelandic saga hero Gunnlaug Adder-Tongue, who refused to limp despite a boil in his instep that was leaking pus all over the Earl of Orkney's hall.

'Why are you not limping, Icelander?' demanded the Earl.

Gunnlaug retorted: 'Men do not limp, sire, while both their legs are the same length.'

It was a rejoinder Magnus used freely to deflect all fussing and any enquiry about his health. Now, however, he looked dreadfully ill. He didn't complain – it was part of the code not to acknowledge anything so piffling as pain – but when he rose to walk over to the desk he stumbled getting out of his armchair. When I kissed him on the forehead it was wet and clammy.

I gave him another kiss when it was time to go. His cheek felt soft: he had made a point of shaving for the doctor. There was something soft and crestfallen about him too. Suddenly I could not bear to let him go. I slipped my arms around his neck and hugged him tight.

Later that day you and Topsy drove him to hospital. You were fiddling with his briefcase and overnight bag, a little distracted. The consultant assured you they would do a scan in the morning to see what sort of blockage they were dealing with, and then they would fix it.

'The one thing we want to be sure of,' he added, 'is that there isn't an abscess there. That's the worry, because we don't want it to rupture.'

Which is precisely what happened. Before the scan could be completed next day, a giant ulcer on his colon burst, sending toxins flooding into his bloodstream and around his body. Kidneys, liver, heart and lungs all started to fail.

When Topsy rushed to the hospital, he was lying on a gurney with an oxygen mask over his face, chest heaving, fighting for breath. He was drenched in sweat and his skin was mottled. You were holding his hand and speaking softly to him. Your cheeks were bright red and your eyes tiny, like a bird's.

'I haven't left him for a second,' you told Topsy. 'I wouldn't leave him, even when they asked me to. He didn't want me to go and so I stayed. I just kept talking to him through everything.'

As the medical team began attaching him to a battery of machines, you whispered, 'Dearest, hold on. Remember a man never limps while both his legs are the same length.'

He tried to say something, his eyes fixed on you. Then they took him away. Topsy called the rest of us in London, where Margaret and Jon both live. I was in a recording studio near Oxford Street. We met up within the hour at Heathrow Airport.

And now we are in a waiting room at a different hospital, where he has been transferred after the operation to mend the ruptured colon. Our father has systematic organ failure and septicaemia. He may not make it through the night, the portly intensive care consultant tells us. But he is alive. And you, our mother, are keeping us going. Your optimism, even though hardly warranted by the doctor's careful phrases, cannot be dented. It is irrepressible. We find ourselves, like children again, following your lead.

Throughout the night we are allowed, two at a time, to sit by his bed. You refuse to leave him and we take turns to join you. To our delight his eyes flicker open when he recognises our voices, his hand returns our squeezes.

You remind him it will be your fiftieth wedding anniversary in a few weeks' time and you want him there for it. You lay your cheek against his arm and begin to hum the Icelandic lullaby 'Sofðu Unga Ástin Mín' (Sleep, My Little Darling), written by his great-uncle, the poet Jóhann Sigurjónsson, as part of a typically depressing Scandinavian play. The mother in the play croons it just before tossing her baby over a cliff-edge, something better forgotten when singing it, but the melody is haunting. My father's eyes remain closed but he grins from ear to ear. And he stays alive.

As the week goes on his condition improves, worsens, improves and then deteriorates so dramatically that Margaret, keeping guard overnight in the dim waiting room, calls us all in at four o'clock in the morning. His heart is in trouble again. We should come and say goodbye.

In the sickly dawn light we climb once more to the fifth floor. This is the place, I am thinking, where our family goes to die.

*

You look across the cramped office and see a young man urgently scanning the shelf of newspaper files. He has blond hair and a reddish beard and is wearing a blazer, grey slacks and tie. He stands out at once among the rumpled hacks of your acquaintance, not least, you note at once, because he is glowing with golden good looks.

'Who's the character with the beard?' you ask a colleague.

'Magnus Magnusson,' he whispers.

'What? Nobody has a name like that.'

You are told he is from Iceland, a country of which you have never heard and are not the first to confuse with Greenland. You wonder why he doesn't look like an Eskimo. You are definitely interested.

Someone calls this chap over and introduces you. He speaks with a soft Oxford accent, which you rather like. You turn away to speak to someone else and mention you are heading out for lunch to Poppins, a small restaurant around the corner. You have just sat down there when this fellow bursts in. As he explains eagerly, he has followed you. He joins you at the table and the pair of you chat non-stop through the meal. By the end of it he has asked you to join him for dinner that evening before taking in a late-night show. You tell him you have your piece about the festival to write up and will be late in finishing. Fine, he says.

It is hard to think of another job in the early fifties in which a girl from your background could have ended up in the same office as an Oxford graduate like him, earning not only more than him (not particularly difficult at the moment, it's true) but considerably more than the other men too. In journalism the nose for a story was valued more than a university degree and writing ability took precedence over gender. There were not many of you, but with luck and determination it was possible for talented women to make their way, blazing a trail for generations of female journalists to come.

You were there to cover the 1953 Edinburgh International Festival for the *Scottish Daily Express*. Magnus was back from Oxford, living at home and trying to fund his post-graduate studies through freelance writing.

His family had moved to Edinburgh from Reykjavík in 1930, when his father, Sigursteinn Magnússon, was sent by the Icelandic Co-operative Society to open an office in the port of Leith to handle the country's fish exports to Europe. Magnus was eight months old when they carried him off the steamer *Gullfoss* to make their new home in Scotland. It was a home almost as Icelandic as the one they had left behind, even down to the young maid who came with them on the boat. Leather-bound editions of the medieval Icelandic sagas lined the walls, symbol of a nationhood sustained through the centuries by words alone.

Sigursteinn was deeply absorbed in the political struggle for full independence from Denmark, which was finally achieved in 1944. He instilled in his four children a passion-ate attachment to the homeland and in his younger son a reverence for the sagas almost as great as his own. His chief concession to British culture was to standardise the family name to Magnusson, thereby abandoning the Icelandic patronymic style which should have made his sons Sigursteinnsson and daughters Sigursteinnsdóttir, a move for which his new countrymen were no doubt grateful. Magnus himself spoke barely a word of English until he started school.

The Edinburgh Festival found him mooching around the *Express* office in Jeffrey Street to see whether any of the festival reviews on which his precarious solvency depended had made it into the paper. Although he had started a doctorate on Old Norse in Copenhagen, he was proving a tad rowdy for the academic life and felt increasingly attracted to the more buccaneering realms of journalism. Meeting you would be what decided him.

That evening Magnus turned up at the Greek restaurant in Rose Street with two exotic friends from Oxford in tow. He was wearing his blazer and carried a smartly furled umbrella. During coffee you noticed him in eager conversation with the proprietor, a man he addressed improbably as Mr Hustacles. It transpired afterwards that he had not a farthing to pay for the meal and was inquiring whether he could settle up at the end of the week.

Afterwards neither of you could remember which show you saw that night. 'We had really fallen for each other,' you said. 'Instantly. Just instantly. We were going about Edinburgh in a kind of *dwam*.'

He accompanied you to the station to catch your train home to Rutherglen, and arranged to come and see you the following Saturday.

'I remember just as the train was moving out he leapt up and kissed me through the open window. It was wonderful. He was clean and nice, with lovely dry lips. That was my lasting impression of him.'

You grinned as you recalled that moment. 'I thought to myself, there and then, that this is the kind of person I would like to be with for ever.'

*

Margaret opens the waiting room door to greet us and you stumble towards her with your arms out.

She grabs you and says, 'No, no, he's still here. They gave him another drug a few minutes ago and he's started to respond. It's okay.'

After that you refuse to leave the hospital, even for a minute. We stay with you in shifts, forgetting work and partners and even our own children as we revert to the old family unit again in our waiting-room bubble, bickering, joking and weeping as the moods ebb and flow, but being continually buoyed up – we raise our eyebrows at each other, we can hardly believe it – by you. When one or other of us starts to drift into despair, you simply will not allow it.

'Mum's back,' we whisper to each other.

I realise now it was never as simple as that. You had not miraculously returned either to full mental vigour or to what we routinely thought of now as your old self. Rather, the gradual 'pulling apart' of your selfhood was serving you well as a coping mechanism. It blunted the sharpest edges of reality and tamed those parts of the imagination that make hope a struggle. Cold medical fact, the grasp of atrocious odds, the imagining of what might so easily come next: these are what make a person despair. Dementia dooms you to an eternal present, but there are some situations where the present is a better place to be. When emergency jolted you into full engagement, the inconvenient medical niceties went straight over your head but the old optimism, strength and fight that had always served you in a crisis surged back. And on that wave you carried us through.

Soon Dad was off the ventilator, heaving himself into consciousness through a sedative stupor and raving about drowning in a herring boat and being tortured in a slave-trading vessel. He said later that he spent most of that period believing he was playing a dying man in a film. At first he talked in Icelandic. When he asked what day it was I got mixed up between Thursday and Friday and blurted out *Föstudagur* when I meant *Fimmtudagur*. I rushed out of the ward to whoop that he had rolled his eyes at me.

After just over a week the tubes began to be removed one by one. He changed wards. He sat up. He described the weird and scary places he had felt himself to be in and even started making notes while he could remember. He indicated that both his legs were indisputably the same length and that he could do with his pipe. You were exhausted, but gay and merry and always at his side.

On the thirtieth of June you and he celebrated your golden wedding anniversary. That morning you drove together up the road to the old kirk and renewed your marriage vows, quietly and alone. Later we cooked a meal in your house and everyone was there: children, partners and all the grandchildren. Still a little shaky with relief to have him with us, we took dozens of photographs in the garden with you and him in the centre. In all of them you are beaming with delight at the life and colour around you.

But there are things I remember about you both that day that are not in the photos. Dad, although enjoying himself, was thin and pale, and there was a look in his eyes of someone on the way back from a distant place. You, too, had an absence about you, for all your smiles. It was a different sort of absence from his and, sadly, it was the kind we recognised. You had led us triumphantly through the crisis but now we were on familiar ground again. You were not on your way back at all.

9

Grey havens

J.R.R Tolkien, *The Lord of the Rings*

Going away. Taking your leave. A boat slipping into the mist. A personality dissolving round the edges. An identity melting. A tattered mind. How language struggles with dementia. We clutch after metaphors in the hope that words will offer a sort of shape and a kind of meaning. Sometimes the poets manage it best.

> *The brain's*
> *black holes into which memories have fallen*

is Lorn Macintyre's attempt in 'Dementia', a poem about his mother.

And we are right, it turns out, to reach for images of falling and fogging and clogging and clouding and loss and absence and the desperate dying of the light. It turns out that this is exactly what is happening in the brain when Alzheimer's disease gets underway. The Christmas lights that enchanted me in St Andrews become grimy with plaque, their connections to each other are cut and they start to go out. Neurons, to change the metaphor, are departing; memories are going.

The plaques and tangles classically start in an area of the brain known as the entorhinal cortex, located just outside the hippocampus, which curls through the centre of the brain like the seahorse it is named after in Greek and is responsible for memory and emotion. It is once the disease reaches the hippocampus that the first signs of memory loss are detectable. It then spreads through the other regions, killing cells and affecting behaviour, judgement, personality and functionality as it goes.

This is where the detached language of science should take over, as I get my head around the twin bogeymen of amyloid and tau. But I don't feel detached. Those plaques and tangles terrify me. I see them advancing on you like black riders, my sweet mother, and I am scared of what they might do next.

And yet – calm down – they are only clumps of protein, the sort we all need in our brains to function normally. Amyloid and tau. Perfectly natural. It's just that something is turning them bad. In the case of beta-amyloid too much of the protein is made, so that the nerve cells finally kick it out to gather in the toxic mass of plaque that Alois Alzheimer saw in his microscope. Meanwhile tau, the protein normally involved in providing the structure and transport of molecules inside the cell, becomes corrupted by several extra molecules of phosphorus, loses its structure and folds into a twisted mess of tangles.

Why either of these processes starts going wrong, how they are connected and whether amyloid or tau takes precedence in triggering the disease remains a matter of vigorous debate. So-called 'Tauists' compete with a bigger group of beta-amyloid believers who call themselves 'Baptists', those names hinting at the degree of quasi-religious faith that sustains scientists in a research field where nothing much is certain. There are also those who think the answers lie elsewhere, perhaps with the free radicals, toxic molecules that inflame neurons and disrupt the energy-generating mitochondria within them, ultimately killing the cells.

In general scientists of all shades of opinion are cautiously optimistic. Most believe that the years spent developing research techniques are starting to pay off and they are at last beginning to penetrate some of the mysteries of Alzheimer's; vascular dementia has attracted less scientific attention. It will in most cases be up to pharmaceutical companies to take the research to the next stage.

This, however, is the sticking point. It has proved so difficult to make effective drugs that there are still only four capable even of relieving some of the symptoms. Four drugs for a disease that somebody in the world gets every four seconds.

Not so long ago pharmaceutical companies were piling into the race to locate more effective treatments for this desperate and potentially lucrative market, yet time and again an apparently promising solution has been tried on real people and found not to work. These setbacks have proved costly for the big pharmaceuticals, many of which subsequently cut back their research programmes.

Governments have been slow to adjust their own funding priorities to support the scientists. Having picked itself up after a late start, dementia is still way behind other nasty and fatal diseases in the global race for research money. While comparing diseases is invidious, it would seem to make little economic sense to be spending £12 on cancer and £3 on heart disease research for every £1 on the hunt for a dementia cure.

A UK government pledge to double dementia research funding has been largely honoured, but there is still a long way to go to rectify the chronic underfunding. In the USA President Barack Obama has championed a public-private brain-mapping initiative that he describes as the challenge of the century.

'We can identify galaxies light-years away, study particles smaller than an atom,' he said at the White House launch of the Brain Activity Map, 'but we still haven't unlocked the mystery of the three pounds of matter that sits between our ears.' Quite.

This question of how we reason, memorise, learn, move and have emotions is a different mystery from the one the molecular detectives are pursuing. William Newsome of Stanford University, one of two neurobiologists leading the initiative, believes the great questions about how behaviour and cognition emerge from the nervous system will be answered only by looking at how thousands or even tens of thousands of neurons at a time are engaging in coordinated activity and coordinated computation.

'It's like looking down at the US from a satellite, seeing the grid of lights at night. You can infer certain things: here's a city, here's a city. But really to understand the interactions between those cities you need to get down to the level of individual people moving around in cars.'

Newsome's brain map will ultimately feed data into the most ambitious initiative of all – the Human Brain Project, run from Switzerland by Professor Henry Markram at the École Polytechnique Fédérale de Lausanne. It aims to collect every kind of data from neuroscientists around the world and integrate it into a massive simulation running on a super-computer. Funded to the tune of 1 billion euros by the European Commission, it brings together eighty research institutions across Europe. The rhetoric promises 'the most accurate model of the human brain ever produced'.

Clearly nobody is going to 'solve the brain' any time soon. But it does look as if the goal is getting nearer.

'There is hope,' says Frank Gunn-Moore, whose team at St Andrews has developed a 'decoy' to protect vulnerable sites inside the cell where the amyloid first binds itself. 'I'm not going to tell you that my own drug *per se* is going to work – there is so much hype – and even assuming I can get the funding at each stage you're still looking at seven to ten years. But for my work and that of others, yes, there really is hope.'

Hope is a banner to wave at the dark riders of the imagination, and we could do with more of it. Sadly, though, it's not for you. Nothing will happen in time to bring you back from the empty places where dementia is taking you, my mother, or from the grey havens towards which you have set your lovely white sails.

10

Catch the moments as they fly

Robert Burns, 'A Bottle and Friend'

There are times in life so sweet and so precious that even as we live them they have acquired the lustre of memory, even as we exult in them we are pierced and shaken by the knowledge that they can never come in quite that way again. The keynote of the experience is not just drinking in the joy of it, but registering in some deep, sad place that we have already lost it.

Two years, near enough. A golden two years between the ulcer that nearly killed my father in May 2004 and the cancer that actually did. Two years when your mind still more or less held together. A gentle enough time, in which he voluntarily slowed down for the first time in his life and, to our astonishment, discovered how to relax.

At precisely the same time each morning he would down his books, send his computer to sleep and announce his readiness for departure to a café in the nearby town. Into the car the two of you would get, eventually, after you had taken an age to fuss around locating your coat and bag and he had hung around at the front door waiting for you with what for him was a passable imitation of patience. You would laugh and joke as you settled into the front seat, soothing any tetchiness with practised ease. Then the car would slide off, my father driving the country roads at such a snail's pace that he was regularly overtaken by cyclists, while you blethered beside him, blissfully secure in his company. After he died you said wonderingly that you could not believe he had gone without you, since you had assumed you would both expire together in a car crash on the way to that café. At the speed Dad was driving, this was possibly the least likely joint-death scenario you could have devised.

Once the car was parked, he would march up the town's steep underpass, his 'mountain' as he called it, for the exercise the doctor had ordered, with you on his arm. Then the pair of you would settle at a table in the central precinct – in the open air so that he could smoke – and sip tea and coffee as the world wandered by. A motley collection of local figures began joining you, among whom Dad held court, puffing thoughtfully on his pipe.

You were in your element at his side. Your stories wandered with impunity in this company. You basked in the attentions of an undemanding audience and the reassuring nearness of my father. And, most importantly, this excursion gave a purpose and focus to your day that helped counter the feelings of lostness. You felt you were tending to him, while he was in reality quietly looking out for you. He knew you were at a loss in the house while he was closeted in the study. He understood the comfort you felt in being with him.

You, on the other hand, did not sense what was happening at precisely the same time to him. You did not notice, as once you certainly would have, when he began to show signs of a different kind of weakness. It escaped your attention that it was becoming difficult again for him to climb his mountain. You were not aware of the way his favourite tweed jacket was starting to hang off him as he sat, chin cupped in his right hand, pipe and ashtray at the ready by his left, contemplating the passing scene.

This is how he is sitting the day I walk around the corner and am shaken by a gust of both happiness and loss, each emotion chasing the other, as I catch sight of your group in the distance.

From here I can see the tweedy deerstalker my father has taken to wearing in the chill breezes. I can tell at a glance how many members of what he calls 'the Club' (chairman: M. Magnusson) have braved the elements to join the table. You are next to him as usual, chic in the creamy woollen Icelandic coat he bought for you many moons ago on a trip to the homeland. You are leaning towards him, laughing. Even from this distance I can see your head flung back, mouth wide with an uninhibited merriment that makes me want to laugh with you.

I linger on my corner, drinking in the scene, the sight of my parents together, happy and, from a distance, whole.

And yet I know. Of course I know. At the very moment the happiness bubbles into my throat, I know it is about to end.

*

Despite the sheen with which memory has burnished those two years, your dementia did progress. You were often list-less, your get-up-and-go, as you complained mournfully, having determinedly got up and gone. Instead, your energy was directed into angry outbursts against your bewildered twin. You became easily frustrated and quickly agitated. All of a sudden, out of nothing it seemed, you would become 'het up', as if stoked in a furnace of irritation.

It came out as a rash on your skin. Itching built up in the course of the day, until your back, arms, chest and scalp were a mass of red blotches that creams were powerless to clear up. You scratched and scratched, clawing at your head and tearing at your arms until they bled.

After returning from the café, my father would head off to write or read in seclusion and the itch would hot up as the afternoon crowded in on you with its unformed worries and nameless agitations. The more you scratched, the more bothered you became about how much Anna was annoying you with her whirring vacuum cleaner and her fussing over domestic details in which you no longer took even the most perfunctory interest. And the more she annoyed you, the more the two of you argued.

Many a day one or other of us would call in to find the household sagging with misery and at the same time electric with tension. Like many relatives in her situation, Anna could not help arguing. She was not to know that dementia causes a progressive lowering of the stress threshold. You having been quite the least stressed person any of us had ever known, it took a leap of imagination for her to grasp that a little-understood brain disease was making you overreact to what the experts call 'stress stimuli' – a noisy vacuum cleaner, a feeling of constraint, your wishes being resisted, a loss of control – by becoming agitated and at times verbally aggressive.

For your children, popping in and out, it was easy enough to soothe these anxieties and redirect your latest obsession with a quip, but Anna, on hand all the time, was quite unable to stop herself correcting you and becoming upset in turn. While she was in constant despair at how difficult you were becoming, you in turn would be clutching at your fiery skin and complaining vociferously about her. Increasingly we sisters had to place ourselves in the middle and find the words to calm and divert.

Anna phoned Topsy one day to say she had had to lock the door to prevent you storming out and now you wouldn't stop shouting at her. Topsy raced over to find you wild-eyed and red-faced. She sat you down under a pool of light in the kitchen and made you a cup of tea and toast spread with banana. You took a bite of toast and a sip of tea while she sat opposite, leaning close in, holding your hand and talking and making you laugh. Suddenly the cloud went and you were back again, eating ravenously, turbulence soothed.

Toast and tea, Mum. The family comforter. You used to do the same for Topsy when she was young, filling the kettle and sitting her down and smoothing away her fears and worries. Now she was being regularly summoned from her flat in Glasgow to offer back to you that same capacity to make the world right again.

Another morning, a Saturday, she answered a plea from Dad: 'Can you come over? Your mother is upset and fretful and she's asking for you.'

She cycled over, enticed you out of bed and made your day harmonious. As she left to go back in the evening, you said to her, 'You know, you're the strongest person, the most comforting person, I've ever met in my life.'

Who was the parent and who the child here? 'It was so entirely the reversal of how things used to be that I felt quite disorientated,' my sister says. 'Everything had flipped.'

Of course it hardly takes a parent with dementia to sow confusion in a middle-aged soul. Many of us are pinched so hard between two generations that we have trouble locating an identity of our own anyway. Perhaps dementia only intensifies the inevitable process of becoming a parent to the person who used to parent us.

I suspect the real problem for my sisters and me at this time was that we simply did not expect, and could not bear, that Shakespeare's vision of the last stage of life

– 'second childishness and mere oblivion' – should have started to apply to someone as strong and vital and young at heart as you.

*

My father said he began falling for you the moment he read what you had written about the opening of the Edinburgh Festival. The piece started, so he said, something like 'So-and-so the Polish violinist was in the middle of such-and-such a concerto when the rain started. He put his violin away in its case, shut the lid and walked back to his digs. The 1953 Edinburgh International Festival had begun.'

I have never managed to locate this article, which seems to have evaded your joint cuttings collection. Recently I waded through old *Express* files on microfiche in the public library to look for it, without success, although I was in a hurry and there were so many stories packed into every page that I may have missed it. Perhaps I was subconsciously not trying very hard, since I suspect my father's memory may have gilded the genius of the piece and I would rather not be disappointed. But its effect on him was real enough.

He described it to me the day I at last managed to tie him to my cassette recorder at the beginning of the 1990s. I had already collected your memories, but he was proving harder work. I was beginning to despair of enticing anything very personal, when suddenly we reached 1953 and he turned instantly, dreamily voluble.

'I was so struck by Mamie's sheer effortless brilliance and lucidity and compassion, all mixed up into one,' he said, gazing out of the study window with a faraway look most unlike him. 'This way of seeing the festival in terms of human beings and not the arty-farty nonsense that most people were writing at the time. I was terribly taken with it.'

'What was she like at that time?' I asked.

I find myself reading my transcription of his answer now with a kind of longing. Yes, this is you, Mum. This is how I remember you, too.

'Oh, immensely dishy,' he was saying. 'She had a wonderful freshness about her, an open, merry, gleeful way of looking at life. She never took herself seriously – or indeed us, which was a good thing. I liked her eyes, always open, and the way her nose crinkled when she laughed.'

He laughed himself, took a brief suck at his pipe. I was sitting on the windowsill beside him, willing him to continue.

'Also it was the first time I had met a girl who was actually working, who wasn't a hothouse Oxford plant. Although Mamie was so marvellously unworldly in so many ways, she had been earning her living for some time. If she had a job to do she would say, "All right, sorry, I've got to be off." I admired that.'

He was into his stride now, still gazing off into middle distance. I had never heard him talking like this before.

'She was the externalisation, also, of the tremendous love-affair I was starting with journalism. I suddenly discovered what a marvellous thing it was to do. It just got into my blood, and after that festival I asked for a job on the paper full-time. It was a mixture of wanting to be near this wonderful creature, who wrote like an angel and looked like one too, and also wanting to be a journalist. She was the muse, the goddess of journalism, and I had become a devotee of both.'

He really did talk like this, my dad, didn't he? Talked the way he wrote.

'I think that by the end of the festival I had already decided to marry her.'

His reminiscing flagged a bit after that and he began to look meaningfully across the room at his computer.

'I'm afraid I don't have a very good memory,' he sighed, which is ironic, all things considered. 'I do remember her coat, which was bluey-grey, very loose, tucked in with a belt and big collar. She always looked terribly cuddly in that. And she had the most marvellous legs.'

There, Mum, I thought you would like that. Not, as I write, that you are exactly sure who Magnus is any longer, although you smile at the name. But I think our attempts to evoke him still make you feel comfortable and peaceful in some deep way that is beyond words and certainly beyond what we normally think of as memory.

*

What did it feel like to be you, in those last months of sharing your life with him? Although you resisted every attempt to discuss it and hotly denied that anything was amiss, you must have known your mind was not as it should be.

I found a clue in a Dick Francis paperback you left on your bedside table. You had lost interest in reading and we were trying to encourage you with easy novels. This one showed no sign of having been read, but on the inside cover and continuing across the flyleaf containing the author's biographical note, you had written the words of a poem.

I was shocked at first to see that you had defaced a book, even a cheap paperback: unspeakable sacrilege in a house where books were revered. But your graffiti moved me to tears. Not so much because it was evidence of further slippage in your brain, although that gave me a jolt, but because of the words themselves. They were scrawled in short lines of capitals, the letters you were now most comfortable forming. And, although I could see at once that the line-breaks were in the wrong place, the words themselves, no doubt committed to memory in the English class at Rutherglen Academy, were better than any you would have found printed between the leaves of this particular book:

I WANDERED, LONELY AS A CLOUD
THAT FLOATS ON HIGH
O'ER VALES AND HILLS

WHEN ALL AT ONCE
I SAW A CROWD –
A HOST OF GOLDEN DAFFODILS
BESIDE THE LAKE BENEATH
THE TREES,
FLUTTERING AND DANCING
IN THE BREEZE
THE WAVES BESIDE THEM
DANCED, BUT THEY OUTDID
THE CHATTERING WAVES
WITH GLEE,
A POET COULD NOT BUT
BE GAY, IN SUCH A JOCUND
COMPANY
I GAZED AND GAZED BUT
LITTLE THOUGHT
WHAT WEALTH THE SHOW TO ME
HAD BROUGHT.
FOR OFT WHEN ON MY
COUCH I LIE
IN VACANT OR IN PENSIVE MOOD
THEY FLASH UPON THAT
INWARD EYE
THAT IS THE BLISS OF SOLITUDE
AND THEN MY HEART WITH PLEASURE FILLS
AND DANCES WITH
THE DAFFODILS.

You hadn't recalled the correct adjective for Wordsworth's 'sparkling' waves: 'chattering', you thought. But you were very nearly there. As you lay in bed in the dim hours of the early morning you must have been working your mind. You were trying to hold on to memory.

Much later I picked up the book to read myself one idle afternoon. A slip of folded paper fell out, and my throat caught again at the sight of it. You had captured there, in the same untidy capitals, a rather less poetic piece from your speech-making days:

LADLES AND JELLYSPOONS, NAILS AND SCREWNAILS – I STAND UPON THIS SPEECH TO MAKE A PLATFORM. I'M HERE TONIGHT BECAUSE I CAN'T BE HERE TOMORROW NIGHT. AND THE FIRST SONG IS A DANCE.

You may have insisted nothing was wrong, but here again was the evidence that you were hanging on for dear life, scrabbling for memory before it went.

Although my father knew you were struggling, he remained reluctant to bestow solidity on the monster by giving it a name. There were only hints and unspoken understandings. Once he took me aside to ask if I could buy you a dress to wear to a posh function. At the official dinners to which he was forever being invited, as chair of Scottish Natural Heritage or chancellor of Glasgow Caledonian University or patron of this charity or that, you had always been an asset. You could talk to anyone, remember the names of acquaintances he had forgotten, remind him surreptitiously of the punchline to any joke upon which he had recklessly embarked and be relied upon to start up a song if the table needed enlivening. Although you never had more than a functional interest in clothes, you knew what suited your rangy figure and kept it simple. You always made the effort and he was proud of you.

Now he said there was a dinner coming up at which you would be, just a little, on show. I remember how hesitantly he said this. At the time I was too obtuse, too busy, or perhaps too afraid of peering under a scab he was clearly keen not to open, to say more than: 'Yes, of course I will.'

How long had he been worrying about you on those public occasions? How long had he been quietly rescuing you from conversations in which you had lost your way? And when did he start noticing that you had not bought yourself anything new at all for a very long time?

Tempting you out shopping was a trial. You could not be bothered, did not see the point and were not even impressed when I told you we were doing this for Dad, which normally did the trick. Still, I propelled you to the shops at last and we bought a floaty summer dress in which you looked fantastic. I was the one who made you try it on but it was you who chose it in the end. You still knew what you liked and you could never abide granny clothes.

When the night of the dinner came around, Topsy and I laid everything out for you on your bed, made sure you did not forget your lipstick and led you downstairs like a bride. Dad was waiting for you at the bottom. He beamed when he saw you.

That summer, July 2006, we all spent a few days in Iceland. 'Unforgettable' days I was going to write, before I remembered that this is one of the most useless words in the language and that anything can be forgotten, even, as you know, that holiday, the last occasion our whole family was together on this earth.

You and Dad, with your children and our partners and offspring, joined a mass pilgrimage to the old estate of Laxamýri in the north, which my grandmother Ingibjörg's branch of the clan had owned long ago. It was the kind of hearty reunion in which Icelanders specialise, bringing together scores of relatives whose common ancestors had once lived and toiled on this fertile stretch of farmland.

My father revelled in his role as clan patriarch. He looked thin and not very robust but immoderately joyful to be here where his family story began. Radiant with satisfaction, he walked along the lupin-fringed path to the waterfalls in the company of nine jostling grandchildren and 160 assorted kinsfolk, pointing out the harlequin ducks in their exotic plumage and the blue mountains still laced with snow.

Six months before you were parted, that is how I like to remember the two of you: Magnus the saga man, squinting into the sun on a summer's afternoon on the farmlands of Laxamýri, with a breeze ruffling his hair and you at his side, happy.

11

O' Mice and Men

Robert Burns, 'To a Mouse'

There is no way of opening up a living brain to study Alzheimer's disease. Which is why every question I ask of the scientists who are trying to figure out where and why memories go, and how we stop it happening, seems to lead in the end to mice. Possible cures, hopeful stabs at vaccines, the latest theory for which someone somewhere has managed to land a research grant – sooner or later they all have to be tried out on a mouse.

My father used to call us children his 'mice', which has long given me fond, sisterly feelings for the species. As you know, Mum, if I had to wish dementia on any living creature it would emphatically not be a mouse. But sometimes needs must.

In the natural course of life mice don't get Alzheimer's, but they can be genetically engineered to develop a disease similar to it and lose their memory. Among their more promising research activities has been aiding the development of a vaccine, testing out a decoy drug and drinking vast quantities of coffee.

First it had to be established that mice do have a memory. In the 1980s neurologist Professor Richard Morris devised an ingenious water-maze that has since been used in thousands of experiments. A mouse is slipped into a round, high-sided pool of milky water which contains an escape platform hidden a few millimetres below the surface and a number of clearly visible clues, such as coloured shapes. The mouse swims around looking for a way out, until it locates the platform and scrambles to freedom. Every subsequent time it is put in the pool the mouse finds its way out more quickly, which suggests it has learned and remembered where the hidden platform is relative to the visual cues. After enough practice it will swim from any release point straight to the platform.

Richard Morris showed that this mouse is using spatial memory located in the hippocampus, the area vital for making new memories and one of the first to be affected in Alzheimer's.

Through genetic selection mice can be bred to produce too much amyloid and tau, until there are enough of them with bad memories to experiment with. Those are then given the water-maze test before and after receiving treatment and the effect on their memory measured.

In the 1990s a group of these mice were immunised with injections of beta-amyloid at the age of six weeks. At 13 months all their amyloid deposits had gone, while the brains of untreated mice were still littered with them. Unfortunately the first trial of this vaccine on humans had to be stopped in 2002, when several people trying out the vaccine developed brain inflammation. Scientists are still trying to develop a human vaccine that will avoid this dangerous reaction.

Attacking an earlier stage in the disease process, researchers in St Andrews and Kansas universities have given another set of mice a protein they believe can block the degeneration of a neuron from within by acting as a decoy for the amyloid inside a cell to attach to. After being injected with the decoy, the mice found their way to the hidden platform more easily than before.

In these experiments, and hundreds of others, the fightback against dementia around the world is advancing. At the neurological level it really is like a war, conducted around a three-pronged defence of the neuron. Right inside the cell is the move to protect weak targets. Outside the cell is the battle to stop or reverse the formation of toxic amyloid once it reaches that point. Then, disappointingly far from the real action, are the drugs currently on the market that aim to protect the function of those cells that are left as damage is wreaked around them. This last is the weakest flank, but it does have the honour of being the only one currently on the battlefield at all.

Meanwhile caffeine has joined the field. Researchers in Florida gave a group of elderly mice with impaired memories the equivalent of two cups of coffee in their drinking water every day – also equivalent to fourteen cups of tea or twenty soft drinks – while a control group received their water neat. When the mice were tested again after two months, those which had been given the caffeine performed as well on memory tests and a mousey version of 'thinking skills' as mice of the same age without dementia. Those on plain water continued to do poorly. During autopsy the brains of the mice given caffeine showed almost a 50% reduction in levels of beta-amyloid. The caffeine also appeared to suppress inflammatory changes that may be implicated in the over-production of amyloid.

The million-dollar question in all these trials is whether the same effect would be seen in humans. In Florida a team has been monitoring a group of over-sixty-five-year-olds in Tampa and Miami who already suffered mild cognitive impairment, a condition normally expected to lead to full-blown Alzheimer's in about 15% of cases. Every one of those with higher blood caffeine levels reportedly avoided the onset of Alzheimer's disease during the years they were being observed.

There is still too much the scientists don't know here for immoderate excitement. Even so, as the great battle of the brain rages around us, anyone worrying about their own might do worse than raise an espresso or two to those gallant mice on the frontline.

12

A man himself must also die

Hávamál ('The Words of the High One')

Anna takes me aside one day in October 2006. She says, 'I think your dad's failing.' That word 'failing'. As soon as she says it I know he is going to die.

They call pancreatic cancer the silent killer because the symptoms are so often put down to something else. In the months since our return from Iceland he had been getting ever more thin and pinched, but we thought we knew why. On a filming trip to the remote island of St Kilda, he was thrown backwards in a motorboat and painfully damaged some ribs. The doctor prescribed paracetamol and stoicism: nothing to be done with ribs, he said. As usual, Dad made no complaint.

Now it is Anna who notices what has eluded his children, dropping in and out, always busy; Anna who spots what you, devoted but cloudy, attached but disengaged, have not. And the moment she puts her disquiet into words, I see too.

I suggest he consults a specialist, and my father agrees with such little demur that I realise he too must have started to wonder. It feels odd to be colluding to sort out his health without you.

You join us at the hospital, though, to receive the results of his scan: a probable tumour in the pancreas with likely spread to the liver. It is 'worrying', says the consultant behind the desk, choosing his words with care. My father sits with hands folded, looking, all of a sudden, very small. He is listening intently. Perhaps his heart is thudding, like mine. Perhaps he too is feeling sick. This is the worst it could be.

'So I'm riddled with the damn things,' he observes pleasantly.

He bares his arms for blood tests – 'tumour-spotting'. How could I not have noticed how angular they had become? His wedding ring hangs loose on his finger.

You are sitting beside him, saying little. Not understanding when the doctor says essential fatty acids might be good to boost his system, you leap in to protest that you would never dream of giving him fatty foods. The doctor nods politely.

After the consultation I collect the car and drive to the hospital entrance. You are waiting together at an outside table. Dad is in his raincoat the colour of milky tea, staring straight ahead. He looks unutterably bleak. You spring across to the car and hold the door open for him. A spasm of irritation crosses his face.

'See,' he says to me, *sotto voce*, 'the kid gloves are out already.'

'I heard that,' you say, settling yourself in the back seat.

'What did you hear?'

You're laughing. 'I know what you said.'

And he laughs, too. You two were always able to make each other laugh.

Back at your house, I go and perch on my favourite spot on the radiator in the study, next to his leather armchair.

'I don't want to be treated with kid gloves,' he repeats. 'I just want to carry on as normally as I can.'

He sits there. Just sits there. What else do you do when you have just been told your life is ending?

Looking straight ahead, I say to him, 'You knew, didn't you?'

'Yes, I knew.'

'Because of how you were feeling?'

'Well, you get to know your own body. And as Thor said, you can't fart against thunder.'

'Did Thor really say that?'

He laughs. 'Well, I may have embellished that one.'

Next day I compile a press statement for him. He has had to cancel an appearance at the Cheltenham Literature Festival to talk about his latest book, *Fakers, Forgers and Phoneys,* and the Gloucestershire news service has released a story on the wires referring to a 'critical medical emergency', which has had the phone ringing all morning. I write something to the effect that broadcaster Magnus Magnusson has had to cancel his immediate appointments because of a recent diagnosis of cancer. 'He is currently undergoing tests and is in good fettle.'

Dad murmurs, 'Yes, good fettle, I like that.'

'I had hoped you might have had a little longer to absorb it all.'

'Oh, I've absorbed it. I absorbed it right away. It's shit. Then you have to get on with it.'

I love him.

The papers next day are full of 'Magnus Magnusson has cancer' stories and the phone hardly stops. 'Who needs counsellors when you've got friends?' Dad muses. He is warmed and touched by the outpouring of public and private affection. And he really is in good fettle this evening, full of fun and calling for music. Jon and Topsy, the family pianists, are both here to bash out Scottish ballads and Icelandic drinking songs. You, in turn, catch his mood. Out comes your mouth organ, its jaunty whine the accompaniment to every family ceilidh.

A day or two later he goes into hospital for the tests. His hair has been freshly cut at the barber's and is neat and silvery smooth. He has forgotten to have his eyebrows trimmed and they beetle over his eyes like sunshades. When I bring you in to visit him, he is waiting for us in the foyer in his tweed jacket bearing a yellow badge from the previous week's seventy-seventh birthday proclaiming 'Best Grandad in the World Ever'.

He takes us to his four-bedded ward, which is otherwise empty, and eases himself into an armchair, while I sit on his bed reading a newspaper. You perch for a minute at a little table, but you can't keep still. You keep getting up and fluttering around to check that his pyjamas are in the drawer and his bed covers straight. I look at him out of the corner of my eye for his reaction, but your dementia-induced tendency to fuss over nothing shows no signs of riling him today.

Later he and I are standing in front of the window, and he tells me he is looking forward to the spring.

'Everything always feels better in the spring.'

I am convinced he will never see the spring, and I wonder if he suspects it too. And yet, if only he could. One more spring with the curlews calling and the breeze rippling through the mighty pine tree in the garden. Just one more spring.

*

The Saturday after you met he came through from Edinburgh as promised. You were waiting for him at the station in Glasgow. He was dressed in a pin-striped suit, the one his parents had bought him for his twenty-first birthday, and a shirt with an immaculate stiff white collar. He was carrying the rolled-up umbrella again and his pair of yellow pigskin gloves. His hair was beautifully combed. He managed to maintain this unruffled air even when you revealed you had planned a bracing five-mile hike in the country.

You walked him up the muddy slopes of Cathkin Braes in his polished shoes. When it started to rain you asked him why he didn't put his umbrella up, which forced him to admit it was full of holes, a mere front to keep up the dandyish Oxford image. You laughed, he said later, but kindly, trying not to embarrass him.

Afterwards you took him home to tea at Milrig Road, well aware that if your ferociously protective father had been alive this dashing suitor, a foreigner to boot, would never have been allowed across the doorstep. Still, you thought your father would have been impressed by his education and good manners. Your mother was so used to your bringing boyfriends home to tea and nothing ever coming of it that she didn't take much notice.

Before this your most intense romantic involvement had been a passionate holiday fling with a young Austrian courier; since then you had fended off a number of enamoured reporters and were currently seeing a six-foot quality engineer you had met at the Plaza Ballroom. You had gone dancing with a group of girls from the office in your sleeveless nylon dress. The engineer, a member of the Communist Party, invited you to dance and had been taking you out to the pictures ever since. When you told him you had met someone else, he burst out that he had been working up to asking you to marry him and was just waiting to be sure. You pointed out somewhat heartlessly that he had waited a bit too long.

Your mother took Magnus in her stride. He in turn appreciated the lack of pretension in Milrig Road, even if it meant, come Hogmanay, that his beer was served in a jam jar, which would have given his own mother a fit. Ingibjörg, later to become my other adored grandmother, had gone to a renowned 'finishing' school in Denmark, where she learned the elegant home touches with which Magnus had grown up. The only time he annoyed you in those early months was when he suggested packing you off to the same college for a quick course in the household arts. Perhaps the jam jar had hit home, after all.

'No way was I going to any school in Denmark,' you reported, with some heat. 'I said I wouldn't even go to a housekeeping school here, never mind in Copenhagen.'

You were the first to agree that if you had acquiesced in this suggestion you might not subsequently have thought it such a good idea to spread the icing on my first birthday cake before placing it in the oven. Nor would your daughters have been sent into the world better able to turn a limerick than an omelette. But you preferred to look on the bright side of your many culinary catastrophes: they kept you in copy for years.

Anyway, Magnus gave up on the finishing-school idea and the pair of you remained thoroughly smitten.

'He was a great hit with my family,' you said. 'He had a lovely mixture of seriousness and a sense of humour. In some ways he seemed older than me, though he was four years younger, and much more worldly, despite my being a working girl. He had an air of having been around. Oh, I just fell hook, line and sinker.'

You were cautious, though.

'I thought I mustn't let myself get too involved: he's younger than me, he's foreign and our backgrounds are so totally different. Here was I, a working-class girl living in a council house and helping to keep my mother. And here was he. Although he never played it up, his father was consul-general for Iceland, he lived in a big detached house in Edinburgh, he had been at a fee-paying school and then Oxford, and he had even got himself engaged to Princess Astrid of Norway. He didn't have a job. He was supposed to be still doing his BLitt and I was determined that he wouldn't interrupt his education for me. Whatever way you looked at it, it was just no good.'

For his part, Magnus had no qualms whatsoever and set about disposing of yours. He announced that he had made up his mind and would not be returning to university. He managed to talk himself on to the staff of the *Express* in Edinburgh and eventually engineered a transfer to Glasgow. You found him digs near Milrig Road, and he sauntered over every evening for a meal cooked by your mother.

He took you to meet his own parents. His father was disappointed that he had abandoned an academic path that could have led to a professorship in Iceland and his mother was still smarting, just a little, about the princess. It was plain they both thought their golden boy could do better, although Ingibjörg was always kind and you won over even the gruff Sigursteinn in the end.

Magnus himself had not an ounce of snobbery in his make-up. Talking about him at the kitchen table all those years ago, you looked for a moment as misty-eyed as he did when he talked about you.

'He had this mixture of youthful enthusiasm, your dad, almost childish at times, so sure of himself that he would rush in where angels feared to tread, and at the same time he was tremendously mature and could speak to all sorts of people of all ages. I loved his openness with people. He never stood on ceremony with anyone. His weaknesses and his strengths were almost the same thing. He never did anything in moderation, whether it was drinking, eating, working, having a good time, being serious or being generous. He went at life with everything he had, as he still does.'

You were engaged by December and fixed the wedding for June.

*

Dad and I hold a competition to see who can spell 'diarrhoea'. There has been such a lot of it that we feel we ought to know. He wins with only one letter wrong. Four weeks on, the cancer is showing no sign of retreat. He has begun a course of chemotherapy, which we are warned will not be 'curative' but may give him a small hope of remission. His medication stands sentinel on no fewer than four shelves of his study, below the Penguin Classics, above his spare tobacco, and he is finding it hard to remember times and dosages.

Anna knows the medication off by heart, but you will not let her near him. I see now that you must have felt jealous of her ability to minister to Magnus's everyday needs in a way you so badly wanted to yourself but simply could not. The advancing invasion of your brain was interfering with your ability to think through and execute the simplest tasks. It must have felt inexpressibly frustrating. You fussed and interfered, but were of no practical use. This added to Dad's nursing a tension the rest of us could have done without. You could not grasp how vital it was that he received the right number of pills at the right time from somebody. Topsy or I had to make sure we were on hand every day.

Soon the oncologist tells us the disease is progressing. Dad is weary, sinking a little each day. All he can eat is poached egg. His eyes seem the biggest thing about him now, huge in his face. His skin hangs in loose folds around his neck. But these eyes, when he is listening intently, still sparkle with fun and interest and intelligence.

One day, while waiting at the hospital for a bed in which to receive his latest shot of chemo, he and I wander out to the smoking shelter. Rain is driving against the glass. What a desolate place it is, with the water creeping in and wind hurtling through and fag-ends littering the floor. There is one seat, which a man courteously gives up. There my father sits with his raincoat around his shoulders, tweed jacket open as always, trying to light his pipe. The lighter splutters in the draught, so he tries holding it under his jacket. I create a wind-shield on the other side with my hands clad in his gloves (real Vikings, I am led to believe, do not wear gloves) and he gets the pipe going at last.

As he smokes I ask what he hates most about all this.

'The indignity.'

I suppose he means the indignity of hearing his bowel movements endlessly discussed. Of wearing pads. Losing control. Not being able to walk where he wants or climb his mountain to the café. His precious MacBook Pro being commandeered by a daughter he fears will wipe his latest opus while attempting to answer his emails. His life being run for him. The daily regimen of pills. Hospitals. Symptoms. Being asked how he feels. Having to stay seated now in a forlorn smoking shelter while I stand.

And yet in what he calls indignity I see only dignity. Feeling a little self-conscious, I blurt out: 'You've taught me so much about grace.'

He looks baffled. 'Who's Grace?'

'Your grace,' I mumble, embarrassed. Now I sound as if I'm addressing the Archbishop of Canterbury.

He shrugs it off. Says nothing. Draws on his pipe.

I watch him later as he waits to see the consultant, one wasted figure in the midst of a quiet mass of illness: people without hair or leaning on sticks, people drained of colour, waiting. He sits with his legs neatly crossed, clad in baggy black sweatsuit trousers, hands clasped in his lap. He is lost

in himself, eyes in some far place, so composed that I want
to weep.

While he is having the chemicals pumped into his arm, I
take you down the road for a cup of tea. You drop your
butter, spill your tea, tell stories and enjoy yourself hugely.
Just as during his previous illness, your disengagement
from the full medical picture is enabling you to remain
cheerful. But this time it feels strange and unnerving. Your
husband is dying and you have no idea.

*

> *My dearest, my darling Mamie*
>
> *I've been looking forward to this moment all
> day, when I draw the curtains in my room, turn
> on the reading lamps, enclose myself in the
> privacy of my communion with you. The house
> is (or should be) asleep. Nothing stirs, nothing
> disturbs. Only, far far away, a train – a frequent
> visitor. And even further away, you, my sweet-
> heart, asleep. But you are very much with me in
> here, in this room and in me.*
>
> *I do not need to close my eyes to see your eyes
> – your lovely, lovely laughing eyes, shining with
> your love.*

A letter from an ardent twenty-four-year-old plighting his
troth. He wrote it on ten sides of thin white paper and

posted it from Edinburgh to 53 Milrig Road, Rutherglen, on 9 December 1953.

> *All my life, Mamie, I shall love you with all the*
> *strength and feeling I possess – and, loving, recreate*
> *strength and feeling that I may love you even more.*
> *Your happiness will be my happiness (I never used to*
> *believe that word meant anything). Ahead of me I see*
> *– fulfilment. And I know now, as you also know, that*
> *our means to fulfilment lies in each other.*

Ahead lay much else he didn't see right then. Ahead, too, was dementia, with its insidious losses and the inexorable retreat of so much that made you the laughing, carefree girl to whom he pledged his eager heart. But you knew that heart and he knew yours.

Magnus's wallet didn't stretch to an engagement ring. In 1994 he presented you with a ruby one instead on your fortieth anniversary. You wear it still, beside the slim gold band inscribed with the date 30-6-54.

*

It is a mid-afternoon in December. The log-fire is crackling and the lamps are on as the light outside seeps away. The room comes into its own at these times, all gold and mellow. Dad loves it. He is sleeping on the couch here at night now because he cannot manage the stairs to the bedroom; one of us siblings bunks down nearby to be on hand. The other night you slept on the floor beside him on a mattress yourself. Dad complained fondly of 'a lot of footering and pottering', but I think he liked having you there.

Out of the blue he turns to me now and says: 'Isn't life great?'

At first I don't realise what he is getting at.

'I suppose life might be greater if you felt better.'

'I feel all right,' he says. 'All right. Just very tired. And my legs don't work very well.'

It took me a while to understand that living itself was what my father wanted to celebrate. He never wondered aloud about what dying might be like or showed any interest in organising his affairs or planning a funeral. Death, I began to see, was a no-go area for him, a bit like dementia.

Icelandic saga heroes are not much given to self-expression. Only in one paragraph of one saga does a character express a softer emotion. My father, who began translating them from Old Norse into English in the 1960s, loved the spare lyricism of the moment when the outlawed Gunnar Hámundarson in *Njál's Saga* realises that he cannot bring himself to leave Iceland and his beloved farm, although staying must cost him his life. As he rides away towards exile, his horse stumbles, forcing him to leap off. In that moment Gunnar glances back towards the farm on the slopes of Hlíðarendi, and knows he cannot go.

'How lovely the hillside is,' he murmurs to his brother.

'More lovely than it has ever seemed to me before, with its golden cornfields and new-mown hay. I am going back home.'

Rather than dwelling on death, my father marvelled, like Gunnar, at the wonders of life: the dance of sun and shadow on the Campsie Fells, the lethal swoop of a sparrowhawk, the smell of wood-smoke on a damp afternoon, the wind pouring through the trees outside his window. With his head bowed in fatigue, he could still breathe the words, 'Isn't life great?'

Life was what had always mattered to him. One of the poems closest to his heart was from *Hávamál*, a collection of Norse sayings from the Viking age, supposedly those of Óðinn, chief god of the pantheon:

> *Cattle die,*
> *kinsmen die,*
> *a man himself must one day die;*
> *But one thing never dies –*
> *Word-fame, if truly earned.*

Word-fame. A man's reputation. The only form of immortality in which he truly believed.

*

That first Christmas Eve, before joining the rest of his family for the traditional celebration, he lit a single candle for you in his bedroom and put your presents to him around it as if it were your own little tree, yours and his.

He had always loved the Icelandic Christmas Eve. Scots at the time underplayed the festival, but his parents had always insisted on the full Scandinavian glitz. Magnus adored the sensuous theatricality of it: the swish of his sisters' long dresses and the scent of his mother's perfume, the carols sung around a tree flaming with candles against a dark window, the gorgeously presented meal and leisurely haze of cigar smoke.

You embraced the tradition with as much aplomb as you did the rest of his Icelandic heritage. As you pointed out in a talk, it hadn't taken you long to realise that a real live Icelander was a force to be reckoned with:

> You might find yourself married to an English-
> man or a Norwegian or a Frenchman who had
> spent all his life in this country and hardly notice
> the difference. But when an Icelander has
> breathed his first life-giving gulps of air straight
> from the glacier peaks of his own mountains, he
> is a marked man for the rest of his life. Wherever
> he goes, whatever he does, he is first and fore-
> most an Icelander. He thinks Icelandic. He feels
> Icelandic. He acts Icelandic. He is fiercely
> nationalistic, hopelessly sentimental about his
> country's past, inordinately proud of its inde-
> pendence, protective of its rights, and given to

frequent bouts of hopping on the first plane to
Reykjavík to recharge his batteries with fresh
supplies of mountain air and large doses of
conversation in his native tongue.

In this speech you described your first visit to Iceland in
1955, the year after your wedding, and the culture that
awaited you: the food ('every kind of fish I'd ever heard
of and many I hadn't', your favourite being *harðfisk*,
'dried fish which looks like an old loofah but tastes deli-
cious'), the duvets made from the fine down of local eider
ducks, the cheap central heating straight from the boiling
earth, the hot springs and volcanoes, the no-tipping rule
in taxis, the no-dogs rule in Reykajvík, the high propor-
tion of home ownership, the ubiquitous love of literature
and the fact, as you put it (with a sense of humour dangerously near the edge where your husband's reverence for
the sagas was concerned), that 'the place is lousy with
poets, all descended from men who would stop in the
middle of hacking somebody's leg off or cleaving a chap
from head to toe in order to, as the sagas say, "utter a
verse".'

At home you entered gaily into the Christmas Eve rites,
never carrying it off with the formal grace of your mother-
in-law but keeping the tradition breezily intact for us.
Magnus always led the singing of carols, the carving of the
turkey and the dispensing of presents, just as his own father
used to do.

This Christmas Eve it is the same ritual that carries us through.

We dress up to the nines for him, we cook, we murder 'Silent Night' in Icelandic and go wild with the candles. He has insisted on struggling up the stairs to put on his dinner suit for 6.30 p.m. sharp as usual, but it is such an effort that on his return he almost collapses on to the sofa beside the tree, and sits there with his eyes shut, the log-fire darting at his feet. When I stroke his back and shoulders I can feel every bone.

He says we should go into the other room and have the meal without him and you insist on staying beside him. The rest of us troop off obediently to give Christmas dinner our best shot without either of you. But no sooner has my brother-in-law begun carving the turkey than the door suddenly opens and there you are, the pair of you, walking slowly in together, arm in arm. Dad seizes the knife and regales us with the old joke his father intoned solemnly every Christmas before him. 'Can anyone tell me, by the merest chance, how a carving knife travels?' As tradition dictates, no-one knows the answer. Neither, it transpires, does he tonight. Punchlines were never his forte.

He sits with us throughout the meal. He cannot eat and says little, but his eyes glitter with pleasure. He stays for the exchange of presents, exclaiming in delight at the calendar Topsy has made of Laxamýri photographs from our summer expedition, revelling in the attentions of his immaculately groomed and preternaturally well-behaved grandchildren and even joining in the singing of a last few carols. Perhaps because we expected so little and certainly because he led the way, it was the happiest of Christmases.

This, I thought that night, is what it is to live. This is what it means to experience joy: to will it, taste it and be grateful for it. We cannot beat death itself, but here perhaps is the way to trounce the miserable business of dying.

And perhaps it is the same for dementia. Our only hope of not being defeated by this disease may be to learn to tilt with willed joy at a different kind of dying. That is what my father taught us on his last Christmas Eve.

*

On New Year's Day our bouncy blonde district nurse arrives to find that his blood sugar has dropped dramatically. She calls out the paramedics to administer glucose. She also notices a sudden change in his colour, a sign, she says, that he could be nearing the end.

I decide it is time to take you aside and explain, as gently as I can, that Dad does not have long to live. You react with a flare of anger that shakes me.

'How can you say your father is dying? I know he's seriously ill and it's going to be a long haul, but we're helping him through it.'

I gaze at you nonplussed. Then try again.

'Mum, I know it's a shock but you need to be prepared for this. It's what the nurses are telling us.'

Your voice rises in a howl of pain. 'You mustn't talk like that. Dying? DYING? That's a wicked thing to say. Your dad will be fine.'

That old optimistic verve of yours that had rallied us so effectively last time had come to this: an unshakeable, demented (forgive me, Mum, but I even said that word to myself) inability to grasp what was going on. All that made sense to you was the steady love to which you held fast when everything else was shifting, a love that insisted he could not die.

(Less than a week later you said to me: 'I feel such a fool. I had no idea. Everyone seems to have known except me.' And I tried to assure you that you were not a fool. Never that. You had just tried to will him through it as you always used to.)

When the nurse left that day, I called Margaret, who was on a post-Christmas break with her family. She caught the first plane back. Jon and his Australian partner Dale, soon to be his wife, had also arrived. All Dad's mice were here.

That evening, sitting on the hospital bed that had replaced the sofa by the fire, he was thinking of old times. He asked if I remembered the two old men who had lived next door to us in our first house in Garrowhill. One of their names was Bob, I said, and I could still see the brown leather mat over the table and almost smell the pipe smoke that filled the room. You chipped in to say they were brothers-in-law, the other one was called Jimmy and they grew tobacco in their back garden.

'One of them fell once and got his pipe stuck up his nose and it had to be surgically removed,' you remembered. Dad grinned. You could still make him laugh.

We had long talks that night until the murky dawn was almost upon us. We remembered the hilarious family newspaper Jon had started printing at the age of twelve. Jon went to his room and found a copy. Dad rocked with soundless mirth as I read out this precocious parody of the *Sun*. He took a sip of the enhanced protein drink we had foisted on him and offered us a taste. Jon said he had been waiting all week for his father to offer him a drink.

There followed a couple of golden days, bonus hours granted like injury time at the end of a hopeless match, which gave us the fleeting illusion that we might yet pull it off and win the game after all. Our father was energised. He felt strong enough to insist, all of a sudden, on a trip to the café, where the Club greeted him rapturously. He sat beside you in their midst, saying little and bundled in a blanket, but happy. When we got him home, all but carrying him from the car, he sank on to his bed and fell instantly asleep with a beatific smile on his face.

And then, just as suddenly, the pain came. He was in an agony that only massive injections of diamorphine could ameliorate. The responsibility of nursing him at home ourselves, in his beloved room with the pine tree outside the window, began to weigh on us. Should we hustle him for safety into hospital or, better still, a hospice? But you were adamant: Magnus was going nowhere. And, trusting to your instincts if not your medical grasp, we took our lead from you again.

When the nurse asked if he had been feeling bad, Dad himself managed a wry 'Slight discomfort', which was one up from 'Bugger all wrong with me'. But his breathing was slowing. We spent the rest of the day sitting around his bed, the watchful silence broken only by the sigh of collapsing logs in the fireplace and your frequent requests for tea. You had a wistful 'Is there something I should know here?' aura about you. Ever since your violent reaction a few days ago, nobody had tried to explain again. But you must have grasped it in that room at last, as we sat around his prone form hour after hour, holding our breath with his as we waited to see if another would follow.

In the morning it seems to take ages to become light. Rain lashes the windows, while little grey fingers of light appear slowly over the fields in the distance. Dad has been stirring a little and keeps bringing his arm up to his face to peer at his watch. Topsy and I are blethering to him in a way that would normally drive him up the wall.

He is lying with his head propped on five pillows of uncertain vintage and a bizarre variety of hues, from bright orange to patterned navy. His hands with the long, elegant fingers are resting on his chest, slightly puffy now but soft and smooth. His broad forehead is warm to the kiss and his hair has gone flat with stroking. His eyebrows, I notice, are looking unwontedly neat. He must have had a trim when Margaret took him to the barber a couple of weeks ago.

He stretches out his arm and brings his wrist close to his eyes again. It is so like him to want to keep an eye on the time and a grip on the narrative. We sing him 'Sofðu Unga Ástin Mín' and I keep expecting him to raise a quizzical eyebrow, as if to ask the meaning of all this racket when a chap is trying to get a wink of sleep.

You have been sitting nearest him all day, stooping over to blow on his face if he seems hot, stroking his hand, dropping kisses on his forehead. Nothing will induce you to leave his side.

Fifty-three years ago, in the bedroom of a quiet house where nothing could be heard but the distant rattle of a train, he signed off his letter:

> One last long day-dream of your lovely face and
> form, one last recalling of the soft touch of your
> mouth and hand – and then goodnight.

Dementia has not stolen the soft touch of your mouth and hand. Not that.

His breath becomes light, light as air, a soft, pittery wisp of a thing that is barely there. And then it is not. You are holding his hand. You look stricken.

13

The Child is father of the Man

William Wordsworth, 'My Heart Leaps Up'

Cognitively my father had been ageing well. Catastrophe might have been approaching elsewhere, but there was no problem with his brain. In the year of his seventy-seventh birthday he was writing, lecturing and broadcasting as nimbly as ever. He gave every indication of enjoying (and it's exactly the right word) what is formally described as 'good cognitive ageing'.

But why him and not you? Why your twin sister and not you? Why the Queen and not Margaret Thatcher? Why anyone and why not anyone?

For something that happens to all of us, it really is remarkable how little is understood about the ageing brain.

This much we do know. Some people age well, others (a number with estimates as wide as between 5% and 20% of older people) develop 'mild cognitive impairment' and a third group of poor sods (between 10% and 15% of those in the second group) go on to develop dementia. Probe further, though, and we discover that not only are we a long way from finding out why, but the categories themselves cannot even be defined without a baffling circularity.

What, I ask one expert, is natural ageing?

'I would define normal cognitive ageing as that amount of decline in cognitive ageing that is not severe enough to make the criteria for mild cognitive impairment or dementia.'

Okay. So what is mild cognitive impairment? Ah, says the Alzheimer's Society, it's a decline in brain function 'greater than the gradual decline that many people experience as part of normal, healthy ageing'.

Um. Just remind me what normal, healthy ageing is again?

'Well,' says Ian Deary, director of the impressively named Centre for Cognitive Ageing and Cognitive Epidemiology at Edinburgh University, 'we are studying brain structure to find aspects associated with the amount of cognitive ageing. When we complete the current wave of testing we'll have the added advantage of being able to look at the changes in brain structure. These include brain atrophy, white matter lesions, white matter integrity, the thickness of the grey matter in the cortex, the amount of iron deposited and so on. To date, we've found that most of these features are associated with cognitive functioning. That gives us leads to look further at the causes of the differences in brain ageing that underpin some of the differences in cognitive ageing.'

I think that means they don't know yet.

So, let me hazard a different kind of description. Being forgetful is as normal as deteriorating eyesight, luxuriant nostril hair and making an inadvertent sighing noise on rising from a chair. (This kind of forgetfulness may include failing to recall the names of acquaintances, missing appointments and blowing kisses down the phone to the British Telecom engineer in the momentary illusion of being married to him.) On the other hand, an inability to remember what happened yesterday or the name of someone close is not normal.

Becoming slower with mental calculations is normal, but suddenly being flummoxed by the household finances after decades of managing them successfully is not. Searching occasionally for a word, even a simple one, is normal, while frequent pauses and verbal substitutions are not. Being worried about our memory and convinced we have dementia despite a partner telling us not to be so silly is normal; being unaware of any problems, as one relative after another starts to feel uneasy, is not.

As Ian Deary suggests, before researchers can work out why some people age well and others not, they need data, preferably from the same people for seventy or eighty years so that they can measure changes. At his centre in Edinburgh he has access to just that, because Scotland is the only country in the world to have been collecting it for that long. The brains that Deary is studying belong to 1,500 or so elderly members of the Lothian Birth Cohorts.

*

Spruce and purposeful, Robert Forsyth marches through the foyer of BBC Scotland's headquarters to meet for coffee. He greets me with a firm handshake and clear blue eyes so disconcertingly sharp and appraising that I quail under their gaze.

'There was no need to offer me a disabled parking space,' is his opening gambit. 'I can walk, you know, and it's good for me.'

Ninety-one-year-old Robbie Forsyth is a member of the Lothian Birth Cohorts. He is undergoing tests that could one day shed light on the kind of ageing you are missing.

In 1932 he was among 87,498 eleven-year-olds who took up their pencils in primary schools across Scotland for a timed verbal reasoning test. Almost every child born in 1921 sat it, as part of an inquiry into how education could best be delivered for children of different levels of ability.

The practice test contained questions like:

> Underline the ONE of the four answers to this statement which seems to you to be correct: Bath-brick is used for (making baths, building houses, cleaning, cooking).

And:

> If H comes before K write X unless S comes before Q, in which case write Z.

In a series of ledgers in copperplate handwriting are preserved the scores of every child, school by school. These were used for comparison fifteen years later, when a similar survey was made of children born in 1936. Both are now gold-dust for academics trying to understand what happens when we age. In the late 1990s, first in Aberdeen and then in Edinburgh, they began hunting down the people who had been tested at school all those decades ago.

Robert Forsyth volunteered at once. He is among 550 from the 1921 cohort and more than 1,000 from the 1936 one who are recalled every three years to be tested for just about everything, including memory and thinking speed, eyes, walking ability, grip strength, lung capacity and cardiovascular health. Their DNA is also tested on 610,000 genetic markers and they receive a brain scan. Robert has completed the original test a further three times now, and has the satisfaction of continuing to do better than he did at the age of eleven.

I look at him sitting across from me in his checked shirt and gaily striped jumper, sipping his BBC coffee and telling me about leaving school at fourteen, navigating Lancasters for Bomber Command during the war and earning his architecture degree at night school while working in an office by day. I see there what your own old age might have been – curious, busy, alert – and what anyone's might be if we could only understand what happens to send so many brains off course. I feel a swift stab of an emotion I can't place. I fear it might be jealousy.

*

So why, Mum, has your own cognitive ageing been so different from Robert Forsyth's? I have approached Ian Deary's office with high hopes. As the man who has been testing these people since 1999, Edinburgh's professor of differential psychology might have an answer.

However, it transpires that measuring what has happened to the Lothian Cohorts is one thing; working out what has moved their scores up and down is another.

What Ian Deary can tell me is that people who were bright as children stand the best chance of being bright in old age. Getting more education and a more professional job seems to confer a small cognitive advantage (although that may be because intelligent children are more likely to be drawn to education in the first place). Not having 'the e4 version of the *APOE* gene' is a modest help. (I make a note to look into that one.) Not smoking is conclusively useful. Staying physically fit seems to help. Keeping your brain active is probably worth it.

In this minefield of cause and effect Deary says he got excited about red wine, coffee and vitamins for a while, until he realised that drinking lattes and red wine could simply be the lifestyle choices of brighter children who have gone on to exhibit the tribal behaviour of professionals.

Rather than being with-it in old age because of a lifetime of red wine and vitamins, they could be quaffing Châteauneuf-du-Pape for dinner and blueberries for breakfast because they were smart all along.

In any case, says Deary, all these effects are in themselves small and none constitutes the magic bullet that predicts good cognitive ageing. He doesn't believe there is one.

'We think part of the story will be to do with having good brain vascular supply, but that's as far as we can speculate at the moment.'

He has also concluded that slightly less clever children at the age of eleven are more likely to develop vascular dementia. Findings like this have led to the belief that higher intelligence may act as some sort of protection against dementia.

But it's also the case that people who started out more intelligent may simply have further to fall when it comes to cognitive impairment and therefore survive better than others who, through no fault of their own, started out with a lower level of cognitive ability but developed the same pathology in the brain. One theory is that people who scored higher as children are able to call on mental strategies and other forms of what is known as 'cognitive reserve' to act as a buffer against changes in the brain.

This is where I perk up. Bright child as you were, might not cognitive reserve be what you have been employing? Like Iris Murdoch, in fact, whose ultimate decline into Alzheimer's is thought to have seemed as fast as it did precisely because she had exercised her mind so productively for so many years before the disease was finally diagnosed.

I see you doggedly writing out poems and jokes in the grey morning light, using mental strategies to remember. I see you continuing to work out the answers to crossword clues, devising strategies to hang in there, not giving up. Cognitive reserve makes sense of your ability to function as well as you have under what has already been a long assault on your mind.

I find it comforting to imagine you with reserves to deploy against the enemy. This is not something I am going to mention to the professor, who is rather stern about basing an inference about an individual on aggregate data from a group. It's called the 'ecological fallacy' and not to be encouraged. But it makes me happy.

Pioneering work on ageing is being done at this centre and more definitive conclusions will come in time, but I realise now that no epidemiological study is going to tell me why a teetotal non-smoker with a glowing school record, strong heart, low blood pressure, lifetime of walks, agility at crosswords, lean figure and vitamin-rich diet ended up with an old age like yours.

Robbie Forsyth emails later to say he has had another battery of tests and is relieved to report that everything is 'normal'.

I know, Mum. There is absolutely no point in feeling jealous.

14

Well, hello Joe

Grant Clarke, 'Ragtime Cowboy Joe'

G rief owes so much of its traumatic force to memory.
As the American physicist Austin O'Malley has said,
'It is yesterday that makes tomorrow sad.'

You mourned my father's loss with a sadness at times
acute but more often – so it appeared from outside – muffled
and distant. Your yesterdays were going, and with them a
clear sense of the husband who was no longer there.

On the night he died, Margaret slipped into your bed to
cuddle you and was struck by the way the trauma of the day
had already lost clarity. You had no desire to talk about
Magnus or what had happened. Lying beside you and holding your hand until you fell asleep, she realised that this was
now the only kind of comfort that really counted. From
now on communication at the most profound level would
increasingly be based not on words or explanations but on
physical balm. Grief would be, and to an extent could be,
kissed away.

I often wondered how much you were aware yourself of
this blunting of the sharper edges of bereavement. You gave

me the answer one day after you became upset over misplac-
ing your hat, the pink woollen one he had bought for you.
With an insight that rocked me on my heels you said, 'I
made more of losing your father's hat than I did of
losing him, didn't I?'

I wondered then if you sensed that in some inexpressible
way you had let him go too easily, the love of your life, without responding as you felt you should.

On the surface your mental energies seemed to be
directed less into grief than into resenting Anna for her
attempts to look after you. Perhaps that is how your cloudy
sense of loss played itself out: with the person you ached
for gone, there was only a sister on whom to pile your form-
less unhappiness. Together in the family house without my
father's genial presence as a buffer, you twins rubbed
against each other with mounting friction.

'I could strangle you, Anna,' you tell her one day, teeth
clenched as she urges you to eat up your porridge.

'I wish you would – and get it over with,' Anna retorts,
oscillating between trying to ingratiate and losing her
temper. She has slipped *de facto* into the role of carer and
in her eighties herself is ill prepared to deal with this
hostility. Although it has been building for years, she is
continually shocked to find herself the butt of your fierce
frustrations.

Afterwards, I ask why you spoke to your sister like that,
you who were always the peacemaker, the smoother of
family tempers.

'I'm used to being independent,' you say, looking sheepish.

We are all, Margaret and Topsy and I, ashamed now of how often we upbraided you in this fashion, as if you could help what you were saying, as if we could somehow argue you out of speaking in a way you never would have before your brain came under attack. I wish we had understood earlier that venting our feelings about your behaviour was not only pointless but cruel. All our protestations ever did was to make you feel guilty.

Nevertheless you were spot-on in your analysis of the problem. You were indeed used to being independent and you could not be any longer. You were not safe. You kept falling. After you had plunged headlong on a country walk for a second time and had to be whisked off to casualty to have your arm set again, we had begun casting around for help to keep an eye on you. Although you remained polite to the strangers who began turning up on your doorstep, you knew perfectly well that they were on guard and you resented it.

Ours was the same problem that besets every family trying to look after someone with dementia whom they want to allow to be themselves for as long as possible: how to keep your independent spirit flying and help you to feel like a free agent capable of decisions, when the decisions you made were so often disastrous (like insisting on walking out on a road shiny with ice) and the decisions you increasingly could not make (to get up, to dress, to eat) were so fundamental.

I know we occasionally encouraged you to fly a little too high. My heart still lurches as I remember your last public speaking performance. Eight months after my father's death you were asked to give the address at the funeral of an old friend. My sisters and I had misgivings, but you were so keen that we thought, well, why not? Why not let you feel the exhilaration of interacting with an audience again? So we solicited your stories about the late university professor and I typed up a tribute in your style. All you had to do was read it.

On the day of the funeral you and I set out for the church. I was nervous. I knew we were on the edge of the possible here, but I wanted so passionately to give you the chance to be yourself and feel the adrenaline of performance pumping through your veins again. As your moment approached, I was on the edge of my seat with trepidation. This was worse than waiting for the entrance of my firstborn at the school nativity. Still, everything was going swimmingly. Up you marched to the front, revelling in the attention of dozens of friendly mourners. And you did well. You looked up from your script like a pro and engaged the audience, who laughed in all the right places at my carefully crafted reminiscences. You made it to the last sentence without a tremor and I relaxed. Almost there.

And then, to my horror, you started again. You turned over page 3 and started again seamlessly on page 1, reading it with precisely the intonation and professional enthusiasm you had given it just a moment ago. And on you went, delivering exactly the same speech all over again. I was going to have to go out and lead you away, but when was the right moment to embarrass you? Perhaps you would stop when you reached the end a second time, but there was always a chance you would not. Perhaps you would go on and on and on, instantly forgetting what you had just read.

I was aware that people around me were gazing at you with anxious concentration, breaths held, willing you to stop. One more sentence and then I would act. No, just one more. Any second now.

And then the minister stepped forward. Quietly, swiftly, he grasped you by the elbow and, as you paused for breath with the last page looming again, edged you hurriedly down the stairs. The congregation erupted in most unfunereal applause, and you looked thrilled. I should have realised that embarrassment had flown to the same place as many of your social inhibitions. Everyone, especially the widow, understood. But as I steered you between these sympathetic faces, I felt sick with guilt. This was not how you should have left the public stage.

My father, as I realised with a stab, would never have left you exposed like this. Too late I remembered that as far back as 2001, a full six years previously, he had taken discreet action to draw your public speaking to a close. He must have noticed that your off-the-cuff Burns Suppers addresses – those traditional replies to the toast to the lassies to which you applied an original take and a mocking wit – were starting to ramble a little, or perhaps that your reception had been falling short of the rapturous acclaim you were used to. In any case, having nudged you gently to call it a day and make this your last Reply, he typed up one final speech for you. You probably concocted it together but it was certainly in your style. I found it on his computer after he died.

'Tonight I have decided to sober you all up by announcing that this is to be my swansong,' you began.

You went on to remind the audience what Burns Suppers used to be like 'in those heady days when men were men and women put up with that sad fact fairly quietly' and then offered an elegant riff on the poetry supposedly locked within the soul of the inarticulate Scotsman and unleashed only on Burns Night with the help of his hero the bard. I can shut my eyes now and see you, tall and beautiful in a long evening skirt (the bright red crêpe one, perhaps, that Dad bought for you in some hideously expensive boutique you would never have entered yourself), delivering your speech with a panache only slightly constrained by having to keep your eye on a printed note for once, and hear the laughter in your voice as you slip in and out of Glaswegian dialect to evoke the acutely observed social encounters you had made your trademark.

Surely that was the right way to go, amid what I like to imagine were gales of laughter and clamours for more? Not messing up. Not having to be led back to your seat among a congregation aching with sympathy for the speaker when they should have been thinking about the departed one. I let you down badly at that funeral, didn't I?

Or might it be the case that none of that actually mattered? Serenely unaware of gaffes and social expectations, you drank in only the appreciation. Perhaps it is my own embarrassment I am lamenting today.

But at least at the time of that fateful last hurrah you could still follow the words on the page. Soon that facility too was receding. The concentration and the visual coordination needed to move quickly from one line of print to the next was failing you to such an extent that on Sundays you would lose your place in the church hymnal almost as soon as you began. Not that it bothered you unduly there, because you could still sing the tunes, your harmonies floating to the eaves and your final amen held for so long that Tony the organist had to extend his own note until you finished.

But I grieved for your lost pleasure in words: the writing of them, the reading of them, the agile dance of them on your tongue.

Day to day you were still functioning well enough, as long as you were surreptitiously guarded and had plenty of company. Dementia is such a long journey and it is important to remind myself how many good times there have been along the way, how long and how often you were able to taste happiness. It is a mercy of this disease that there are so many bright days to be relished before winter closes in, if only people can be helped towards living rather than dying.

I remember how you and I sat in the lounge with the fire lit and the sweet smell of wood-smoke, doing crosswords at which I am so notoriously bad that you were still able to shine. We walked arm-in-arm down the hill to the farm road, plucking brambles in late summer to test for ripeness and whistling a walking song to keep us in step. I remember how we relished our car trips together, even just to see the doctor, laughing all the way. I loved to watch you putting your lipstick on before we went out, the way you smacked your lips and looked instantly glamorous.

In the days before they became terrifying, those excursions brought you joyous bouts of in-the-moment happiness. Topsy used to take you up the winding road to the Campsies, stopping on the way for tea from a flask and a chocolate biscuit. You would lie back in your seat, shut your eyes and lift your face blissfully to the sun. Other times she would drive you to the seaside, down the Clyde coast to Largs perhaps, for an ice cream on the promenade with the wind whipping your coat.

'I've been all over Scotland today,' you reported happily to Anna on your return from one of these afternoon excursions. As Topsy tucked you into bed that night, you told her, 'I'm the luckiest person in the world.'

Those were the days when it was relatively easy to turn a bleak afternoon into what you regularly pronounced to be 'the best day of my life' by snatching you out and away, even just to the end of the road or into the garden for a bonfire to break up a long evening. On bonfire nights, wrapped up like an Inuit, you would bask in the glow of the flames while munching a Mars bar, exclaiming delightedly every time you saw a plane overhead, 'Oh, there's Margaret on her way.'

Margaret herself would arrive at the weekends in a blast of energy and hopefulness, armed with fresh ploys to keep you engaged: muffins in town, a new DVD to try and spark your interest, crosswords and songs and funny stories about her life in the south. Sometimes you went back with her to stay in London to give Anna some respite.

One way or another you managed to fit in a lot of best days of your life in the couple of years after our father's death. But there was trouble ahead.

In January 2009 Topsy accompanied you to London for a stay at Margaret's. Five days later I took a call as I was about to go on air with the 10 p.m. headlines. It was Margaret.

'Is anything wrong?'

'Well, yes and no.' Slightly hysterical giggle.

'Not another break?'

Silence.

'Not her arm again?' You had broken the same arm twice in the space of six months. You were just out of the second sling.

Small gulp. 'No, not her arm. She's broken her hip. She's in hospital.'

I made arrangements to absent myself from the next day's shift and booked a pre-dawn flight to London. My sisters and brother were there already. At least all your children would be on hand to see you through this next crisis.

*

You took to having children with enthusiasm, although it meant leaving your job to get on with it. That's what a girl did in the fifties: left work, got married, had babies. My father joked that he only married you for your job, and he had a point. No sooner had you exchanged a typewriter at the *Express* for a desultory vacuum cleaner in Garrowhill than he replaced you as their leading feature writer.

Except that you did not quite leave, and nor did you abandon the typewriter. Once again you found yourself in a working arrangement ahead of its time for women. The editor was so keen to keep you that he offered your full salary on a retainer. All you had to do was the stories that suited you if the paper rang.

When the first baby arrived, you wrote about the trials of apprentice motherhood, forging a relationship with readers that had them responding in their thousands. Under the gargantuan headline **MAMIE'S BABY** I gazed out winningly from page 3, a media babe at three months.

The following summer you and Magnus were sent around Scotland to report on the misadventures of a holiday with baby in tow. 'Express Family Magnusson', as they dubbed you, operated as a double-act, taking turns to write, although his contribution seems mainly to have consisted of going fishing. He ended one piece from the Isle of Arran:

> And if your conscience troubles you, you can tell yourself that if you're anything like me, it's a holiday for the wife merely to be rid of you for a little while.

Not that his conscience ever did trouble him unduly when it came to leaving you alone on holiday. He loathed sand, sunshine and anything that involved hanging around, opting to work at home while you took the whole gang of us on your own to a farmhouse in Argyll or a guest-house in North Berwick. He would swoop in and visit from time to time, and then be off.

At the end of his Arran piece, in which he boasted cheerfully of having caught fourteen fish including a 5-lb cod, you added tartly:

> It should be pointed out in the interests of strict accuracy that the number of fish alleged to have been caught is not the one I was told originally. Nor was any brought back home, even for evidence.
>
> Transport difficulties, he said.

Soon after this you decided you were not doing enough to justify your retainer and handed in your notice. The editor, Sandy Trotter, replied at once:

> *My dear Mamie,*
>
> *Thanks for your letter. I realise your problem and I accept your decision.*
>
> *But I do not regard this in any way as a parting. You have done magnificent work for us in the past and despite your domestic ties you will do more magnificent work for us in the future. We shall certainly be using you on a freelance basis.*

The *Express* did use you, and so did other papers. The *Evening Citizen* ran 'Life with Poggles', a series describing my antics as a toddler. Decades later I am still assailed by strangers keen to rehearse my adventures at eighteen months. If only you remembered them. The last time I read you one of the pieces, thinking it might stimulate your memory of those halcyon days of young motherhood, you smiled and looked blank.

You continued to report from an increasingly crowded domestic frontline, often driven to the typewriter less by your own desire than my father's determination not to let your writing die in a hail of babies. When Margaret was born, he marched into the maternity hospital with a pad and pencil and a hearty 'Come on, the *Citizen* wants an article on what it's like to have a baby'. You told him to write it himself if he was so keen, and his column duly appeared under the byline *Mr* Mamie Baird. You were much better known than him in those days.

By the time your third daughter was born you did not even put up a fight. You were still scribbling your piece, flat on your back, in labour, as they wheeled you into the delivery room. Back home a couple of weeks later, you kept going:

> Just 18 days to National Baby Week, but in this house it's baby week, baby fortnight, baby month, baby year, babies all the time.
>
> The place seems to be littered with babies. On actual count there only seem to be two, but when one is aged 14 months and the other two weeks the general impression is of an awful lot of baby. Baby clothes, baby cries, baby powder, baby talk – and prams everywhere.

You explained in this article that I was refusing to countenance the Icelandic names given to my sisters, Margaret Ingibjörg and Anna Snjólaug, and was calling them Little and Tiny. I had also chosen Big for myself, which at least put an end to Poggles – a lucky escape considering the fate of tiny Anna Snjólaug, who somehow became Topsy for ever.

Three weeks after her birth we all moved from Garrowhill to a semi-detached sandstone villa in Rutherglen, on to which my father immediately built a study where he could retreat from the domestic chaos. Within a year the first boy arrived – Sigursteinn after his grandfather, a name at once contracted to Siggy. Then came Jon, called after your father John but spelled the Icelandic way and pronounced 'Yone', bestowing on him a lifetime of explanations.

Jon was born while his father was in America for the BBC's *Tonight* programme, reporting via the pioneering Early Bird satellite that had been launched the previous month. I sat at home on our stylish sixties sofa in charcoal grey (a Magnus choice, for sure), watching in amazement as presenter Cliff Michelmore announced the birth of my brother on air. Anna was there too, keeping house and minding the children while you were in hospital.

Your hands were so full with five children and a peripatetic husband that the right moment for Anna to return to her own career in hotel management never quite arrived. She loved us as her own and rejoiced in the satisfactions of housekeeping with a zeal that made her more a woman of her time than you ever were. You, meanwhile, were freed to continue what really did interest you: mothering us, dancing sparky attendance on our father when he was around, dashing off articles and columns to a variety of newspapers and enjoying a budding sideline as an after-dinner speaker.

Two mothers, we used to think. What could be better?

These two mothers of ours are now so often at each other's throats, inchoate frustration squaring up to uncomprehending defensiveness, that most of our energy is spent keeping you apart.

*

On the day you are about to leave for London I invite a local lady to the house to meet you both. She has replied to an advert for someone to pop in for a few hours a week to give Anna a rest. We have been trying a succession of companions from a local agency, but you both loathe the intrusion.

The interview at the kitchen table is faintly surreal. Anna asserts, less than helpfully, that she doesn't need any help at all. Your contribution is smoothly to write off Anna's role by assuring the poor woman that the only person required is a 'housekeeper'. Later, to nobody's surprise, the kindly applicant calls to say she is not sure she has the time to spare after all.

Neat and combed for the journey, there is an air about you today that I cannot put my finger on. An aura of insubstantiality. A wispy, evanescent sense of something not there, of someone passing. I want to leap across the table and crush you in my arms and stop you from leaving.

Before you depart for the airport with Topsy, we stand for a moment at the front door to say goodbye.

'I'm just your daft mum,' you say, as I lean in to straighten the pink hat I have clamped too heartily over your ears. I stroke your smooth cheek and bury my face in your neck.

I love you, my daft mother, but I cannot stop you from going.

*

Your bed is one of six, right next to the window looking high over London. Armies of rust-red chimneys patrol the skyline, out towards the high-rises of Canary Wharf in the distance. As I arrive hotfoot from the early flight, the lights of Harrods are still twinkling garishly in the blue half-light of dawn. From here I can look across at the yellow windows of a thousand lives just like ours, up one minute and down the next, trying to deal with whatever life throws at them next.

At your bedside Topsy has been describing how you and she had been striding arm in arm along a street near Margaret's house singing 'I love coffee, I love tea' at the top of your voices, when you tripped over a crack in the pavement and were down before she could grab you. A Burmese registrar in blue scrubs is now explaining the form of the operation to replace your hip.

'What's your name?' you ask as he pulls the curtain back.

'Joe,' he smiles shyly.

'Well, hello Joe, and what do you know?' you chant at him, quick as a flash, 'I just got back from the rodeo.'

Topsy heads you off at the pass, just as you are moving from the preamble into a full performance of 'Ragtime Cowboy Joe'. The registrar remains charmed, if bemused, until, confusing him with the Japanese hairdresser who gave you a trim in Chiswick yesterday, you offer him the sum of your knowledge about the Tang dynasty in China. He backs off.

The operation does not happen. As the day wears on with nothing to eat, you become more and more confused. Night approaches and your agitation is increasing. Topsy asks if she can spend this one at your bedside to soothe you and keep your mind tethered to the familiar. She is refused.

We feel helpless. Leaving you to face the night alone in this strange, noisy place, frightened and achingly vulnerable, is like abandoning a scared child. No parent would do it. No parent would be expected to. Can anybody tell us the difference?

Topsy returns next morning at 8 a.m. to be told that you have been shouting and raving all night, trying to pull your hydration drip from your wrist and haul out your catheter. When she approaches your bed, you don't recognise her. By the time I arrive a couple of hours later Topsy is weeping in a side room, as traumatised as you.

I find you sitting up in bed, stony-faced and belligerent.

'Sally, I'm surrounded by mad people,' you declare by way of welcome. Well, at least you know who I am. 'These mad people did terrible things to me in the night. And they're all women. Where are the men?'

This, incidentally, is the first manifestation of a phenomenon that will become familiar. You have always flourished in the company of men, having spent so much of your life beating them at their own game, but why this aggressive demand for more of them? Like most of the acute confusion that develops in hospital, it is a sign of trouble to come.

We stay at your side all day. The NIL BY MOUTH sign is still prominent by your bed. After waiting all yesterday for an operation, another day is in full swing with no prospect of action. The doctors have been on their rounds without stopping at your bed and are now in theatre, working on other people.

I accost a nurse. 'I know my mother may not be a medical emergency, but she is deteriorating mentally. Does that not necessitate any kind of urgency?'

'I'm afraid it happens all the time with elderly patients,' she says.

Statistics suggest that if surgery for a broken hip is not done within 48 hours, around a third of patients will have died within a year. It will be 72 hours before you receive your own operation.

You keep trying to put together a sentence.

'Did you ever grow up with the thought . . . ?'

Yes?

'Did you ever grow up with the thought . . . ?'

Plenty of time, Mum. What are you thinking of?

'Did you ever grow up with the thought that tall people . . .'

You stare out of the window, face tight with effort, struggling to nail . . . what? A thought? A word? A memory?

'. . . that tall people move something . . .'

Your shoulders slump and you give up. 'No, I can't think. I don't know what I'm trying to say.'

*

Nobody told us at the time, but you must have been suffering from a state known as delirium, which came to a head in the crucial night you so badly needed someone familiar with you and were instead left alone.

Delirium was described thousands of years ago by the ancient Greek physician Hippocrates and first recorded by the Roman author Aulus Celsus in *De Medicina*, the surviving volume of his encyclopaedia. Unfortunately delirium's antiquity seems to have made no difference to the state of modern knowledge. Only now are real efforts being made to remind medical staff about the symptoms and effects of the most common complication affecting elderly people in hospital.

As I now learn, delirium can involve changes in levels of alertness, perception and awareness, confusion about time or place, loss of short-term memory, wandering attention, speech that doesn't make sense, anger, agitation and anxiety. You had the lot. Overnight, wrestling with those invasive tubes and in terror of the touch of strangers, you had plummeted to new depths. We thought your mind had gone for ever. Some people never recover.

Since that time the National Institute for Health and Clinical Excellence (NICE) – now charged with evaluating social care as well as medical treatment in England and Wales and renamed the National Institute for Health and Care Excellence – has said that patients should be assessed within 24 hours of admission for clinical factors contributing to delirium. There should then be 'a multi-component intervention tailored to the person's individual needs', to be delivered by 'a multi-disciplinary team trained and competent in delirium prevention'.

If only. Patients are supposed to get enough food and water, too, and be taken to the toilet when they ask.

Still, nice work, NICE. Delirium is on the radar now. Just too late for us.

*

How your reporter's eye would have gleamed in this ward. Two beds to your left is a large woman in violent pink pyjamas, her head wrapped in a multi-coloured patchwork blanket. She is yelling incomprehensible instructions at the nurses in Croatian. 'Hallo. Hallo, sistro,' she roars. 'Sistro.'

Pauline, our attentive Irish staff nurse, comes running and tries to figure out what she wants. 'A drink?' She passes her some water. 'Oh dear no, don't eat the tissue. Would you like a sandwich?'

Alongside every damning report of the neglect of the elderly in hospitals, we should remember there are also nurses like Pauline, whose care is impeccable. We next catch her trying to make herself understood to a stroppy deaf patient, who has been shuffling around with a tea-cosy affair on his head.

'No, no, no, Mr Browning, I only said you'll get a chest infection if you lie in bed all day. I NEVER SAID I HOPE YOU GET A CHEST INFECTION.'

By mid-afternoon it is clear there is to be no operation today. The female registrar, hair escaping from a harassed ponytail, comes to apologise and explain there have been a huge number of emergency admissions, mainly children, and there is only one theatre at the weekend. She says you should start eating, but all you can manage now is a few spoonfuls of soup and a potato crisp.

That evening Margaret marches up to the nurses' station and informs them she will be spending the night with her mother whether they like it or not. She sits down beside the bed and takes your hand. Pauline is off duty and the overnight staff are not friendly. Margaret glares back. But the difference in your condition next morning is palpable. Soothed by her presence you wake without distress.

Soon your eyes, so lost and empty the day before, start to register interest. You beat me to a crossword clue for *diplomacy*. 'Tact,' you shoot back. A six-letter word for *piles*? 'Everyone's got that in here.'

It looks as if our own version of 'multi-component intervention tailored to the person's individual needs' is paying off.

A young anaesthetist in scrubs has floated in to discuss the operation, which may or may not happen tonight. A sweet, dark-haired girl with tiny, black rectangular specs and three studs in each ear, she sits down and scares the life out of you.

'There are two options for you, Mrs Magnusson,' she says. 'One is to have a general anaesthetic. This will put you right out for the count while the operation is done. There is a small risk that we may damage your teeth . . .'

'My teeth?' That's torn it. 'I don't want anything to happen to my teeth. I definitely don't want that one.'

The doctor takes a breath and ploughs on. 'We can also give you a local anaesthetic, which would mean a needle going into your spine. I have to tell you there is a 25 million to one risk of some paralysis here . . .'

Your eyes are narrowing dangerously.

'Excuse me, doctor,' I say, 'could you possibly go easy on the risks here? My mother has already given her consent to this operation and she's going to obsess now about damaged teeth and paralysis.'

'I have to tell her the risks,' the doctor says nervously. 'Really 25 million to one is nothing at all. In fact 25 thousand to one wouldn't even be an enormous risk,' she adds recklessly, as you start to look agitated.

Do their training manuals not teach doctors how to speak to people with dementia? There is no use abandoning the does-she-take-sugar approach of talking over a patient's head if instead medics simply read the rulebook to someone whose speciality is missing the point.

You are not remotely in a position to weigh up the options, but you do have the nous to understand why she is bombarding you with a terror list.

'Don't worry, dear,' you tell her gently. 'Nobody is going to sue you.'

*

They finally operate at 7 p.m., three days after you were admitted. Before settling you to sleep afterwards, we sing the Irving Berlin ditty that will become our anthem.

> *It's a lovely day tomorrow*
> *Tomorrow is a lovely day.*
> *Come and feast your tear-dimmed eyes*
> *On tomorrow's clear blue skies.*
> *If today be sad and dreary*
> *And every little thing looks grey*
> *Just forget your troubles and learn to say*
> *Tomorrow is a lovely day.*

Jon taught Dale to sing it as a party piece for their wedding celebration, jauntily accompanied by him on the piano. She is being treated for breast cancer now, diagnosed, in a cruel twist, the week of our father's funeral. So some troubles are hard enough to forget. But to hear you singing the song in a quavery voice, word-perfect, does make us feel that it might, just might, be a lovely day tomorrow all the same.

And it is. You begin to walk again. With the help of the physiotherapist and his assistant you shuffle to the edge of the bed and take three steps.

'Excellent. Some people don't manage that for two days,' he says. 'Being so light is good for you here.'

You are left with instructions to do ten bottom squeezes and ten football kicks from the chair every hour, which of course there is not the slightest chance of your remembering to do. Again I wonder how people with dementia are expected to manage in hospital without someone to listen, ask and remember for them.

When I return from a flying visit home a couple of days later, I find you already able to shuffle painfully down the ward on a zimmer. You turn at the bottom and begin the long journey back, mouth set with determination, nostrils flared. You are walking, and you are doing it alone.

The physio makes his way next to the bed at the bottom of the ward, where the loud Croatian lady has been replaced by Janet, who has a few brown teeth, a cut-glass accent and advanced dementia. Behind her curtain we hear him conducting a not-so-discreet mental test.

'Do you know what hospital you're in?' he asks.

No reply.

'All right. Do you know the name of the Prime Minister?'

You are listening avidly.

'Arthur?' the poor woman ventures.

'Not Arthur,' says the physio, raising his voice like Dickens' Mr Podsnap encountering a foreigner. 'DO YOU KNOW WHO THE PRIME MINISTER IS?'

The rest of us wait with bated breath. Not having a clue yourself, you hiss, 'Well, *you* hurry up and tell us then if you're so clever.'

Even as I try to stifle the giggles, I know that Janet represents our future.

Later I catch you gazing intently at the bed opposite. 'What is that cat doing over there?' you remark after a while.

'What cat?'

'That cat. Nice ginger cat, like Margaret's. In fact, I think it *is* Margaret's.'

'No, Mum, it's that lady's catheter bag. To collect her urine. You've got one, too. Look.'

'But mine doesn't look the same as hers.'

'No, hers has got more in it.'

'But what about those ears? That cat has got ears.'

It was probably the delirium, but who cares? It was the best laugh we had had in days.

15

Thanks for the memory

Leo Robin (sung by Bob Hope)

Robert Burns never wrote about dementia, although he could be tender about old age. But he did have important things to say about happiness:

> *Then catch the moments as they fly,*
> *And use them as ye ought, man:*
> *Believe me, happiness is shy,*
> *And comes not aye when sought, man.*

It's the end of January, 2009. You are due back from London any day and I am on my way home from a Burns Supper in Alloway, where the bard was born exactly 250 years ago. Driving down the dark Ayrshire roads, I think about moments that can be seized as they fly, if only we know where to look and how to value them. I think of you and Dad side by side in the café, your head flung back in laughter. I think of him gazing wistfully at a flock of pink-footed geese gusting off home to Iceland in the spring. I remember a recent moment in the London hospital when you wearily reached out from your bed to stroke my face. Beautiful moments caught, like those geese, on the wing.

There is another the night you do return to Scotland, although this one is mixed with pity and anger. You have just arrived by ambulance at a drab rehabilitation ward for the elderly in a hospital near Glasgow, discharged from London into the care of this one for more physiotherapy before being allowed home. With Topsy having kept you company all the way, you appear, as ever, invigorated by the adventure.

'The binmen were so kind,' you confide, indicating two burly ambulance drivers.

A young doctor comes and sits by your new bed and suggests she might ask a few questions. You look alarmed. Questions, questions. They induce panic and humiliation.

'Do you know what day it is today?'

'Saturday?' you guess. The doctor places a small cross beside the first question. She seems to be following a version of the so-called Mini Mental State Examination that bamboozled Janet.

'And the date?'

'The third of January?' Another tiny cross on the sheet.

'Do you know what year it is?' persists the doctor.

'Would it be 1946?' you answer politely. I feel tears welling up. Don't do this to her. Please stop.

'I am going to write something on this paper. I'd like you to do what it says on it.' She writes CLOSE YOUR EYES in capitals. You glance at the paper and obediently screw your eyes up tight. Go for it, Mum. Topsy and I give you an ecstatic thumbs up behind the doctor's back. The examination receives its first tick.

'Now,' says the doctor, 'I want you to write down a message for me.'

I could think of a few. You take the pen and start to write. It is wobbly, not the even, confident hand of old, but bold enough. You know what you want to say. The doctor takes it from you and smiles. Topsy and I lean over to read and then shout with laughter. Oh Mum, our wonderful, smart mother. You may think this is a Saturday in 1946, but who else would be quick enough to write, 'Thanks for the memory'?

We hug you and congratulate you and your eyes shine. And I catch that moment in flight, that spark of your old wit, the glitter of achievement in your eyes. I have it still.

But asking questions a person is doomed to get wrong is a strangely heartless way to establish someone's cognitive ability in an alien place when she is already confused and uncertain. It seems almost as mean to measure bafflement in this way as it would be to confirm a weak heart by giving someone an almighty shock. Boo! Yes, as we suspected, heart failure.

The test does at least establish your mental impairment, although to what end is not clear. In the days to come no-one will take the slightest account of your dementia at all.

*

It is a daily battle to be allowed in to keep you company outside visiting hours. It seems extraordinary that wards devoted to children actively encourage close family, while in old people's wards, where there is the same need for a familiar face and touch, relatives continue to be considered a nuisance.

'She's perfectly all right,' says the staff nurse icily when I approach at 9.30 a.m. a couple of days later to ask to see you. 'She's been no trouble at all.'

I want to snap, 'That's because one of us was with her all day yesterday and she's secure and happy, eating her food and doing her exercises – none of which would happen if we hadn't been here.'

Instead I say quietly, 'I'd be really grateful if you would let me be with her. She gets rather confused.'

'We have a lot of patients here who get confused,' retorts the nurse, 'and we can't have all their families coming in.'

And is that likely? Not everyone is a position to do this; not everyone would feel it necessary. But if they do want to, then give us a system that lets them, for heaven's sake.

The staff nurse relents in the end and waves me in resignedly. You greet me with boundless relief.

'The absolutely worst thing is when I don't have one of you with me. I can't describe the . . . what's the word?'

'Desolation?'

'Yes, that's it. I'm desolate when you or Topsy or Margaret are not here. I can't explain what it's like not having you.'

Big, blowsy Jessie in the next bed tells me that when you asked for us before I arrived, you were told, 'We can't have your daughters traipsing in all the time. This is a hospital.'

But next day comes alarming news from your ward mates.

'Mamie has been going round without her walking stick,' big Jessie tells me. 'She walks so well,' she adds admiringly.

This is horrifying. One trip or bump and you will be over again: you should not be walking alone for a second. I look around for the wooden stick you were given in London but it is nowhere to be seen. It is eventually located on a bed in the next ward, where it transpires you have been wandering around, making friends with everybody. It seems crazy to discourage watchful relatives while having nobody on hand to monitor the movements of mentally fragile patients who are learning to walk.

Fortunately you are doing so well with the daily physiotherapy sessions that you will be out soon. Teeth clenched and with an air of fierce concentration, you kick a football at a bar, step forwards and back when asked, stand up and sit down. You are pink with either achievement or the satisfaction of a spot of light flirtation with your latest physiotherapist.

When I ask how you are feeling, you send my spirits soaring with your careful linguistic command. 'I feel a continued indebtedness to the people who are helping me to perform these things, but a little tired.'

All afternoon I chant to myself, 'A continued indebt-edness, a continued indebtedness.' I must remember this the next time you announce with confidence, as you did the day before: 'It was the straw that broke the camel's egg.'

In the quiet of the evening, before the tea-trolley trun-dles in, the ladies on the ward begin to talk about themselves. A couple have been in one hospital or another for months, chronically infirm with nowhere to go. Little May is a tiny gnome with a deformed back, red sunken eyes and straggly grey-brown hair. She takes trouble with her appearance: black leggings today and a light blue cardigan. She wears perky gold-hooped earrings and is telling a tale so appal-ling I am speechless.

'I speak oot and the nurses don't always like that. This other hospital I was in, I didn't do what the nurse wanted me to. It was just too sore, I couldnae. We were in the bath-room. She put me in a cold bath. Put me right in and pulled my hair. It was that cold my teeth was chatterin'. I think that's how I lost some of my teeth.'

She has a total of six teeth: three at the front, one on the right and two sentinels on the left.

'I says, "I'll get you for this," and she says, "You're just skin and bones. You can't do anything." But I could do something all right. I reported her and I didn't see her again after that. That was at another hospital.

'Mind, the other night here a nurse that doesn't like me put my bed way up high and left it like that deliberately. It was there till midnight and nobody came to put it down for me.'

'Surely not?' I say, looking at Jessie, younger than the others, acknowledged leader of the ward gang.

'She's right,' nods Jessie. 'I rang my buzzer and rang and rang to get them to come to her and they didn't come. The rest of us were all in bed. I think some people have taken agin her. But she's someone's mother, isn't she? She's a human being.'

What the people who can articulate their feelings resent most about their treatment here is not cruelty – which no-one is really alleging, in this place at least – but the endemic thoughtlessness that stems from not seeing the individuals behind the zimmers.

'See last night,' says Jessie, 'I woke up and needed the toilet.' She is a heavy woman with a new hip and diabetes but a brain firing on all neurons.

'I've got these bars around my bed at night in case I fall out, so I can't get out by myself. So I rang for the nurse. "What's wrong with you?" she says. "I want to go to the toilet," I says. "Oh," she says, "you're just at it. You were at the toilet a wee while ago."'

Jessie flushes with indignation. 'Well, what a cheek. I woke up and I needed the toilet. I just wanted that bar down so that I could get myself there. But that nurse, she just banged the bar down and marched off. They shouldn't talk to you like that. They treat you like a baby.'

This is a problem for the nurses. Some of their patients

are like babies, or at least they possess the same needs and insecurities and frustrating habits as young children. You won't mind my saying, dearest mother, that you are one of them. But others are not. And even the ones who need to be encouraged and helped like children are entirely different from one another. Your dementia is not as advanced as Joan's, a former primary school teacher with a soft Aberdeenshire accent who spends much of the day weeping; Betty, dapper in a peppermint dressing gown, is deaf, which makes her appear less on the ball than she actually is.

But here the prime motivation seems to be control. Joan is crying again in her armchair. When I go to comfort her she says she wants to have a sleep in bed. 'But I can't get out of my chair.'

Like you, she has no clue how to press the red button for assistance. My policy is not to risk the wrath of the nurses by interfering in an obvious way, but to act as a fifth column, ringing the buzzer of the person who needs help and then darting back to my seat beside you to wait for action.

A nurse comes at last. 'What's wrong, Joan?' she asks in a loud voice. Joan is not hard of hearing. I often catch her smiling to herself at something someone has said at the other side of the ward.

She says nothing. Sits with her head bowed and eyes tight shut.

'What's wrong, Joan?'

'She'd like to have a sleep,' I pipe up from beside your bed. 'She told me she'd like to get into bed.'

The nurse ignores me. 'What's the matter, Joan?' she roars. 'Why did you ring your bell?' My heart pounds. I last felt like this plucking up the courage to confess to vandalising a maths jotter.

'I think she's tired,' I hazard again nervously in a squeaky voice. This is ridiculous.

'What do you want, Joan?' bellows the nurse, as if I had never spoken. No response. I bite my tongue. The ward holds its breath.

Eventually the nurse asks, more softly, the yes or no question most likely to elicit an answer from someone with dementia. 'Are you tired, Joan?'

Joan nods.

'Would you like to get into bed?'

'Yes, please.'

This nurse is a pleasant woman and no harridan. I know perfectly well that she and her colleagues, with so many dementia patients and little, if any, dementia training, are on a hiding to nothing most of the time. In fact, I am even starting to wonder if this might be a disease that turns all but the most saintly carer into a kind of monster in the end. It is something I will have cause to consider in the months to come when I stare into my own mirror.

But we could do without the power game here. If there is help to hand, it should be used. According to her daughters, Joan had few signs of dementia at all when she arrived here a few weeks ago to be treated for constipation. Now she is at a more advanced stage than you.

These people are too important for games.

*

The night before you leave the hospital, diabetic Jessie smuggles in a couple of chocolate cream buns the size of two Hebridean islands. Her attempt to hide them from the staff is thwarted by May, who accepts the offer of one and plasters it all over her face, adding with a smack of her lips: 'They'll never know I've had a thing.' Jessie laughs so much that she chokes on her own bun, is immediately found out and has to be brought a sick bucket. When peace is restored you get everyone singing.

Next day, as you say your farewells, Jessie leads the assembly in 'Three cheers for Mamie!' You depart the ward like a monarch, responding to the hip-hip-hoorays with a wave as gracious as the one you offered the crowds on the day you followed the real Queen to Rutherglen after her coronation.

As the royal procession rolled along Main Street you were a couple of cars behind, hearing the cheers swell up ahead as the crowds lining the pavements surged forward to snatch a glimpse of the young Elizabeth II. It had happened that way in every town on the tour. But this day was different. It seemed to you, as the press car inched along, that the excitement was rising up afresh. You sat there listening to the din, puzzled. It was a full minute before you worked out that just about everybody you had ever known in your life was out that day, packing the broad pavements of Rutherglen, and that they were cheering for you, you in your best black dress and fancy white straw hat, as enthusiastically as they had for the Queen a moment before.

After a while you began to feel silly, sitting primly in the car without doing anything. So with an airy twirl of your gloved hand, you began to practise a graceful wave towards the overflowing pavements. You kept it up all the way to the town hall where, in the hush that descended as the Queen stepped out, one of your old neighbours was heard to screech: 'It is *so* Mamie Baird. And to think I used to wipe her nose with my pinny.'

That grin of yours, that merry acceptance of popularity, that regal flick of the wrist – it is exactly the way you are waving to Jessie and the girls now as you shuffle out of the ward on your stick, leaning on my arm.

I feel an enormous rush of relief and exhilaration. You are leaving hospital without having fallen again, caught a fatal infection or entirely lost your mind. Since it's now well documented that older people take their lives in their hands when they enter any hospital, you really are very lucky. I asked the expert who first alerted me to this what on earth people are supposed to do.

'Stay out,' I was told drily. 'If your relative has to go in, make sure you get them out as fast as you possibly can. It's the only way you can stop the hospital from turning your loved one into a basket case.'

The public ought to know this, but when were we ever told? Perhaps a notice at every hospital entrance might help. 'STAY OUT!' it would say. 'Entering may endanger your health.'

My sisters and I vow that, if we can possibly help it, you will never be in another hospital again as long as you live.

16

Let them eat cake

Attributed (probably wrongly) to Queen Marie Antoinette

Two hospitals at opposite ends of Britain. Two random experiences of how older people fare in them.

I saw no serious neglect in either, nor any direct example of the degrading treatment that has been reported both anecdotally and by one official body after another in hospitals the length and breadth of the UK. But in both places, with honourable exceptions, the lack of empathy for confused patients and knowledge about their condition was staggering.

Dementia specialist Professor June Andrews says this remains a fair reflection of what happens in hospitals. 'In fact,' she sighs, 'it is only too fair.'

She should know. As director of the Dementia Services Development Centre at Stirling University, the first of its kind in the world, she visits a lot of hospitals and has some grim statistics at her fingertips.

'You need to be pretty smart to survive a hospital admission, and if you are cognitively impaired and a bit frail you face double jeopardy. You are more likely to be sedated, more likely to fall over, more likely to have a urinary tract infection and in general more likely to be treated in a way that implies your condition is hopeless and you are on a fast track to a care home.'

Older people occupy up to 70% of acute hospital beds, of whom around half will have dementia and delirium. Andrews is withering about how they fare.

'I was in an acute hospital in the north of England last week and I've never seen so many frightened, distressed old people in one place as I saw there. The standards are so, so poor.'

What can be done? Robert Francis, who led the final inquiry into the cataclysmic failure of care at Stafford Hospital, called for a new 'patient-centred culture' in hospitals. We are a long way from that, but awareness of the need for one is at least growing. There are nudges from governments, action plans, improvement programmes, care standards and a swelling band of 'champions' charged with spreading the word about dementia, all of which it would be churlish not to acknowledge. Alzheimer Scotland now funds nurse consultants across the Scottish health boards in a bid to improve awareness of dementia in acute settings; there are other moves in different parts of the UK.

But everyone understands that none of these steps is likely to have more than a marginal impact on patient care unless they are followed through at the highest level of NHS policy-making. If acute hospitals are ever to become places that people with dementia can enter safely, big, bold, top-down culture change is needed.

But where, if anywhere, has this actually started to happen?

*

The garden of ward C22 has clematis trailing over the fence, tubs of pansies in one corner and a couple of tables set with chairs and an umbrella pole. The area, taking up two cars' worth of space, was only wrested from the New Cross Hospital car park after a fierce internal wrangle. Person-centred care doesn't come easy, it seems, even when the chief executive of the Royal Wolverhampton NHS Trust is leading the charge himself.

The dayrooms that open on to the garden, one for men and one for women, are flooded with natural light and sport cheerful red gingham tablecloths. In the men's ward a nurse is writing up a report at a small work station right inside the bay, within sight and earshot of patients who may struggle to articulate their need and could certainly not locate a call-bell. There are pictures of flowers on the walls and an air of calm. Well past breakfast time, one man is being fed a bowl of porridge beside his bed.

The building of this twenty-bed ward for patients who, as well as a broken hip or a respiratory infection or some other acute clinical condition, also have dementia, was sanctioned from the top. But it still created a shock within a hospital used, like every other, to saving space, squeezing in beds and removing homely extras in the name of efficiency.

CEO David Loughton, responsible for one of the largest acute providers in the West Midlands with 700 beds and almost 7,000 staff, found the change of mindset unsettling himself.

'I've been a chief exec for an awful long time and I've lost count of how many dayrooms I've closed and how many pastry chefs have fallen by the wayside,' he tells me cheerfully. 'Now we're opening dayrooms and serving cakes.'

Giving New Cross an expertly staffed and innovatively designed ward, along with an outreach team to take best dementia practice into the rest of the hospital, has required leaders who are passionate and, he says, don't mind bending the rules. 'People like *her*.' He raises an eyebrow across the table at Cheryl Etches, his immaculately groomed chief nursing officer, who gazes innocently back.

Etches had read all the damning official reports. She knew that their hospital, along with every other, was harming a large group of people in their care through ignorance.

'But it did feel overwhelming,' she says, 'because you just don't know what to do about it at first. There was nobody in the organisation who knew what to do.'

She started by hooking up with the King's Fund, sending staff on their Healing Environment programme to learn how to turn an ugly old ward in a prefab into a place where people with dementia would feel calm and secure.

Design can seem an airy-fairy concept until you see the small nurses' station inside every bay. Or the bright dayrooms. Or the slender see-through glass lockers. Or the shower-room without a billowing curtain to frighten anyone.

But it is more difficult to change a hospital culture than a shower curtain. That's being tackled through teaching the staff – everyone from doctors to porters – that they are dealing with individuals with a condition that can be understood, a life that can be learned about (every patient has a booklet about themselves filled with information from relatives or carers) and a personality to be valued.

Matron Karen Bowley arrived at the beginning of the project and has presided over the changes. The first was in herself.

'I thought I knew how to look after someone with dementia. If you had told me I was supposed to be caring for them as an individual, I'd have said, "I do. Of course I do. That's what I always do." But now I know I wasn't – not properly.'

'Tell me the difference.'

She brings her fist down hard on the coffee table between us and begins a rhythmic thump.

'If we'd had a patient before who was continually tap-tapping on the table like this, I'd perhaps have thought they were bored and that it was just a habit. I might have gone to try to distract them. But now I know it probably means they're trying to communicate something and it's our job to find out what. It might be that they want to go to the toilet. Or that they're hungry or thirsty.'

Relatives, it turns out, are welcome here. Fancy that, Mum. The ward is not overrun by 'traipsing' families and nor has infection control been compromised.

Because C22 is able to accommodate only a third of the hospital's acute patients with dementia, a new computerised flagging system identifies the others in different wards and the outreach team systematically visits each person. The team's job is to act as role-models to other staff, showing by the way they talk, listen and respond to patients how it should be done.

Academic evidence suggests that doing dementia care well costs less in the end than doing it badly, by reducing falls and complaints, for instance, and the toll on staff. However these first moves to turn around the acute care juggernaut at New Cross are proving expensive, with the cost of running the dementia ward half as much again as a normal medical ward.

'Let's not beat about the bush here,' says David Loughton, a man for whom one suspects bush-beating has never held much attraction. 'It's been difficult. Our commissioners felt it was costing too much – until an independent report confirmed we were providing better care to this group of patients than any acute hospital anywhere in the UK.

'But there's no appetite among other chief executives to tackle this one. They're just battening down the hatches financially.'

He doesn't sound very sanguine, I murmur, about the future of the kind of care he is pioneering here. What does he think should be happening?

'I would like to see in a short space of time every acute hospital having at least three dementia wards, plus an outreach team to go elsewhere. But that will only happen if there is a will at the highest level of government. It will not happen, frankly, unless it becomes a target.'

He picks up his coffee cup and wanders back to his own office, leaving his lieutenant to outline her own belief about where the ultimate answer lies.

'I think we need to find alternative ways of delivering acute care in the patient's own home,' Cheryl Etches says. 'At the moment it goes something like this: Patient with dementia has urinary infection. GP refers into A&E or the acute medical unit because they'll need intravenous antibiotics. Patient is moved to hospital, gets distressed, pulls out tubes, catches other infections. So we need to consider how we can deliver IV antibiotics to this patient in their home.

'And we can go beyond that to ask what we are doing to keep this group of patients healthy at home. Who is working in the community with the relatives to prevent that person getting the urinary infection in the first place? If a loved one won't drink regularly, we need to be giving caregivers the skills to persuade that person to drink every hour to keep them well flushed through. If necessary, the next stage would be acute care at home. Only at the final stage would there be an admission to hospital.'

Etches acknowledges that persuading the public that genuinely person-centred care can best be delivered at home will be tough, but she doesn't pull her punches on why new ways of doing it are so vital.

'The public's perception is that the best place to be when you're ill is in a hospital bed,' she says. 'They have no conception that a hospital bed is the most dangerous place to be of all.'

This is becoming a theme.

All the same, Mum, if people like you have ever got to be in one, there are worse places. New Cross has a way to go, and nobody there would claim otherwise, but it's part of a trust where worthy rhetoric has been followed up by the determined, rule-bending, pugnacious, wily action that serious change to the system does actually require from leaders.

I do believe that if you had tripped and broken your hip on a pavement in Wolverhampton, C22 would have done nicely.

17

Give sorrow words

William Shakespeare, *Macbeth*

The night Siggy died you slept in his bed with his school jumper on the pillow and your face buried in the smell of him. Next day you put the books that had been with him in his satchel into the drawer beside your own bed. Sigursteinn Magnusson 1B2. You had forced yourself to discard the most badly damaged ones, trying not to be silly about it. You closed the drawer. It would be thirty years before you opened it again.

Those exercise books are still in your bedside drawer, the slim stack of them tucked neatly beside his striped blue school tie. I made myself take them out the other day. On the cover of each jotter are his name, class and subject – ENGLISH, FRENCH, HISTORY, GEOGRAPHY, MATHS – inscribed in felt-tip over a test run in pencil and then underlined with a ruler. I had forgotten how fastidious an eleven-year-old boy could be back then.

In the English one I find meticulous essays in blue fountain pen, which flicker still with his personality. In 'A Memory of Mackerel' he remembers a holiday drama on

Arran in the summer just past, a fish-hook caught in his finger and how sickened he had felt, not so much by the pain as by 'the smell of the strip of mackerel, and the sight of it hanging from my hand'. In casualty he had waited to have it removed in an agony of nervousness. 'But it was all over in a few minutes – a jab with a needle, the snap of pliers, and a tug which seemed to last for ever. All that was left were two tiny holes in my hand, two pieces of metal lying in the doctor's wastepaper basket, and the smell of mackerel.'

The teacher had given him 18 out of 20 and a 'Vivid' in red pen.

A speech he had been asked to prepare for homework at the end of those same school holidays begins 'I love sport'. It describes the 'feast' he had enjoyed on television all that blissful summer of 1972: tennis from Wimbledon, Test cricket, the British Open and, best of all, the Munich Olympics, in which the performances of the seventeen-year-old Russian gymnast Olga Korbut had entranced him.

'I don't know which moment was most exciting – when she won her gold medals, or when she failed to win another through making three terrible mistakes on the uneven bars.' He ends with an earnest declaration that he has returned to school 'keener than ever to take part in as many sports as possible'.

The last sentence of all makes my eyes swim. 'I don't intend to be an onlooker all my life,' my little brother had written.

That eager life had only a few more months to run.

I think of you reading this, all by yourself, thirty years later. You told me about it one day, turning to me out of the blue to say, 'I steeled myself to look at those jotters again.'

It was a fine spring morning, I remember. We were at the kitchen table. Your mind was failing somewhat by then, but there was no sign of it as we spoke. Your eyes were clear and your voice steady as you explained, 'I had never been able to look at them before. I just cried and cried and cried for two hours. It was a kind of expiation.'

Siggy was on his way home from the school sports field when he darted off a bus and across a busy road without pausing to check for overtaking traffic. A lorry hit him. It was May 1973, just a couple of weeks before his twelfth birthday. Terribly injured when the lorry struck, he seemed nonetheless to be pulling through. Three days later I was in a hospital side room with you and Dad, waiting to visit him, when a consultant tapped on the door and asked if I would wait outside. He told you there had been a sudden deterioration. Our Siggy was gone.

As my father brought the car to a halt outside the house, I saw Margaret, Topsy and little Jon rush to the window. Surprised to see us back so soon, they looked suddenly hopeful. Any minute now they would rush out of that door to greet us and we would have to tell them. You lingered in the passenger seat for a moment, quite still, arming yourself to face the rest of your life.

You did your weeping in private. I only learned from you many years later that you used to sit howling on your bedroom floor with one leg flung against the door in case a child should burst in and discover you. At the time it was not your tears or your words or even your demeanour, all carefully guarded, that screamed your agony but your legs, so shockingly thin in your garden shorts that summer that they reminded me of the Biafran famine. Your hair also gave you away. Jon, only eight at the time, remembers noticing that it seemed to turn almost instantly grey, as if the very pigmentation of your body had been shocked into dying of grief. Your eyes, too, held so much pain that for a long time I literally could not bear to look into them. Yet by a monumental force of will you continued in all other respects to be our cheerful, laughing mother.

You were researching a book my father had been commissioned to write about the history of his old school. Day after day you immersed yourself in the stories yielded up by old records and registers of Edinburgh Academy alumni (including the writer Robert Louis Stevenson, who kept you going for weeks), and for those hours you were almost able to lose yourself. The hard part was surfacing again.

'If I had to stand up to go to the bathroom or make a cup of tea or answer the phone, it was like being kicked in the stomach,' you said. 'I just got up and did whatever I had to do and then plunged right back into the book again. It helped.'

Even as a teenager I looked on with awe at the way you dealt with the grief that crashed upon our family that summer, showering us with glass and splinters that remain stuck under the skin. It was our father, you said, who had found the words to help you shore us up.

'These children have lost their brother,' he told you. 'Don't let them lose their mother too.'

Now I wonder what it cost you to remain so fully a mother to the rest of us, not to retreat, not to allow grief to consume you, not to seek refuge in pills or alcohol, not to take to your bed and never leave it, not to give up.

What *did* it cost you? There is always a cost.

*

To reach psychiatrist Sube Banerjee's office I have to walk down a flower-scented path through the leafy grounds of the Institute of Psychiatry at London's Maudsley Hospital. The name on the plaque is Memory Lane.

Dr Banerjee is an experienced clinician as well as professor of mental health and ageing at Kings College, London. (Not long after this he would move to the chair of dementia at the Brighton and Sussex Medical School.) He was the expert entrusted with writing a pioneering national dementia strategy for the UK's Labour government in 2008. The following year he published a searing investigation into the overuse of antipsychotic drugs. I am told he is one of the best people to approach for a straight answer to any question about dementia.

Well, I have a question. I want to ask him about the mental toll of bereavement and other forms of sustained psychological trauma. Some of the academic papers I spend so much of my time wading through suggest that stress can play a part in the onset and progression of Alzheimer's disease. It causes changes in cortisol levels, which can mean an increased risk of strokes, which in turn are a risk factor for Alzheimer's. Could grief, along with the superhuman effort you made to suppress it, have made your brain vulnerable to attack?

Like most of my questions, this one is both urgently personal and of wider significance in a research field where new theories are being proposed all the time. The death of a child may be at the extreme end of life's most stressful experiences, but there are plenty of others.

Comfortably large and bespectacled, with dark curly hair spilling over his shirt collar, Sube Banerjee thumps back with a lightning series of questions of his own.

'Was your mother a footballer in the 1950s?'

Er, no.

'Did she head a lot of wet, heavy balls?'

Well, maybe one or two, knowing her, but no, not really.

'Was she a professional boxer?'

Well, obviously, um, no.

'Did she work with power tools a lot, including large hydraulic drills?'

Erm, no again.

'Did she smoke?'

No.

'Did she have a nasty car accident that left her unconscious with a head injury?'

No, she didn't.

His point is that physical trauma to the brain can certainly give a person dementia, or, to be accurate, reveal the dementia process earlier by bashing away neurons and reducing cognitive reserves. 'More and more American footballers of a certain age, those big fit black guys who were playing forwards in the 1950s, have been getting dementia because they've had repeated head traumas.'

Yes, but what about prolonged psychological and emotional trauma?

He fixes me with one of those unsettling expert looks with which I am becoming familiar. 'What age was your mother when she lost her child?'

About forty-eight.

'And when did she show signs of dementia?'

Early seventies.

'Nearly thirty years later, then?'

Less probably, but yes.

He pauses. His voice softens. 'Well, that had nothing to do with her dementia whatsover. Honestly. Not when she was forty-eight. I'm very seldom as definite as this, but it's really going to be nothing to do with it at all.'

I left with my heart lighter, relieved not to have to face the thought that one hurtling lorry might have cost you not only your son but your mind itself.

But nothing in dementia studies is ever as definite as we might like it to be. Geriatrician Dr John Starr, honorary professor of health and ageing at Edinburgh University, points me to a large population study by him and four colleagues that did find an association between elevated psychological distress and an increased risk of dementia, even when that distress may have occurred decades before.

'Ne'er pull your hat upon your brows,' Shakespeare's Malcolm urges the bereaved Macduff, stunned by the violent deaths of his children:

> *Give sorrow words: the grief that does not speak*
> *Whispers the o'er-fraught heart, and bids it break.*

It looks as if the part played by your own o'er-fraught heart in the assault on your mind is one I must be content to lay quietly to rest for now.

*

But now come words I hear with a thud of horror.

We are walking downstairs together, a few weeks after the hip replacement. You are moving well now, but your confusion has manifestly increased.

'Here's Jon's room,' I say as we pass the door of his old bedroom. 'Jon had it until he moved away to university, remember? Before that it was Siggy's. He's the one who stuck all these plastic football club badges up. Look, they're still here on the door. He sent away for them from a magazine. You would never take them down.'

You look at me searchingly for a long minute.

'Now remind me,' you say pleasantly. 'Who is Siggy?'

The blow nearly winds me. The pain I feel is not just for me or even for him, my lost little brother, but for you. You who could not bear that your firstborn son should be forgotten, you who would never tell people you had four children, but always that there had once been five. What terrifying new milestone are we passing now?

I should have remembered that dementia does not do milestones. It bumps along, doubles back, plunges down, gets lost in a hollow and straightens out for a while, so that only later do we look back and notice the miles travelled. That's why the words of the Irving Berlin song are so apt. No matter how dramatic the intimation of a new phase and another loss, tomorrow can still be a lovely day. (And vice-versa, of course, but we don't need a song for that.) The important thing to understand is that the Christmas lights flicker before they go out; the neurons don't give up without a struggle.

I should also have realised that forgetting a name, a voice and even a face is not always the same as forgetting what a person means to you. It may even be that Siggy, who has remained an eleven-year-old boy for ever without undergoing Jon's disconcerting transformation into a middle-aged man, will hold a more secure position in the end than any of us.

Anyway, two days later you volunteer his name. You remember everything. You remember too much.

Sitting on the bed beside you, I have drawn your attention to his photograph in the frame on the wall, the one where he looks like a shy waif, all arms and legs in his white athletics vest and shorts. You look at it and burst out: 'I have to push that memory away.'

'What memory?'

'That day. When Siggy died. It was all so unnecessary.'

'Do you lie here thinking of that in these mornings, Mum?' I ask, my stomach tight with ancient dread. 'His accident?'

'No,' you say. 'No, I don't.' You are clear and focused. 'I had to push the thought away. I couldn't go there. I just keep on pushing it away.'

You told me long ago that you and Dad had banned the words 'What if?' because that way madness lay. What if he had not rushed out from behind the bus at just that moment, what if the lorry had been passing more slowly, what if, what if. You pushed the aching sense of waste and futility away by force of will.

That morning, as we looked at the photograph, you were still pushing it away. It was a revelation to discover the extent to which, even as the plaques and tangles were advancing through your brain, you still had mastery of your mind.

18

I thought this was yesterday

Mamie Magnusson

Your younger son breezes in on a visit from London. His greying curls and beard are a puzzle, although you are instantly comfortable with him and sure you know him. You wonder vaguely if he might be your brother.

It's a Sunday afternoon and you have come to my house for lunch as usual.

'I thought this was yesterday,' you exclaim wonderingly as you ease yourself down the two stairs into my kitchen.

What a strange world you are inhabiting, this planet beyond time. 'I can't believe this is the day it is,' you will say. 'I really had no idea this was today.'

I keep trying to imagine what it is like to be eternally surprised by the arrival of a new day, each one encountered as if for the first time. It's certainly not as exciting and energising as one might hope. With nothing to measure today by if you have forgotten yesterday, it is a scary, disorientating place in which to find yourself. It means the violent onset of loss and desolation if you are left alone in a room, even just for a couple of minutes. You are losing the security of knowing that the person you are with will return; one based, like all our securities, on the memory of what has gone before and the assumption that it will continue.

Soon after Jon has dropped in on this perplexing planet, you and I go for a walk. The roadside is littered with snow-drops and bulging clumps of daffodils. A weak sun alternates with spits of rain. You are stumping along with your stick at a fair old speed, still worrying over the guest from London.

'You know the funny thing?' you muse. 'I can't seem to remember that man when I was working on the *Sunday Post*. He doesn't seem to have been around then.'

'Listen, Mum,' I say. 'Joni is your son.'

You stop dead and gaze at me open-mouthed, the way a cartoonist would depict amazement.

'*Is* he? My *son*?'

'Your youngest son, Mum. Your baby. Number five.'

'But I have no memory of him on the *Sunday Post*.'

'No, he came a long time after that. Remember the little boy you used to take to the art class? Remember the way he outwitted the piano teacher by learning all the pieces by heart? Remember how he refused to go to the orthodontist?'

Remember this, remember that. I wince now to recall how often, with the unthinking superiority of the memory-secure, I said that to you in those days. You look at me in continuing wonderment and glumly state what should have been obvious: 'I don't remember any of that.'

Jon sees much less of you than the rest of us do. His wife Dale's struggle with cancer keeps him in London, consuming his time and attention as it must. He first became aware that his absence was starting to affect your ability to recognise him when, during an earlier visit, you wandered into his old bedroom and demanded to know what he was doing in Jon's bed. Yet none of us can know how much he lives, like Siggy, within your mind, surfacing in dreams we cannot share and thoughts we have no means of accessing. Who knows, we may all find ourselves consigned to the staff of the *Sunday Post* before long.

So much becomes explicable once I understand that not only were the neural memory pathways of your brain being affected by then, but also those responsible for the interpretation of visual signals. Damage will have been spreading through all the different lobes that make up the cortex: the *frontal* lobe that takes up the front third above the face, responsible for insight, planning, organisation, personality and initiative; the two *temporal* lobes situated at each temple, where some of the most basic memory functions lie, along with the processing and interpretation of sounds and the formation and understanding of speech; the *parietal* (meaning wall or side) lobes at the top and back of the crown, which integrate input from vision, touch and hearing; and the *occipital* lobe at the back of the skull, responsible for the processes of vision themselves.

While I am away on holiday the neighbouring farmer holds a wedding reception for his daughter in a marquee in the field next to your house. Topsy takes you as a guest and reports that you enjoyed yourself. But new experiences like this are becoming baffling, not least this enormous flapping canvas construction that had rendered a familiar field alien.

'I've been thinking for a long time,' you tell me on the phone that evening, 'that there must have been a boat in there.'

Ah. I hang on tight. 'What kind of boat would that be, Mum?'

'Well, you know, a ferry. The kind of boat young couples go away for their honeymoon in.'

At the other end of the phone I am struggling with the usual multitude of reactions. Laughter, because, let's face it, it's funny. Admiration, because it's so obvious you are continuing to think, worrying away at a memory you sense is not quite right. Unease, because it still feels like a betrayal to enter into your fictions, as if I have given up paying you the compliment of arguing you into sense. And, regrettably, a dash of impatience, because I keep succumbing to the temptation to bash you with superior logic anyway.

'Listen, Mum, the tent was in the middle of a field. Where is the water for a boat?'

'Well,' you retort, with an air of settling the matter, 'we get plenty of rain here.'

I think back to that conversation now and I want to laugh and cry and congratulate you all over again. You were working out a narrative that made sense of innumerable misdirected visual and memory signals and it was an inspired one. Neuroimaging has begun to show that similar neural systems underpin both remembering and storytelling, so it is not really surprising that when memory, mutable enough at the best of times, goes wrong, stories are prone to take over. There is even a name for this – 'confabulation'. When key memory functions are damaged, imagining a possible explanation for an unsettling experience is a perfectly understandable response. Since the monitoring systems in the brain that would normally reject an explanation as implausible are also playing up, the explanatory story is likely to be experienced as a genuine memory. Why not a ferry in a marquee?

Topsy describes being with you as like listening to random lines of obscure poetry and trying to unpick the imagery. Or like listening to a foreign language.

I imagine rather that it is we who are speaking the foreign language and you who are trying ever more dispiritedly to penetrate the meaning. I think of the countless times I have listened to Icelanders speaking in a tongue in which I am far from fluent. I grasp the gist but miss nuances, fail to follow whole chunks of dialogue and may pipe up with a hilariously inappropriate intervention based on a contribution I have misunderstood.

In both those senses you must feel like a foreigner in your own tongue, struggling in that heavy-tongued, cloth-eared way many of us experience in a foreign language to express what is in your mind and to understand what others are saying. How hard, how unthinkably frustrating must this be for someone who had such an effortless ability to hold a room with words.

And all the time your mind is protesting that this is not the way it should be, that nothing about your life is the way it should be.

'I used to be doing all the time,' you told me that spring. 'Always busy or' (this with a grin) 'in trouble. I think I'm just bored to tears.'

Bored to tears yet unable to initiate a single activity. Not reading. Not television, which has to be foisted on you. (Both of these are dependent on the parietal lobe, one half of which is concerned with things we have to put together into an order or structure, like reading and writing, and the other half with receiving visual information.) Not crosswords any longer. Not making a cup of tea. Not able to relieve your frustrations by striding out on your own and filling your lungs with country air, or by dashing out in the car. Not even able to get up in the morning without someone to say, 'Pyjama jacket off now, Mum. Vest on. Leg up.'

'It's your memory,' I say. 'That's what makes everything so difficult for you.'

'Yes,' you say, 'it *is* my memory. I can make decisions, but it's so difficult. Anna says do this or take that, and I have to school myself to do it in the time.'

I love your use of the verb 'school'. There is effort in that word. In situations where we see only your inactivity, your apathy, your flick of irritation at being pestered, you are telling us of discipline silently exercised and willpower put to work. I am thrilled at the confirmation that this disease has not yet beaten your will, but sad to realise how painfully conscious you are of what is wrong with you.

I used to think the one saving grace of dementia, as it progressed, might be that you would become less aware of what was happening to you. But you know. You certainly know. And the knowledge is hell.

*

You have been doing a series of psychiatric tests at a place they call the Memory Clinic, by which of course they mean the opposite.

When I bring you back for the results two weeks later I am amazed to hear you being asked, in a friendly way, how you found the tests. If you could remember the tests you took a fortnight ago you would be unlikely to have failed them so abysmally. There is no harm meant by it, but I wish someone here knew how you hate being stuck for an answer. It is the problem with the system. Nobody knows you at all.

The psychiatrist beckons us in. A small, kindly Asian doctor, she delivers your results: a total of 46 out of 105. 'Severe mental impairment' it says on the record sheet.

Interestingly, your scores for Language are relatively high. The doctor shows me the sentence you had written on the day of the test when asked to describe how you felt.

You had written: 'This has been an awful experience, softened beautifully by a lovely lassie called Israela.'

'We could tell from that that she had been a writer,' says the doctor. Impressed by the language, she doesn't appear to notice that you had found the tests 'an awful experience'.

Your other scores are pathetically low. 0 out of 4 for Memory (Recent), 2 out of 9 for Calculation / Attention, 4 out of 17 for Memory (Learning), 3 out of 10 for Orientation, 3 out of 9 for Perception, 3 out of 8 for Abstract, 7 out of 12 for Praxis and 3 out of 6 for Memory (Remote). The 14 out of 20 for Language (Expression) and 7 out of 9 for Language (Comprehension) are by far the best.

I feel strangely humiliated on your behalf, hurt by the implicit assumption that these scores somehow sum you up, that you in your infinite variety and complexity can be reduced to marks out of 105.

As we leave, the psychiatrist turns to you. 'Now, Mamie, do you have any questions?'

You do have one.

'And what is it?' the small lady smiles.

'Can I ask where you learned your English?'

There is just a beat of a pause while the doctor collects herself before replying briskly that she was at school in India, where English was the medium of instruction. I doubt if she bothers much about political correctness in her line of work, although I shoot her an apologetic look, just in case. Still, good journalistic question, Mum.

What we do take away from the clinic is a full diagnosis at last. You have 'mixed dementia', a combination of Alzheimer's disease with its busy plaques and tangles, and vascular dementia caused by reduced blood flow to the brain from a series of 'silent strokes', so small they often pass unnoticed. These have been confirmed by a brain scan showing areas of what the report calls 'brain atrophy and vascular damage'.

So now we know.

*

It is a shock to discover that these mini-strokes have probably been happening for years without our knowledge or yours. A Transient Ischemic Attack – TIA, as we learn to call it – interrupts the supply of oxygen to the brain and damages areas associated with learning, memory and language. You are given medication to suppress the attacks, but they still occur from time to time and we quickly learn to recognise their aftermath. When one happens during the night, we find you in the morning hardly able to open your eyes. Your lids stay heavy and you take a long time to come round and back.

In the middle of March 2009 my phone rings at 7.30 a.m. Anna says there is something wrong with you. You are in pain. You cannot move.

I find you in bed, a ghastly shade of pale, protesting that everything is too painful to move.

'You wouldn't be too sad if I just slipped away, would you?' you say wanly, expressing a sensation that often seems associated with these TIA attacks: the feeling, while it lasts, of a system closing down.

'I'd be sad, but I'd feel better if I knew it was okay with you. Is it okay with you, Mum?'

'Well, I wouldn't do anything to hasten it,' you assure me. No euthanasia for you, then. 'But I felt this morning that I would never smile again.'

You manage a weak smile now, your face so thin that when the skin around your mouth is drawn back to smile, your teeth are bared in a sweet snarl. You stare hard at me. It is as if you are flailing back through mud or lava from a place where the boundary between sleep and death is not obvious. I climb into your warm bed and snuggle into the crook of your neck. Your stroke my leg with your left hand. Rain drizzles against the windowpane and the wind hums a dismal drone. You fall asleep, breathing quietly beside me while I watch the sun struggle over to the patch of distant hill.

When you wake, I call two of my boys over to help you downstairs. You keep lurching to one side. You are starting sentences and then abandoning them, the way you did in the London hospital.

'I've always had such a . . .'

Such a what, Mum?

'What I'm looking forward to is . . .'

Summer? Tea? Going back to bed?

'Oh, I've forgotten everything.'

I wait encouragingly, trying to catch a clue, fearful that the wrong guess will divert you from your thought. Such a precious thing, a thought expressed. My sisters and I are becoming adept at easing them into the world, like midwives.

I keep wondering what it feels like to have your brain under such attack. You help one day by saying it is 'like being on a long road, getting further and further away from myself' – a description I treasure as one of the most vivid insights into dementia I have heard from the inside.

It reminds me of the bleak words of Auguste Deter to Alois Alzheimer: 'I have lost myself.' You too were losing your sense of self, watching it retreating down the road, powerless to summon it back.

But this is not only a story about loss: yours of yourself and ours of you. It is true that aspects of you are receding – the mental strength I admired, the wisdom I coveted, the literary skill I tried to emulate, the intelligence I savoured with such pleasure, the sunny, lighthearted personality I wished I had – and that as you journey further towards the grey havens you are travelling away from us who love you. But it is not the whole story. As we lose you we are also finding you.

My sisters and I are more intimately engaged with you now than at any time since our infancy, when the traffic was the other way. We wash you and dress you, we tempt you to eat and to laugh, we scan your face for moods and listen to your conversation with eager concentration. We keep you alive, protecting you with a fierce love that co-exists with irritation and jaw-dropping horror at the gibes you aim at Anna, unfortunately so much more inventive than anything else you do. We know you, better perhaps than we ever did, even as you know us less.

*

But you and Anna. What on earth are we going to do about you and Anna? Everything you have been to one another is upside down.

I found an old typewritten speech of yours recently on the theme of Talking, in which you were making the case that as a country we did a sight too much of it. You included yourself, of course, which was your cue to explain just how much talking you used to do as a child.

> I talked so much that my twin sister gave up and just let me get on with it. She tells me that it was only when she got shot of me by leaving school at the first opportunity that people realised she could speak. I was the one who proffered the Saturday ha'pennies at the sweetshop and announced whether it was to be one sherbet dab and a pit prop, or two ogo-pogo eyes and a packet of dabbities. I was the one who got the job of taking things back to the shops, a dreaded assignment, especially when our mother had opened the packet of custard before realising it was cornflour. And I had to do the talking the awful day we were sent back to tell the hairdresser she hadn't taken enough off behind the

ears, and would she just straighten the fringes a wee
bit more. Yes, on both of us – and all for 3d a skull.
At school I hurled myself joyously into verbal battles
that frequently ended in fisticuffs, and defended my
taller, sweet-natured, law-abiding sister against
enemies she never knew existed.

That is how life was. You did the talking. You took on the
tasks that required cheek and daring. You made the decisions. You fought the battles. And Anna was relieved to
let you get on with it. That is how life remained, right to
the threshold of old age, when dementia began to turn
the relationship on its head. Now the timid twin is forced
to boss the bossy one. The strong-willed sister fumes as
the biddable one steers her in a direction she has not
chosen to go.

When I arrive after work one night to sleep alongside
you on the mattress, I can hear the pair of you arguing
before I even reach your bedroom. She has been trying to
get you to do something, or not to do something, and is
sounding shrill.

'I'm not the one telling you. It's the girls who say these
things have got to be done.'

'Who are the girls?' I hear you demanding.

'Your girls. Sally and Margaret and Topsy. Your
daughters.'

You ponder for a second, then fire back.

'Then what's it got to do with you, you great galumph?'

We start to wonder whether the two of you are now literally incompatible and what we can possibly do about it. This is Anna's home and she has no wish to leave, but it is also the familiar surroundings where we can best look after you. Anyway, in an *Alice in Wonderland* complication, you miss her as soon as you are apart. 'Anna will be needing me now,' you say as soon as you have been in my house an hour, a sign, I like to think, that the old instinct of looking out for your twin is still functioning enough to kick in as soon as you are beyond her actual presence.

I once became so fed up with the stream of requests to return to Anna that I said I was surprised you wanted to see her, given how badly you treated her.

You were flabbergasted, mouth wide in pantomime shock.

'I do *not* treat her badly. Don't ever say that.'

I have tried to imagine what it would be like to be accused of having been cruel to, say, one of my children. Since I have no memory of it, how bewildering and infuriating it would be to be told that indeed I had been. At least your fierce protestations of innocence confirm that this is not how you want to behave, or think you are behaving.

Still, we are dealing with powerful emotions here on both sides. Anna, rebuffed in an attempt to get you to brush your teeth, cries out passionately: 'What is it, Mamie? Are you jealous of me?'

With perfect honesty you answer, 'Yes, I'm jealous of you. I'm jealous of what you can do that I can't.'

You are at your most childishly exultant when you can get one over her. As I discovered one Sunday, Anna does not even have to be present for you to thrill to the competition. Getting you to the local kirk had become a struggle in which I forced myself to persevere because once there, you loved it. And I loved the way you loved it. Your soaring harmonies made even the stolid melodies of the Church of Scotland hymnal sound rich and layered; your determination to outlast the organ note in the final amen still animated you.

That morning I sat down on the edge of your bed and asked if you might consider a move out of it, bearing in mind the service was starting in half an hour. With the command of language you could still exert on occasion, you replied: 'But what if I shuffle off this mortal coil today?'

'Mum,' I expostulated, thinking that anyone who could quote Hamlet was not likely to be shuffling off anywhere imminently, 'surely there is no better place to shuffle off this mortal coil than in church?'

That got you. Your eyes shot open. 'Sally,' you snapped, 'I don't know how you can speak to me like that.'

'Mum,' I said, 'just give it a try and see how you feel.'

We were late, of course. But you entered the old kirk that morning like the Queen of Sheba, waving and smiling regally to all who caught your eye. Far from expiring, you sang like a lark and listened to the minister with unusually keen attention.

I knew exactly why you were following the sermon more avidly than normal. It was the story of Martha and Mary again, your story. Much as he might have enjoyed Martha's home-cooking, Jesus (as I could see you clocking) had indisputably come down on the side of your idle, story-loving namesake. In blissful ignorance of the oneupmanship behind your rapt attention, the minister ploughed on. At the conclusion you turned to me with a jubilant grin.

'See!' you whispered.

Divine vindication in the hostilities with your long-suffering twin could not come more resounding than this.

19

This great chain of being

Biochemist Walter Gilbert on genes

Genes. It is hard not to wonder about the genes. Will it be me? Will it be him? What are the chances? How long have we got?

These may not be the most noble questions for your children to be asking over a bottle of wine after a hard day – especially when you're the one going through it right now – but the worse your condition becomes the larger they loom. And the larger they loom the more every minor memory blip of our own becomes an embryonic symptom and a dark portent.

Yes, I know. Textbook neurosis. But it's not helped by headlines like 'Twin Study Confirms Strong Genetic Link for Alzheimer's'.

'We're doomed,' goes up the cry from relatives across the land.

But how doomed, really, are those of us with dementia in the family? What is actually known about the risk of contracting Alzheimer's?

This is where twins come in. The interaction between

genes and environmental influences is extraordinarily complicated in Alzheimer's disease and twins are being enlisted to help tease these apart. In the study almost 12,000 Swedish twins aged sixty-five and over were screened for cognitive dysfunction. They included identical monozygotic twins (from one egg), who share all their genes, and dizygotic twins like you and Anna, around half of whose genetic material is shared. In 392 of these pairs at least one twin was found to have Alzheimer's disease.

In the careful language of the study, 'the model that best fits the data' suggested that genetic influence accounted for 79% of Alzheimer's risk in these people. The other 21% of risk was explained by environmental causes the twins had not shared. The genetic risk was the same for men and women after controlling for age.

On the other hand, as the international study's lead researcher Margaret Gatz was quick to point out, even identical twins varied in their vulnerability. When one brother had Alzheimer's disease, the other developed the disease 45% of the time. Among female identical twins, when one sister had Alzheimer's, the other developed it 60% of the time. The difference between men and women is explained by women being more likely to survive long enough to get the disease.

What it all adds up to, according to Dr Gatz, professor of psychology at the University of Southern California, is that genetic influences generally outweigh environmental influences in relative importance for Alzheimer's risk.

Which means close relatives are at a higher risk of the disease than people without such a relative.

'But in no way is having a relative with Alzheimer's disease – even a genetically identical twin – a guarantee that a person is going to get Alzheimer's disease.'

So, a lottery rather than a sentence. Doom, it appears, is not inevitable.

The same message comes from scientists studying the genes themselves. Very few Alzheimer genes have been discovered at all yet, although more are being identified all the time, but four are particularly important.

Three of them are firmly implicated in the rare, early-onset version of Alzheimer's. Dubbed *APP*, *PSEN*-1 and *PSEN*-2, these account for barely one in a thousand cases of Alzheimer's, but the children of someone with just one of these mutations will have a 50% chance of inheriting it. If they do inherit the gene, they are virtually guaranteed to get Alzheimer's disease, usually by the age of sixty and sometimes as early as their thirties or forties.

This is a desperate legacy for families with a history of early-onset Alzheimer's, for whom the rarity of the condition is no comfort. However, it is not what you and 99% of older victims have. The culprits here are 'risk genes', which increase the likelihood of developing a disease but don't guarantee it. Researchers have found several that increase the chance of developing late-onset Alzheimer's, but the one with the strongest effect on risk is apolipoprotein E, or *APOE* – the fourth key gene.

All of us inherit a copy of some form of *APOE* from each parent, but number 4 is the dodgy one. Scientists have concluded that inheriting one copy of *APOE4* from one parent increases the risk of developing Alzheimer's by four times and inheriting two copies from both parents by ten times. However, it's also true that a person can inherit *APOE4* from one or both parents and never get Alzheimer's in the span of a normal lifetime at all.

Neurobiologist Frank Gunn-Moore at St Andrews even argues (though not everyone agrees) that the risk from *APOE4* could be more or less offset by walking a mile a day, balancing the genetic disadvantage with the physiological advantage of exercise.

So how do we make sense of all this? Bluntly, those of us with a parent, brother or sister with the disease *are* more likely to develop it and the risk increases if more than one family member has the illness. But increased likelihood is not, as the Gatz study also makes clear, the same as a guarantee.

All in all, it's probably wiser to make a more enlightened world for the next generation with dementia than to worry about which of us might end up part of it. In the meantime walking a mile a day sounds like a good idea. Selfish gene-botherers like my sisters and me probably ought to get out more anyway.

20

Eviva España

Leo Roozenstraten and Leo Caerts

We have brought you to Palamos for a break in the sun. Four days in October 2009. Three of us to make the going easier. A holiday organised in response to your emphatic insistence that you have never been on one in your entire life.

This is not a conviction to be easily overturned, and certainly not by recourse to memory. Remember, we said pointlessly, all those shivering beaches when you darted about trying to keep us warm under damp, sand-infested towels? Remember when one of us – was it Margaret? – went missing on the windy seafront at Aberdeen, where your brother Archie and his family lived, and your heart almost stopped with terror? Remember the summer Siggy got that hook stuck in his finger, out fishing on Arran, and you rushed him off to casualty? Remember the holiday with Topsy in France and the Cannes toilet that began to hose itself down with you still inside, or the moped you fell off while zooming along behind Margaret in Greece?

No, you didn't remember anything of the kind. Not even photographic evidence of you and Dad beside the Great Wall of China shook your implacable belief that you had never been anywhere. And why should it, when the neural connections that might have placed you there are ruptured?

So we have flown with you to autumnal Spain to let you feel the sun on your face and white sand between your toes for, as far as you are concerned, the first time. It turns out to be the last. Your mobility has deteriorated in ways that have nothing to do with the hip operation. The coordination required to place one foot in front of the other is becoming erratic. Your distress in unfamiliar places is growing. We realise as soon as we embark on it that there can never be another holiday.

You like Palamos, though. Breathing in the balmy night air, you take in the dusky harbour jagged with white yacht masts, the wide, clean promenade bright with tapas bars and chic with strolling Catalans. 'My,' you sigh in admiration, 'it's just like Aberdeen.'

By morning the analogy has changed to, 'This is just like when we had to pay twopence to get into the baths,' a childhood memory we are doing our best to accompany you along until you follow up with, 'and the Icelandic ambassador came, too.'

However we may flounder behind them, these connections are what enable you to anchor yourself somewhere familiar. The dangerous novelty of a Spanish seaside scene can be safely harnessed to blustery beach holidays on the North Sea coast or Saturday outings at Rutherglen's swimming pool. From the memories that do manage to hack their way through the undergrowth, you are creating a narrative path that makes sense of the moment.

It is only the nature of the memories that makes the outcome in your case so eccentric to those who know you. New acquaintances who don't know that your father was not a Flight Lieutenant in the war, or that Anna did not have the family dog put down when your back was turned, come away impressed by your anecdotal verve.

You even declare an improbable interest in a figure called Václav Klaus, whose face you have noticed emblazoned across my *Sunday Times*. The Czech Republic president hit the headlines when he briefly paralysed the European Union by refusing to ratify the Lisbon treaty. Knowing for one of life's more certain facts that you have not the slightest clue who Václav Klaus is, I ask why you are interested in him. 'He's the character who forced your parents-in-law to leave their home and come to live in Scotland,' you explain confidently.

I suspect you have confused Václav's moustache with Hitler's. Either that or we have a world scoop on our hands.

Many of our most entertaining moments are rooted, like this one, in your persistent attempts to build a present reality around fragments of remembrance. As memory falters you are working with what you have. 'The roof is full of clouds,' you observe, gazing at the sky. Driving past a field of cows you enthuse beguilingly about the lovely black and white pigs.

More startling is the declaration, 'Your dad and I went to America, which no-one had ever discovered before,' although even here it is possible to track you across two spliced memories. Yes, you and he did travel to America and yes, he made much of the claim that his Viking ancestors had discovered it long before Christopher Columbus. I was also impressed to hear one evening, as we watched the movie *Apollo 13*, that you had been to the moon yourself in just such a spacecraft. Around the same time my second eldest mentioned he was reading a book about Genghis Khan and you nodded with every appearance of understanding, adding that you had personally worked from the age of sixteen with Attila the Hun.

I know what you are doing. Even in the middle of a gale of mirth, in which you delightedly join us, we all understand what you are doing. You are straining to take part in a conversation by appropriating whatever has presented itself to your imagination by way of a story once heard or a snippet of information absorbed. Delving into your own experience is what made you such an engaging conversationalist. You will not give up without a fight your right to keep saying, 'I did that, I saw that, I remember hearing, I was always struck by noticing, it reminds me of the time when . . .'

All this linguistic remodelling and bizarre memory assembly goes on amid moments of acute sharpness. On a

walk along the track at home one afternoon, I stop to tie
your coat more firmly against a sharp autumn wind. The
belt is too tight and you try to fiddle with it.

'I can unloosen it, if you like,' I offer.

You look up calmly. 'You know there's no such word as
unloosen, don't you?'

I could hug you. Instead I murmur under my breath,
'Not so daft, are you?' which you parry immediately with,
'As you may have thought hitherto' – one of those carefully
literate constructions in which you take continued pleasure.
Touché, Mum.

And you can still quip with the best of them. 'Do you
need a hand, Grandma?' asks one of my boys.

'Yes, and a leg and an arm too, while you're at it.'

When I tug a new jumper over your head and invite you
to feel how soft it is, you flash back: 'Like my head.'

It is the co-existence of so many different and shifting
levels of awareness that makes living so challenging for you
at this stage. Functionally, you struggle. Stumbling in the
direction of a ringing phone, you make to switch on the
heater. As the ring continues, you try the switch on the
socket that controls the standard lamp. Finally you grab the
phone and hold it upside down to say a breathless hello to
Topsy. You spot me trying not to laugh and join in. Topsy,
too, giggles down the phone. But beneath so much of our
laughter there is pathos. You hate feeling foolish and incapable, hate it with a fierce passion that your continuing
ability to see the funny side is not always enough to douse.

I only realised quite how intensely you felt this when you exploded with fury one afternoon in my kitchen when I was trying, unsuccessfully, to encourage my children to clear up after a meal.

'Have you any idea what it's like for me to see your mother needing help and not be able to do ANYTHING?' you roared, shaking your balled fists at them.

Never have teenagers reached for a dishcloth so fast. I forget sometimes that, for all your celebrated domestic disdain, you would without exception leap into action whenever it meant saving a daughter the effort. It is incapacity, not lack of will, which keeps you sitting languidly in my kitchen doing nothing. And when the maternal instinct that is still so strong makes you desperate to lend a hand but you are unable to rely on the brain circuitry to enact it, the rage bursts from you in a torrent. Out pour frustration, longing and the furious sense that this is all wrong.

You are heartbreakingly anxious to sort things out. As we sit in your living room one night after a companionable day together, you remark thoughtfully, 'Sally, I was thinking.'

You are often thinking. You never stop thinking.

'You always seem to have been around. How did I first get to know you?'

'When I emerged from your womb more years ago than I care to think about.'

'Oh yes.' You gaze at me steadily from the armchair. 'Of course.'

'That makes me your daughter, Mum, doesn't it?'

Now you laugh. 'Oh, I'm so daft. Of course you're my daughter. I should have remembered that. It's just that there have been so many wars in between.'

'Well, I'm not quite that old. I was born after the war you're thinking of, the Second World War. Quite a few years after, as a matter of fact.'

'Were you not in the war, then?'

'No, I wasn't, but you were. Don't you remember?'

'No. No, I don't remember any of that at all.'

*

I remember, though. As keeper of your past I have your war memories by heart. In fact I sometimes feel my mind is better stocked with your vivid, reporter's version of them than with memories of my own.

I see you as a thirteen-year-old in the summer preceding the start of the war, watching your father putting up the black air-raid curtains that your mother had just finished making on the sewing machine. It was the only domestic task you had ever seen him undertake: 'He had all the nails and studs carefully laid out so that he could hammer in the special rail. But when he put his hand down for the next one he found that Anna had tidied them all away into a drawer. He was furious.'

You also recalled a trial night for the blackout. The curtains for the bathroom were not ready and you had to take a bath in total darkness, getting the fright of your life when you leapt in on top of a monster bunch of flowers from the allotment. Another scene you remembered was walking from house to house with your father, carrying piles of folded cardboard. Too old to enlist, he had volunteered at once as an air-raid warden. One of his jobs was to show people how to make up a box in which to carry their gas mask.

You had strong memories of the way your mother eked out food and fuel to see the family through the war. The day before the coalman was due she would bend over the coal box outside the front door in the thin house-coat she wore over her blouse and skirt and separate the coal dust, ready for making up into little parcels wrapped in newspaper that could sustain a fire on a weak flame for hours. Then she would push the small coal left from the previous week to one side to make room for the new bag to come, calculating exactly how many big lumps she would need to keep the fire going for another week.

You remembered her meals with mouth-watering precision. The bread roll with hot egg in it for breakfast, switched with milk and fried into a great, thin pancake. The big plateful of lentil soup waiting on the table when you rushed home from school at lunch-time. Lamb on a Sunday, bought cheap from the butcher on a Saturday night and pot-roasted so slowly in a skin of greaseproof paper that it oozed moisture. Stovies on Monday, made from the leftover scraps of Sunday roast layered in a pan with slices of potato and onion and maybe a carrot or two, cooked in the remains of yesterday's thick gravy juices and served with beans from the garden. Mince bulked up with sausages on Tuesday, stew on Wednesday, fish on Friday (any kind, you hoped, except rehydrated ling, which was like eating someone's vest) and on Thursday maybe a slice of the cheap rabbit that tasted like chicken.

During the whole of your childhood chicken itself made only one appearance. That was the Christmas when the fishmonger next to the City Bakeries offered Harriet a spare bird to take home. When your father came in that evening, she held out her trophy with a theatrical flourish and he stared at it for a long moment. Then his eyes suddenly snapped shut and he slid down the wall, collapsing in a heap on the floor.

'Dadda's having a heart attack,' Harriet screamed, throwing her arms around him.

The performance turned out to be your father's idea of a joke, a field in which he was not well practised.

School continued as normal, only closing briefly when a bomb destroyed the cloakrooms overnight. But the war impinged more subtly through constant worry over Archie, who was captured near Tripoli in 1942 and shipped to a POW camp in Italy; he later escaped and was hidden by an Italian family in their farm in the foothills of the Apennines, but it was years before you all knew he was safe.

At night the air-raid siren summoned the rest of you to your Anderson shelter in the garden. Rutherglen's position on the Clyde made it vulnerable to German bombers targeting the shipyards and munitions factories along the river. Hearts beating with what you described as 'a funny, excited, sort of frightened feeling', you would all troop outside to share the six-seat shelter with Mrs Anderson from the flat below (no relation to Sir John, the government minister responsible for the construction of three and a half million of them all over the gardens of Britain) and her son Jackie. Your father and Mr Anderson were out patrolling the streets on ARP duty.

You and young Jackie whiled away the nights playing mouth organ duets by torchlight, to the silent consternation of your mother. Perched uneasily on the hard bench, clutching a bag containing the insurance policies and rent book, she felt that if she were about to be killed she would rather await the fate solemnly, listening out for the deep, ominous wave of sound that heralded the approach of the enemy bombers without the wheezy harmonies of 'I'm in Love with You, Honey' to distract her.

Rutherglen never suffered night after night like London, but there was a period in the spring of 1941 when the Germans did concentrate on the Clyde. It culminated in the Clydebank Blitz, which in the course of two nights in March destroyed most of that town and killed 528 people, the worst civilian loss of life in Scotland. On its way home one of the planes jettisoned three bombs over Rutherglen, killing a whole family of six in a direct hit on an Anderson shelter in Limeside Avenue. Your father had to go and dig the bodies out. One of them belonged to a little girl of three, whose head had been blown off. Your father returned home in the morning, wretchedly pale and unable to speak of what he had seen.

'That was the night,' you said, 'that my father started to die.'

*

Taking the road from Palamos we drive along the winding coast road to Terra del Mar, from which cliffs plunge to the foaming sea below. You begin explaining to Topsy in the driver's seat next to you, 'You girls all came from somewhere, you know. Me. You were born at the same time.'

'Ah,' says Topsy, 'so we're triplets then?'

'Yes,' you say eagerly, 'that's the word. Triplets. Sally was the first and you were the tiniest, Topsy. But Magnus was called away to America and couldn't be at the birth.'

Your own story of being born a twin, your three daughters, Big, Little and Tiny, your husband stuck in America when Jon was born – all are tossed together and joined up to make narrative sense. A clear case of 'coherence over correspondence', as psychologists would say.

In the back seat Margaret whispers to me, 'This is how it will go, you know. First we're triplets and then we'll all become the one person, names and identities forgotten, entirely interchangeable.'

She was right, more or less.

During the Palamos nights the stories desert you. In a

strange bedroom, shared with a different daughter each time, you drift without anchorage, desperately clutching for the familiar. When it is my turn, you obsess for hours about the whereabouts of Topsy, your companion of the previous night.

'She's in the next room, Mum. She's fast asleep. You'll see her in the morning.'

When endless soothing repetitions fail to work, I feel my temper starting to wobble. No wonder you prefer Topsy's company.

'You're being selfish,' I snap, too tired to care that it is the one charge that you of all people should be spared. Not too tired to be aware that, for the same reason, it is the accusation most likely to hit the mark.

'How am I being selfish?' you demand.

'Because you're stopping me sleeping – and if you find Topsy, you'll stop her sleeping too, like you did last night.'

You are silenced. I wish I had felt more ashamed.

After an hour or two I wake to find you staggering around the room declaring you cannot find Topsy. When at last I cajole you back into the double bed we have constructed out of two twin ones, you ask, 'How do I get close to you?'

'Here, roll over here.'

You shuffle over until we meet on either side of the ridge and I enfold you in my arms. I shut my eyes and you stroke my arm, pat my shoulder and run your fingers gently through my hair. But alas, when I look at you in the eerie orange light cast by street-lamps across the bay, the eyes fixed on me are quite, quite vacant. You are wondering who I am.

By the next wake, you have established my identity to your satisfaction. 'In the morning you can tell me how you do all these clever things like get in touch with your dad on the phone,' you announce. 'It's important that you talk to him.'

I gulp, wondering if you have a séance in mind next. Then you add decisively, 'And I really think it would be a good idea if you phoned your mother, too.'

'But you're my mother.'

'No, I'm your grandma,' you say firmly, in a voice that brooks no argument.

Enlightenment dawns. 'You think I'm Anna Lisa, don't you?'

'Yes,' you say delightedly, glad to have a name at last. 'Anna Lisa.'

I leave it at that.

When Margaret knocks at 9 a.m. I answer the door, looking, as she says, like the wild woman of Borneo. You inform her straight away that a strange woman has been sharing your bed all night, intelligence she receives with a hysterical cackle. Leaving her to get you dressed, I bid you as cheery a farewell as I can summon: 'See you downstairs at breakfast, Mum.'

'You notice,' I hear you confiding to Margaret with an air of heavy intrigue as the door closes, 'that woman calls me Mum.'

Later, identities reassigned after copious cups of tea, we go walking on the promenade, you bowling along in the wheelchair. The autumn leaves look out of place under such a piercingly blue sky. The rows of neat, white-clothed tables stand mostly empty in these dying days of the season. Like the lovely hues of your personality, the vivid summer awnings are being dismantled as we watch.

21

Speakingly incomprehensible

Jane Austen, *Mansfield Park*

Your memories. My memories. Your memories that have become my memories. Those bizarre stories you have begun to tell as if they actually *were* memories. What on earth is memory all about?

Like everything to do with the mind it is slippery. Neuroscientists and biologists and psychologists and artists all mean something different by it. Nobody ever quite nails it.

Scientists point to the synapses, those brain connections where neurons talk to each other, and say, 'This is memory.' They ruminate happily over the mysteries of protein synthesis underlying the way the brain stores information. They argue over the precise role of the hippocampus. They wax voluble about the different kinds of memories, the neural circuits on which they rely and the interactions of a vast range of cognitive and neuroscientific mechanisms required to make them.

Yet still the thing itself slides away and hides in the grass.

Psychologists have a set of distinctions of their own. Off we go next with them through the jungle of semantic memory (for facts) and episodic memory (for events), both of which are overarched by autobiographical memory, which, unlike working memory, is a form of long-term memory.

Our memory for the events of our lives involves the integration of the details of what happened (episodic memory) with long-term knowledge about the facts of our lives (autobiographical semantic memory). There is also explicit or declarative memory (accessible to consciousness) and implicit or non-declarative memory (unconscious), which contains a subset called procedural memory primarily involved in learning motor skills like riding a bike or tying shoelaces.

All – and here we learn something pertinent – rely on different neural pathways.

There are several more forms of memory, but we get the point: memory is difficult to fathom and harder to explain. It is with relief that I turn to the writers, who tend to suspect memory can never be fathomed, only wondered at. As Jane Austen puts it in *Mansfield Park*:

> If any one faculty of our nature may be called *more* wonderful than the rest, I do think it is memory. There seems something more speakingly incomprehensible in the powers, the failures, the inequalities of memory, than in any other of our intelligences. The memory is sometimes so retentive, so serviceable, so obedient; at others, so bewildered and so weak; and at others again, so tyrannic, so beyond

> control! We are, to be sure, a miracle every way; but
> our powers of recollecting and of forgetting do
> seem peculiarly past finding out.

Contemporary investigators, to be fair, are making a pretty good fist of finding out, but in many cases they are confirming what the novelists and poets, whose most precious commodity is memory, have known all along. In his 1980 novel *Midnight's Children*, Salman Rushdie writes that it

> selects, eliminates, alters, exaggerates, minimizes,
> glorifies and vilifies also; but in the end it creates its
> own reality, its heterogeneous but usually coherent
> version of events; and no sane human being ever
> trusts someone else's version more than his own.

This, it seems to me, is exactly what your memory has been doing as it fights to save itself. We'll pass over 'usually coherent' for now and enjoy the thought that as far as Salman Rushdie is concerned, your mental activities are entirely sane. With his novelist's intuition Rushdie knew what science is only now setting out to prove, which is that experiences are not recorded as if by a camera and then taken out to watch like a showreel; instead, memories once encoded are freshly constructed every time we reach for them, adapted, embroidered and amended according to the needs of the moment.

Psychologist Charles Fernyhough argues in *Pieces of Light: The New Science of Memory* that a memory is made in the moment and 'collapses back into its constituent elements as soon as it is no longer required. Remembering happens in the present tense.' Being saddled with emotions and perceptions acquired after the event means that distortions can creep in at any stage.

'A coherent story about the past,' he writes, 'can sometimes only be won at the expense of the memory's correspondence to reality.'

This helps me to understand the narrative fictions you have been crafting: your trip to the moon, your matey relationship with Attila the Hun and personal discovery of the New World. It looks as if these confabulations are merely taking to excessive lengths the normal tendency of memory to reconstruct itself.

Granted, the part of your cortex responsible for monitoring the source of memories and differentiating films and history lessons from personal experience is obviously not in good shape. This is reminiscent of Ronald Reagan, later to be diagnosed with Alzheimer's disease, who moved an audience to tears during the American presidential campaign in 1980 with his story of the heroic pilot of a doomed World War Two bomber who had stayed on board to comfort a trapped comrade rather than baling out to save himself. It was later discovered that Reagan had taken the story from the plot of an old war film. Like you, he was a consummate storyteller who got his sources mixed up.

So, you are just doing what we all do, and what, as a matter of fact, I am doing right now. You are making sense of your experience by using narrative skills to stitch memory into a story. And you are doing it in the teeth of a strenuous assault on the delicate neural connections that make memory possible at all.

I am, as so often, full of admiration.

22

Piffle, balderdash and poppycock

Mamie Magnusson

Through the winter and on past another spring we carry on our strange dance. You stumble and we pick you up. You slip to another level and we make adjustments to meet you there. You treat Anna like a partner in a dying love affair – every rejection casting her further into misery, each nervous smile or over-hearty salutation of hers grating on you beyond endurance – and we squeeze between you both, returning dance-weary and irritable to professional deadlines and teenage angst in another world.

My youngest complains I am 'too serious' these days and losing my temper more than I used to. 'You try doing all this, then,' I snap, trying to write a script while ignoring the flicker at the corner of my screen that indicates yet another change to the latest care rota. The online Dropbox file is amended daily as carers go sick, work takes one of us away, Margaret finds herself unable to leave London or someone else cries off for a holiday. Our phones clamour with complaints from Anna that you have refused to get out of bed, sent a visitor packing or been rude to a new carer. You cannot bear feeling that strangers are here to watch you – and yet turning strangers into trusted companions is difficult when it takes memory to build familiarity.

In a way I like your refusal to knuckle under to the care regime. It is a sign of spirit, of rebellion against the fog. It is just bloody difficult to deal with.

Your physical infirmities multiply. Rheumatoid arthritis now, a disabling condition causing inflammation in the joints. The swelling in your knees and feet progressively denies you any pleasure in walking and adds chronic pain to the challenge of dressing you.

The flight from meaning continues, the pauses while you search for a word lengthening. Diversions are increasingly hard to dream up. Your favourite sitting position now is by the window, staring out at the great Scots pine my father loved, delighted when you spy a sparrow flitting by or, best of all, a car rolling up with a daughter at the wheel.

In the evenings we can still appreciate a DVD together, but it is the camaraderie that engages you rather than the screen itself. We are working our way through the detective series *A Touch of Frost* for the third time: you can't remotely follow the plot but as long as I whoop and exclaim and make sarky comments that help you to feel you are participating, you are content. You have developed a particular fondness for David Jason's smile in the title sequence.

When it is time to sleep, you sit on the edge of the bed while I ease off your clothes, a process punctuated by

ouches and grimaces and an increasingly challenging with-
drawal of cooperation. Your back is curved into a perfect
C, your spine bulging out of skin polished to a shine, gleam-
ing like marble. You are so very, very thin.

I often note down our conversations, anxious to capture
what is there before it is gone. You look on, amused, as I
tap away. Once you asked Anna to dial my number at home
and when I answered the phone, thrilled to hear your voice
because it had been a long time since you rang anybody,
you said Anna was driving you mad and you had to get out
of the house. I came to fetch you, ensconced you in my
study, knelt on the carpet, folded my arms on your knees
and asked if you could express what you had needed to
escape from.

'Anna was looking at the television and translating to me.'

'And what was the problem with that?'

'Well, she said what was to be done and what we had to
look at. First I humoured her and then I got a bit fed up.'
(The television is a perennial battleground. You cannot
express a preference of your own but fall back on a default
resentment of hers.)

'Is the problem that Anna is a bit bossy?'

A wry little grin. 'She's as bossy as I would like to be.'

'Is it because you're used to being the bossy one?'

'Yes, but not being interested in anything, I can't be.'

Under continued probing you conceded that you had
made Anna's life a misery today. 'I'm ashamed of myself. I
had no excuse really. I think I was just bored stiff.'

The conversation wandered off here into impenetrable places, but I had caught a snatch of something important. 'I can't do what I want to do' is at the heart of everything. Despite all of us straining every muscle to enable you to do whatever you might want, we cannot discern what that is and neither can you. You know only that whatever it requires to be fully yourself, fully Mamie, you cannot do it.

Yet one lesson we are learning as we support your staggery walk along this long road is that there may be oases of a most unexpected kind.

I pop in to see you on my way to work. You are sitting in your chair by the window, looking happy. Jon and Margaret are staying for a visit with their families. You can hardly wait to tell me a story.

'Did you hear what I did?' you burst out.

'No. What did you do?'

You think for a long time, struggling to lasso the words. 'As a . . . tribute . . . to one of the . . . children I . . .'

'Go on, Mum. Take your time. What did you do?' I am racking my brain for a useful suggestion.

You try again. 'As a tribute to one of the children, I . . . operated . . .' You stop and look at me helplessly.

'Oh Mum, operated what?'

From the couch on the other side of the room Jon's wife Dale, hair growing back in soft tufts after a period of chemotherapy, chips in, 'Operated some machinery?'

You shake your head and have another go. 'Not operated. I remembered . . . how to . . .'

'HOW TO WHAT?' I explode, but we're both laughing. 'Never mind,' I say, 'I'm going to make some toast.'

'Can I come, too?' And we totter along to the kitchen together. Suddenly I remember something Margaret had told me on the phone.

'Was it table tennis, Mum? Was that what you remembered how to do?'

'Yes!' you cry. 'Table tennis. That's what I did.'

Margaret had put a ping-pong board on top of the dining table for her children. 'Want to come and try, Mum?' she had offered, heart in mouth but remembering your demon serve of old.

Now you are bubbling with happiness and a sudden onset of articulacy as you describe the feeling of playing again. 'It was great. I felt free for the first time.'

Oh, Mum, free. 'Free in what way?' I ask, wondering if you can possibly find a way to express it.

Standing there in your green cardigan with sunlight flooding in through the kitchen window, you explain exactly how it felt: 'It was almost as if something just switched on.'

Table tennis. Who would have thought it?

You and I line up on either side of the table. Margaret stands behind you for safety, arms outstretched, and I send my serve over. You skip towards the ball. Skip. Margaret, alarmed, nudges a beanbag closer with her foot, but you are not going to stumble. There is a dogged look in your eye as you reach and volley and adapt to the table's puny length like a pro.

Here, in front of our amazed gaze, is the tomboy back again. Arms outstretched for balance, your back seems less bent. You have cast off the spell of dependent old-ladyness and are showing off again. I can see you now, throwing your head back with delight as you send the tiny ball over with an easy flick of the wrist. In your eyes is a glint from which I cannot tear my own.

Never have I savoured defeat with such euphoria.

*

You always were a tomboy. Scrapes, dares and showing off are how I imagine your childhood. You were Anne of Green Gables in a Rutherglen back-court with songs thrown in, starting with the one you performed in an impromptu tenement concert at the age of three:

> Oh, the bonny wee barra's mine.
> It disnae belong tae wee O'Hara.
> The fly wee bloke, he stuck to his rope,
> And I'm going to stick to his barra.

You also loved a thrill. When the fairground 'shows' came to town you were first in the queue for the ride with the biggest whiff of danger. From my own childhood I remember how you still gazed at the highest, most vomit-inducing ride on offer with a longing never entirely extinguished until the time you nearly dropped one of us into the internal workings of the rib-tickler. Up until a few years ago your most oft-expressed ambition was bungee-jumping. You rather fancied an Australian gorge, as I recall. You would have done it, too.

What an unusual mixture you were of fun-loving nerve and the clean-living steadiness instilled by your presbyterian mother and fearsomely principled father. On Sundays you carried the communion plate, but only after you had outsung, out-talked, out-laughed and outlasted every guest of my father's the night before on nothing stronger than orange juice. Even throwing in your lot with this roving, hard-drinking Viking in the first place was not a venture for the faint-hearted; over the decades it must have drawn deep on your dauntless spirit. But in marriage, as in life generally, nothing much did seem to daunt you.

As we grew older, the combination of common sense and fun made you an engaging source of advice on everything from journalistic assignments, career moves and speech-writing to babies' teething and children's tantrums – although I drew the line at baking, given your history. You even had a clear-eyed and relatively unstuffy perspective on boyfriends.

Against such a mother it always seemed fairly pointless to rebel, although I perfected a strong line in verbal cheek. Perhaps if we had not lost Siggy when we did I might have tried harder to escape your orbit, just to show I could, but you and I spent my remaining teenage years supporting each other. Where other girls confided in friends, I poured it all out to you. It has probably not escaped your notice that I am doing this again, at what is, even for me, unprecedented length.

Even after I moved to London in my twenties your advice continued by post, as it did for all of us when we left home. There is one letter from that period to which I return whenever I want to hear your lost voice. It's more of an essay really. You dashed it off a few weeks before my wedding in 1984, in response to a severe bout of dithering to which my skin had responded with a histrionic eruption of lumps and weals.

I have only the haziest recollection of the visit I spent agonising over the looming loss of independence and the possibility of making a big mistake, but you must have grabbed your typewriter and pummelled out your thoughts the moment I was gone.

I can see you in this letter, hear you in it and sense your presence in every line: the fond maternal bias, the gentle mockery, the undimmed enthusiasm for the adventure of marriage and, above all, the core conviction that mastering the self is the secret of true liberty and the only happiness that lasts.

> *My dearest Sally,*
>
> *Well, now, as to your parting shot which there was no time to go into this morning – Are your lumps and spots proof that you are embarking on something that*

*is fundamentally opposed to your whole make-up, and
is this your body's way of saying 'Stop! Don't do it!'?*

Your answer was no. You wrote that it was not the step I
was about to take that was causing the angst, but the business of choice itself:

> *Even Siggy's death, and all the pain, could be
> accepted because it had to be. There was no other
> way. But choosing to change your life, having the
> choice of abandoning the even tenor of your ways,
> the familiar rhythms, the self-oriented hopes and
> habits, for paths unknown, depths unplumbed, a
> future directed by considerations other than your
> own comfort or ambition or peace of mind or even
> just the whims of the moment – ah, that is an agony
> to concentrate the mind, torment the soul and sorely
> prickle a sensitive skin.*
>
> *Maybe that makes marriage sound like a terrible
> trial to be tackled with fortitude. It isn't anything of
> the sort, but it is a new adventure, and any adventure
> worth its salt has the spice of danger, of risk, of
> treading unknown territory. There is only one immov-
> able rule as far as I can see – that each of you puts the
> other first in all considerations. It's a great system. You
> just exchange egos. He looks after yours. You look
> after his. His whims are yours. Yours are his.*
>
> *I know you think you haven't the necessary*

patience, or selflessness, or whatever other virtues
are required, that it just isn't in your nature to be
calm and self-sacrificing and you'll spend the rest of
your life coming out in lumps in an effort to fight
against your true nature.

Piffle! Balderdash and poppycock! You are the
kindest, most generous, loving and affectionate
person anywhere. I've never known anyone swifter at
coming back to say sorry – I usually reckon about
twenty seconds before the contrite head appears
round the door, and five minutes at the outside for
the telephone to ring in penitence. And you'll be
amazed at how time and practice can cut those times
down until you find yourself apologising before you
leave the room, or even – Heaven forfend and saints
forbid! – some day in the far distant future you might
actually desist from saying whatever it is you're going
to have to apologise for the next minute.

But that will happen gradually, with age and
maturity. Don't try to change yourself overnight. That
man of yours doesn't want to marry a saint. It's you he
loves, with all your impetuosity, flare-ups, deep
glooms, gushes of affection and pangs of remorse.
Don't try to change your nature, or even think it needs
changing. It's you, the Sally we know and love. All
that's required is for you to make, not an emotional
change, but a quiet mental decision to put his feelings
first at all times, and for him to do the same.

It's the good intent that counts, and that comes from the mind, and we all know the power of the mind. Nobody is going to tell me that it was natural maternal instinct or some basic biological stirring of the blood that made me get up at the crack of dawn for twenty years to feed people and see them off to work when body, mind and spirit craved sleep in quantities that only Jon and I can appreciate. I did it because I made up my mind I'd do it, and I thrived on it.

You could have put this step into marriage off. You could keep putting it off. You could opt out altogether from this most challenging of all realms of living, with its heights of joy, depths of despair, its demands on resources of character and personality hardly suspected and maybe never needed in any other walk of life. Many people get through life without taking this step. Many would have loved to do it and never got the chance. You were lucky to meet the right man at the right time, and you made your decision.

What happens on your wedding day is a piece of theatre. Of course you make public vows, but they are no more important than the ones you make in private, and which you go on making, every day, every minute. In fact if you could just promise to love, honour and cherish for a day at a time, renew your vow in your own mind every morning, or every minute if necessary, it would all add up to 'till death us do part'. Don't worry about tomorrow. Just

*concentrate on today. As the wise old Bible says:
'Sufficient unto the day is the evil thereof.'*

*Without D-Day looming ahead, without any choices
to be made apart from the colour of the curtains, you
can relax, cool down, be at peace. If the spots don't go
away, then it must be your washing powder.*

How could I not marry him after that?

But your theme here went further than the pros and cons of wedlock, fascinating though the clues are to how you made a success of marriage yourself to a man possessing the same tempestuous nature you identified in me. Your central theme was the will itself, the quiet making of a decision to act for good and the remaking of it every day and, if necessary, every minute. It was the way you engaged with the world and its troubles yourself.

But how are you to master a self you can no longer locate? How do you exercise the power of the mind when the mind itself is under attack? You must feel as if your very personality is broken.

And how should my sisters and I respond to that fractured personality? Give me some advice again, O wisest of mothers. How would you deal with you?

*

Here is a case I wish to place before you, one I feel sure you would have been able to help me with in other circumstances.

Persuading you to eat is becoming extremely difficult. Caring for that part of you that is regressing to babyhood, while still preserving your adult dignity and independence, is a challenge I am regularly failing.

While infants progress from liquids to solids, and from spoon to fork and so on, you are on your way backwards. Chewing has become anathema and coordinating a knife and fork is beyond you. You do not quite hurl your porridge on to the floor, but meals have become an emotional battleground that Margaret and I thought we had left behind in the nursery. In the aspects of your life where you are becoming like a child, you need unconditional care, endless forgiveness and constant understanding, but you are a toddler we cannot discipline, cannot train and at times cannot fathom. And you are also, in so many other ways, not a toddler at all. You are acute and sensitive and dignified and you are our mother.

I also have to negotiate this complicated landscape in the face of my own self-pity, my own fraying temper and my own unquashable desire to be mothered myself.

'Look at me,' you said suddenly when I was eating soup across from you one day. I had given up trying to get you to eat yourself, but with bad grace. I sat in sullen silence.

'Let me see your eyes,' you persisted. I looked up. 'Where are you?'

'What do you mean?'

'I want to see if it's really you that can sit there and treat me like a number.'

I felt my eyes filling with self-righteous tears. I have been here every day this week, I wanted to say. I have told you the same thing a dozen times with a patience I was never, as you well know, born with. I have washed your sheets and emptied your commode and spent hours trying to motivate you. How can you accuse me of treating you like a number?

What I actually said was, 'Excuse me.' I picked up my soup and stalked into the next room. I may have slammed the door. All right, I did slam the door.

A few minutes later you followed me. You stumbled towards me, just as I used to hurtle across the room to you in a gale of remorse. You threw yourself into my arms and wept on my shoulder, and I held you tight and stroked your face and said everything would be all right, everything would be quite, quite fine.

'Sorry,' you said, over and over.

But it is I who should have been asking forgiveness for not offering the unconditional understanding I had always received from you. I knew in that moment that I would have to start learning to be a better mother to you.

But how? What would you advise me to do about a task for which I feel so inadequate?

I suppose that in the absence of a letter of advice on how to be a mother to my own mother, I will just have to improvise. Suppose I try to put you first in all considerations and see where that gets me. Suppose I find out as much as I can about what you are going through and try to understand better. No more huffs, no more temper, no more battering you with redundant logic, no more playing the child myself.

Pigs, I hear you muttering fondly, might fly.

But suppose I keep on trying. Though I may need to renew the pledge approximately every minute, suppose I just keep trying.

23

The Three Sisters

Anton Chekhov

There are times when we sisters feel we are acting in a play. We are not particularly good at our parts. In fact, as the roles get harder we begin to feel downright miscast. Some days we wonder if we have wandered on to the wrong stage. Oh, I see, Brian Rix. Wasn't this supposed to be Chekhov?

About the production itself there is nothing special. We are acting out a version of the same script thrust before anyone trying to look after a relative with dementia. Off-stage we are mothers, radio producers, journalists, writers – women with no particular aptitude for nursing, no head for business, no talent for sums and a lifetime's gratitude to have avoided running anything more complicated than the school bazaar. Now, as you become more difficult to look after and help has to be found and managed, we are called upon to take the stage as numerate account managers and shrewd employers.

Feeling increasingly out of our depth, we stumble through our parts murmuring, 'How do other people manage, how do they manage, how will we manage?'

The latest act has opened with the recruitment of paid help. We place an advert on the website Gumtree. We interview applicants, try a trial period, hold our breaths and – yippee, hallelujah – we have our first regular carer. Warm, feisty Carolyn banters her way into your heart, cooks her way into Anna's and proves her worth to the rest of us by learning the mouth organ. She takes the weekday mornings, proving adroit at keeping the peace and tempting you out of bed and into your clothes.

As the months pass and your need for care increases, we go on to advertise for afternoon carers during the week. Eventually you will need regular attention at night, and when we can no longer manage that by ourselves we look for people to help there too. Say it that way and it all sounds easy. But nothing is easy, and nothing is cheap, when it comes to caring for someone who has started to tumble a little faster down the dementia slope.

Many people rely for practical assistance on visits from homecare teams organised by the local authority, but this is a service creaking under the twin weights of longevity and financial constraint. To save money, around four-fifths of homecare services in England have been contracted out to private companies, who find it increasingly difficult to run a decent business while maintaining standards. Care workers, low-paid and hard-pressed, are frequently sent into homes with neither training nor time.

A UK survey by the consumer group Which? found missed visits, food left out of reach, medication not

THE THREE SISTERS   257

given and people left in soiled beds. Some of the care was labelled 'shocking and disgraceful'. A Care Quality Commission review of 250 homecare services for the elderly in England found a quarter failing to meet quality and safety standards.

A homecare worker in London held her head in her hands as she described to me the state she finds some isolated old people in when she visits, and her hopeless attempts to sort it out in the few minutes before she is required to dash off to another stranger. Big-hearted carers like her are deeply troubled by their inability to offer anything approaching proper care.

The inconsistency of homecare can also be distressing. Jeanette Maitland made the headlines when she complained to Aberdeen City Council that in a single year they had sent 106 different carers to clean and change her husband Ken. Jeanette was quite sure of the number. She had written down the name of every one.

After his death she complained to the council. The care itself was fine, she said, but someone who needed regularity and familiarity had been offered neither. She was angry that such an intensely private man should have had to undergo the intimate attentions of so many strangers.

'I should have sold tickets,' she said.

As a founding member of the National Dementia Carers Action Network, she has since been urging local authorities to consider how homecare might be commissioned differently. For all those whose safety and dignity depends on it, new thinking on how people are looked after at home is urgently required.

*

We opted instead for a system of direct payments, available across the UK for families to buy in their own homecare.

Social workers assessed your needs and handed us a tightly regulated budget: a set number of hours a week, increasing as your needs are reassessed, up to a ceiling that is a long way lower than you actually require. Unless families can afford to top up those hours or there is a relative living in who is physically and emotionally strong enough to take up the slack, this system also has problems. Uptake has been low, not least because so few people can get their heads around the byzantine, energy-sapping process of administering the payments.

Topsy, who has legal power of attorney, labours over holiday pay, national insurance and pension deduction for everyone we hire. The strain is showing.

We have begun emailing each other back and forwards with drafts of adverts, testing the different ways it is possible to ask for humour, kindness, common sense, flexibility and a thick skin. Later, experience with advanced Alzheimer's will go to the top of our list, along with the ability to hold a tune.

We seem perpetually to be in the middle of recruiting somebody or other. Living 400 miles away with four children, Margaret cannot be there for the daily caring duties (although she does manage to swoop in remarkably often to take charge of entire weekends), but from London she spends hours sifting applications, phoning likely candidates and checking references. Topsy and I arrange interviews in a local café, followed by fingers-crossed introductions to you and Anna if the interview has gone well.

Over time we find good people with a humbling ability to do for you with a calm smile what sends the three of us swiftly to the wine bottle. Some of them hit it off with you at once; some don't and have to leave. Carolyn departs eventually for college and everything collapses again. It is hard to find people with the right skills and personality who are available for as long as we need them. Even though direct payments offer the chance to have the same faces each day, true continuity of care remains an unattainable ideal.

The shift rota, in which we ourselves feature prominently, soon becomes a tyrant. We have a complicated Dropbox spreadsheet to fill in whenever one of us is away or when carers are on holiday or off sick. We frequently forget to add information, get payments wrong and miss shifts. There is so much else to juggle in our lives and none of us feels cut out for the business side of this.

But teeth-grindingly difficult though we find the process, it does give us control over your care and the chance to make it personal. It does enable us to choose our carers and their hours. And by virtue of education, age, income and there being three of us, we are better placed to operate it than many.

Controlling care at home ought to be a choice that any individual or family can make, not just the few who can get round the barriers. A pilot run by Alzheimer Scotland in Ayrshire has shown that families can be better than any agency at choosing care services to link with the natural support at home. Now legislators are starting to catch up. Scotland's new Social Care (Self-Directed Support) Act requires councils to offer a number of other options besides direct payments. The government in England is consulting on improvements, with similar moves in Wales. Information and trained guidance are key.

In the meantime we three sisters will persevere with the current production – the application forms and assessments, the adverts and interviews, the pay-sheets, pay-outs and Kafkaesque chases around local authority departments. Like everyone else we will struggle on with our parts, dreaming of a different script one day.

24

Tomorrow is a lovely day

Irving Berlin

Just occasionally it is possible to shoehorn Anna out of the house. Shy and reclusive, she cannot bring herself to escape the constant abuse and ridicule any more than you can help delivering the barbs. She is too fearful of change, too attached to you. She rarely goes out, clinging to the dream that one day in the ebb and flow of this disease you will want your twin again and the pair of you will see out your lives as you began them, together.

May 2010, and I am asked to launch the seventy-fifth anniversary celebrations at Bankhead Primary School in Rutherglen, where your father (who is hers, too, although you vigorously dispute the point) was the janitor from the time it opened in 1935. I would have liked to take you both, but when the morning dawns you are being so uncooperative that I cannot risk your turning on Anna in public. She comes alone.

Smiling elderly ladies fall upon us with memories of how they used to cling to John Baird's arm as little girls. They describe him in his black uniform with an official cap like the one in the *Beano* and talk of the plasters he found for their scraped knees. They clamour to say how well they remember you both, though you and Anna had been at school yourselves on the other side of Rutherglen and were a little older. One recalls seeing you walking down the field to your house in Milrig Road one afternoon with Magnus in his Oxford togs. The word had zipped around: 'Have you seen Mamie Baird's posh new boyfriend?' Someone else chips in to say how funny you always were, 'a natural comedienne', and what a good singer. Others remember being served by Anna in the City Bakeries.

Anna introduces herself to everyone proudly as 'John Baird's daughter', laying claim to a relationship you are not here to rubbish. No matter that she had found his sternness intimidating. She loved him, as you did.

The school is due to be modernised, but for now it stands just as it was in his day, the solid stone buildings circling a courtyard still noisy with the shouts of children. At last I am able to place in context this shadowy grandfather of mine, stuck all my life in a picture frame on the mantelpiece looking gaunt with thinning hair and a cardigan. I imagine him here ringing the bell in his uniform, adjusting his peaked hat in the rain, handing out small bottles of milk from the big crates he had carried in, lugging sacks of coal to the bunker. Two men who had lived on a farm across the road remember helping him to sweep up coal dust in the yard.

But, as I watch him in my mind's eye, this janitor is taking his time with the brush and shovel, lingering too long over the dead leaves and the coal sweepings. His head is full of political theory from the books he wishes he could discuss with the teachers, library books full of big, difficult words he enjoys rolling around on his tongue. This is a man who would rather change the economic system than a light bulb. He nudges the broom around, mulling over how unfairly the world's goods are divided, working through the ideas.

Your father, as you used to say, was a dreamer. He cared passionately about the lot of the working man but made few attempts to improve his own, beyond providing for his family and insisting on the value of education. He was happiest tending his tomatoes and chrysanthemums in the allotment on long summer evenings, or practising his violin while you worked on school homework at the living-room table, or debating politics with the roaring fervour of a believer. One of your most precious childhood experiences was sitting between his knees of an evening, rapt, while he sat in his armchair beside the fire talking, talking, night after night, about how the world could be run differently and organised better. Then, early next morning he would don his uniform and set off down the road to spend another day filling his lungs with coal dust.

In the old school logbook I scan the pages for his name. Where is he? The teachers are referred to frequently by name, as is a succession of visiting directors of education, but never the man doing the manual labour in the play-ground. Then I turn over a page of sloping handwriting on 14 December 1945, and discover one line, the only reference I can find to my grandfather in the entire school records: 'Mr John Baird, janitor of the school, died this morning.'

You always believed the coal dust had contributed to the lung cancer that killed him at sixty, although I don't suppose the Woodbine cigarettes helped either. By the time of the 1945 general election he was losing his voice. You remem-bered watching him chair a huge meeting in the town hall for Gilbert McAllister, the Labour candidate for Rutherglen. Your father's voice was so quiet that folk in the audience were yelling, 'Cannae hear ye!' You and Harriet were sick with pity for him. A few weeks later he was found to have a tumour pressing on his vocal chords. The cancer was spread-ing.

He never asked the doctors what was wrong with him. When he went for an X-ray, all he wanted to know was whether he was suffering from tuberculosis, the scourge of his childhood family and fear of his life. When the hospital told him it wasn't TB he sighed with relief and satisfaction, and never asked again.

Anna and I drive home and tell you where we have been. At first you declare roundly that it's all 'a load of baloney', you had no such father and it is scurrilous of Anna in particular to suggest it. But an hour or so afterwards some-thing clicks.

'My father worked at Bankhead School,' you muse, out of the blue.

'Yes,' he did, I say. 'And do you remember he wore a uniform?'

'Oh, yes,' you say. 'Yes. Yes.'

And I watch the memory being remade. Sitting on the windowsill beside you, I catch the moment it enters your eyes. It is like watching a herald return from the place where memories go, bearing a message, waving a sheet of paper.

'A black uniform,' you say, seeing it, seeing him. 'I was so proud of him.'

For some months after this you continue to refer to the Bankhead experiences of your father, as if a memory track has been re-established and the pattern of connections that enabled its reconstruction strengthened through repetition. It soon becomes clear, though, that the memory bears no relation to the place itself.

I have been asked back to Rutherglen to open a summer fete. This time I take you with me. On our way home I drive you down Milrig Road, drawing up in front of your old house along from the school, where as late as the 1960s I can remember playing in the air-raid shelter in the garden, overgrown with weeds by then and dark with musty secrets. I remember thumping up the stairs to visit your mother Sarah, who stayed in the upper-floor flat with Anna for years after you left.

'Well, Mum. Here we are. Bankhead. Number 53, Milrig Road.'

You glance at the place without a shred of recognition. It means nothing. I offer some of your own reminiscences to try and evoke your life here, but you have no idea what I am talking about. None at all.

Yet not long after this, sitting at your own window, you observe matter-of-factly, 'This isn't my real house, you know. Once I get back to my own house it will be fine.'

'Where's your own house?' I ask. I have wondered when this would start, how long the forty years you have lived in this one would protect you from this bleakest of dementia delusions. When it finally comes, not even your married life in another part of Rutherglen gets a look-in, the house we lived in before moving here.

'Bankhead,' you say. 'Bankhead, where my father worked as a janitor. That's my home. And I haven't been there for such a long, long time.'

*

Sometimes you call for your parents in the night.

'The only time anything is real is when I go to sleep,' you murmur as you settle back on your pillows, three as usual the way you like it, piled so high you are almost bolt upright. Your hair frames your face like a cloud. A soft, dark fuzz shadows your temple under the hairline, token of an earlier self.

I often wonder where you go in the night. You told me one morning, as I hauled your socks up your legs, that you had been having 'a lovely dream where everything belonged to me rather than somebody else'. It was probably a place where you also put your own socks on. Are you back there helping Anna with her homework? Is your father staring into the fire while he talks of the books that will change the world?

If waking drags you from crystal illusion to foggy reality, then no wonder you hate surfacing in the morning and are so dopey and mixed-up when you do. No wonder you mutter in the night about wanting your mother and missing your brother, so long away in the war, or insist you must go downstairs right away because your babies are crying for you. When you wake up, it is the present that feels all wrong.

Not that I should wax too sentimental about your night-life. Whatever you may be dreaming, it is a nightmare for the rest of us. We have rigged up an ingenious night alarm system based on a bell attached to a child's safety rail. It is a small Alpine bell, painted gold and decorated with Tyrolean flowers, which I brought home long ago from a school exchange trip to Austria. When you shake the rail for attention, the bell sounds, the baby alarm next to your bed picks it up and the sleeper on duty next door has prac-tically to be peeled from the ceiling. With bells like this on her goats Heidi must have been a nervous wreck.

You quickly become adept at these imperious jangles. Long before the first ring I will start awake with a knot in my stomach, waiting for it. Mainly you need assistance on to the commode, or attention to one of the industrial-sized pads to which we now resort. At other times we rush in to soothe a nameless agitation and assure you that someone is near.

Sometimes Anna will come to your bedside. There, deep in the night when the fight is gone and the resentment stilled, the bond is strong again. Sadly it is not quite resilient enough to withstand an unshakeable conviction next morning that Anna has doctored your tea.

*

As another autumn approaches, the pattern of your life continues its roller-coaster course. This disease may be slow, but it makes for a dizzying ride for everyone else, the breath knocked out one day by a plunge in your condition, spirits sent soaring the next by some precious token of normality. Even rattling along on the level it is hard not to live in queasy anticipation of the dip around the corner.

One day you might be refusing to leave your bed and screaming that a new carer, to whose fake tan you have taken exception, is a slut, the next welcoming me to a glade of smiles. One weekend you will entirely ruin Sunday lunch, interrupting your sister's reminiscences with a face like thunder and a stream of put-downs: 'What do you know, Anna? You never went to school. Don't be silly, Anna. You never had a father.' Another Sunday you will sparkle like a candelabra, bestowing your smile on a virile American guest and assuring him you like a man 'with words as well as looks'. ('Wow!' he mutters.)

Best of all, when I announce to the children after that particular lunch that Grandma needs some music to make her spirit soar, you observe cheekily, 'Would that be *s-o-r-e* or *s-o-a-r*?'

I asked Frank Gunn-Moore why he thought you had retained your interest in words, your ability to pun and to spell, despite finding it hard to place two sentences together and having all but lost the ability to read. I thought he might launch into an explanation about why certain synapses survive in one area of the brain or another. But sometimes even a scientist prefers a different sort of language.

'I would guess,' he said, 'it's because words have been the essence of your mother all along.'

*

Which makes it all the more shocking when certain kinds of words – the words we still half listen for, the words we long to hear – do not come.

Our beloved Dale has died. After three years of treatment and optimism, the cancer spread suddenly to her liver. Margaret, Topsy and I went to help nurse her through her last days. Jon brought her home from hospital and we cared for her together in their London home, the four of us and her mother Pam, as she slipped into a coma. She took her last breath in the early hours of a September morning, just minutes before the rest of her Australian family – father, sister and two brothers – arrived in a breathless rush from the airport.

Back home in Scotland you remain oblivious. The news evokes no emotion, our distress no curiosity.

Shortly afterwards you and I are taking a drive along the foothills of the Campsies in the dregs of an autumn day. You sit in the car morosely, wan and depressed as you so often are these days.

'Margaret's coming today, isn't she?' you say.

Rain is starting to pelt the car. I switch on the lights and almost run into a cyclist looming out of the greyness.

'No, Margaret's in London. She's looking after Jon, because his wife has died.'

No response. You continue to look ahead. No change of expression. I spell it out slowly: 'Your son Jon. His wife has died. He's broken-hearted.'

'Oh,' you say, and stare out of the window.

Once you would have found words of comfort, better words than anyone else. I have a thank-you note here, post-marked 1975, from a woman you must have met while in hospital for a minor operation. Her mother had since died and she was responding to a letter from you. Hers ended:

> *I think I was meant to go into hospital that week*
> *to meet you, Mamie, so that you could help me*
> *through my sorrow. I can't thank you enough.*

You have been a great comfort to me. I think of
you often and also of your own sorrows.

Your own experience enabled you to express beautifully
and without glibness what those in grief needed to hear.
Now the death of a daughter-in-law, just forty-five years
old, evokes nothing and the pain of your youngest child
cannot touch you.

I hate this disease. I hate it with a boiling fury. It has
robbed you of the ability even to imagine what you cannot
remember. It has stolen your empathy.

25

The sound of music

Rodgers and Hammerstein

'Take the subway uptown to Allerton Road and turn right at Dunkin' Donuts,' her secretary had said. 'You'll find us two blocks along.'

Beth Abraham Health Services, where the world's leading music therapist Dr Concetta Tomaino co-founded the Institute of Music and Neurologic Function in 1995 with British neurologist Dr Oliver Sacks, is a long way from trendy Manhattan. It's an enormous, not-for-profit nursing home and outpatient centre in the middle of the Bronx, patrolled by a burly security guard who has not been hired for his bedside manner. Most of its patients are subsidised by Medicaid or Medicare. Half have dementia.

It's also the place that has nurtured probably the most hopeful and certainly the most innovative development anywhere in the treatment of dementia. In this teeming centre in one of New York's poorest boroughs personalised music is being used to reawaken memory and restore, for a time at least, a sense of identity.

I'm here, Mum, because amid so much that is letting you down, music is not. At some profoundly mysterious level it's helping to hold your own identity together. It is keeping you with us and tugging you back when you stray. I want to know why.

*

All the time you and I have known each other there has been a song on your tongue. I have to work to think of an occasion you did not consider a legitimate target. No parent-teachers' evening or doctor's waiting room was ever entirely safe.

And if you were able to dodge some practical work while regaling the company with, say, 'The Wee Cooper o' Fife' on comb and paper, so much the better. As we drove through Connel Bridge all those years ago on our journey to Mull, you recalled having once organised a group of women from home to help clean someone's holiday house nearby. You had led the way but not, you seemed to remember, the floor-scrubbing.

'I likely didn't do much cleaning at all,' you mused with a grin. 'I probably sang to them.'

I doubt if there was any 'probably' about it.

Your repertoire includes the hymns your mother sang at the family organ, including a Scots one composed by your grandfather, John Fulton Greig, and snatches of the symphonies your father listened to on the radio. He used those classical pieces to teach you all syncopation, instructing you how to come in behind the beat. He was a proud member of the Socialist Choir and insisted on allocating parts of whatever rousing number he was working on to each member of the family. Since it had to be taken extremely seriously, Archie saw his job as making Anna laugh.

'He could do it just by looking at her,' you said. 'She kept being sent out of the room for laughing. But I remember those songs yet. Father used to teach us things like . . .' And off you went:

> *Truth your standard,*
> *Steady your word,*
> *Be faithful to death*
> *For your freedom and worth.*
> *And right is might,*
> *And might is right*
> *Something, something, something*
> *And fight the fight.*

Harriet, who was particularly keen on singing, brought home the pieces she was learning for the Rutherglen Choral Union and practised them with such verve that she could be heard in the street, where the local kids took delight in mimicking her in the wrong key. Thanks to her we have Hugh Roberton's great choral work 'All in the April Evening' in this repertoire of yours, rubbing up

against 'Tiptoe Through the Tulips' from your trendy
Aunt Betty. Alongside the hits of Glen Miller and the Ink
Spots are the anthems you and Anna belted out in the
church choir, the songs Vera Lynn popularised during the
war and the never-ending stream of Scottish melodies that
raised the roof at Hogmanay. Effortlessly adorned with
one of your harmonies they have all joined the soundtrack
to my own life.

But here is the thing. This soundtrack is still going
strong. Very little has changed. What else in your life is it
possible to say that about? Your songs are as deeply woven
into this part of it as they ever were in merrier times.

We can still rely on you to break the monotony of a rainy
Saturday afternoon with a perky 'Let's sing something'.
Who but you would soften your refusal to get up in the
morning with a rousing burst of 'How Do You Solve a
Problem like Maria?' or sanctify a trip to the toilet with
'The Hills are Alive with the Sound of Music'? I do wonder
sometimes what Mother Superior would think of the places
she finds herself.

Long after your own words have begun to desert you in
droves, these familiar songs deliver an illusion of fluency:
'Java Jive' and 'Do-Re-Me', 'The Skye Boat Song' and
'We'll Meet Again', 'Let Me Call You Sweetheart' and 'The
Northern Lights of Aberdeen'. Silly words, fun words, fat
words, thin words, Scots words, English words, they bubble
to your lips still. We sing them in your bed, in the car, in the
bath, over a meal sitting by the window with a cup of tea.

And it's instantaneous. Like a switch. Someone starts you on one of your favourites and suddenly you are awake again, alive and remembering who you are. Music, I begin to see, is what rescues you from silence and the bars of the prison-house.

For a long time I imagined it must be your particularly song-infused history that had enabled you to retain such receptivity. I imagined we were lucky and thought you might be unique. Then I met Connie Tomaino.

*

Beth Abraham's senior vice-president for music therapy has a round, cheery face and curly dark hair. She greets me from behind her desk in a small office, old like the rest of the building and laden with books and papers. A jazz saxophonist is playing in one of the rooms nearby and the notes drift across our conversation.

Even before she came here in 1980 from another skilled nursing facility, Connie Tomaino had noticed that people deemed 'non-responsive' came to life and showed signs of recognition when familiar music was played. Was there something about music, she wondered, that could engage recognition in people for whom all other kinds of sensory recognition seemed to be damaged?

'Oliver Sacks had already experienced a sort of awakening with music with his post-encephalitic Parkinson's patients. So when I arrived, he and I were like partners in crime. Why is this happening? we were asking. Scientists in the early eighties told us music was too complex for them to study, so we decided to look at the clinical implications – how and why does music affect people, and can we refine some of the protocols to provide more direct approaches to care? That was the start of the Institute of Music and Neurologic Function.'

In the intervening decades neuroscientists have started to look at how the brain processes music. They have shown that because of the many elements involved – rhythm, melody, harmony, pitch, timbre and accent – music involves many different parts of the brain. Its seat is in the stem itself, that deep, primeval place just above the spinal cord where our most basic functions, like eating, sleeping and breathing, are regulated. A pulse of sound comes in and the neurons that receive that pulse fire off, stimulating those primary parts of the brain that only stop when we die.

'It's like when you have a tip of the tongue phenomenon – you would remember if you just had an extra clue,' says Dr Tomaino. 'Well, music, because it involves so many brain areas, is actually providing multiple clues, because a song isn't just melody, it's rhythm, it's emotional and historical associations. That means that just any piece of music is not going to affect a person with dementia – it has to be one with personal importance, at least when you're talking about arousing someone who seems to be lost. Even at the end stage in dementia, if people still have physical ability you'll see them beating to the music.'

It's all down to how our auditory system is wired. The auditory nerve has immediate connections to what's known as the fastigial part of the brain, to the autonomic nervous system, to respiration, heartbeat and the brain stem. Then there's another connection to the fight-or-flight amygdala, the almond-shaped mass of grey matter inside each cerebral hemisphere that's involved with the experiencing of emotions. The word is from the Greek *amugdale* for almond.

'Without any awareness on the part of the person, the auditory nerve is already sending pulses, like pressure pulses, into those very basic nerve areas. Even if the person has no cortex or any ability to process information at all, their brain is receiving information about the sound.'

I lean in towards her, feeling all of a sudden a bit emotional. Here at last is something the plaques and tangles cannot lay waste to. Here is the explanation of music's ability to bring you back, time and again. Here, it may even be, is our hope for the rest of your life.

'So, almost literally until the last breath,' I say, 'everyone is able to respond to music?'

'Oh, absolutely. It's the first sense in the foetus and the last to go at death. It's one of the most robust sensory inputs we can have.'

'And the one thing dementia cannot destroy?'

I am so used to experts telling me to be careful, not to leap to conclusions and clutch at theories that I ask this a little nervously.

'That's right. That's absolutely right. People may not be able to sing all the words of a song, but they'll show you through facial expressions that they recognise it. And many times, up until the very end, people with dementia will still be able to sing the words. Sound and melody are so intricately connected to the words of the song that the words just come back.'

It is hard to overstate the significance of this. Tomaino and Sacks have shown that personalised music works not just as an occasional recreational activity but as a regularly delivered therapeutic treatment that can help to socialise someone, increase verbalisation and reduce agitation and fearfulness. In a dementia landscape where pharmaceutical aids are thin on the ground and a cure a long way off, here is a resource – potentially available to every single person – that can preserve mental engagement and recognition.

As the pair wrote as far back as 1991 in the *International Journal of Arts Medicine*:

> Music acts as sort of a Proustian mnemonic, elicit-
> ing emotions and associations that had been long
> forgotten, giving the patient access once again to
> moods and memories . . . One sees that it is not an
> actual loss of memories here, but a loss of access
> to these – and music above all, can provide access
> once again . . . can constitute a key factor opening
> the door not only to specific moods and memories,
> but to the entire thought-structure and personality
> of the past.

Beyond their own empirical studies, there has been little scientific research into why music operates in this way or what physiological effect it might be having on the brain. Working with his own students, cognitive neuroscientist Dr Petr Janata, associate professor of the Center for Mind and Brain at the University of California, Davis, has made a start. He has shown through functional magnetic resonance imaging that the medial prefrontal cortex (the area supporting a sense of self and the retrieval of autobiographical information) lights up in response to music of particular importance to an individual. His next step is to find out whether the same illumination occurs when someone with dementia hears that type of music.

In the meantime the Bronx pioneers continue to observe some extraordinary effects in practice. Oliver Sacks, author of *Musicophilia* and *The Man Who Mistook His Wife for a Hat*, says he has watched music sparking a response in everyone he has encountered with dementia 'without exception'. He describes as amazing the way familiar songs touch the springs of memory in people who have lost their entire autobiography. He notes how the 'quickening' effect which the philosopher Immanuel Kant observed in music can bring these people back into their own personhood, memories and autobiographies, with a lucidity and pleasure that can last for hours afterwards.

He uses a striking image: 'The past, which is not recoverable in any other way, is embedded in the music as if in amber.'

*

There is no doubt that Tomaino and Sacks are right.

You are lying back in the bath, looking skeletal. The triangle of bone at your neck is so empty of skin that water has pooled in the cavern. I am soaping you with bubbles and trying to calm you down. You emphatically did not want to get into this bath and I know for a fact that in a moment you won't want to get out either. You are upset and frightened by the transition from towel to water, this awful feeling of vulnerability.

I start to hum 'It's a Lovely Day Tomorrow' and in a slightly quavery voice you join in. 'Just forget your sorrows and learn to sing,' we warble together, 'tomorrow is a lovely day.'

You relax. The tension drains from your face. You shut your eyes. You let the water lap around your chin. You begin to smile. It really is a little bit like magic.

*

On my way through New York I visit Dan Cohen, executive director of the not-for-profit organisation Music and Memory. He has put the Sacks and Tomaino findings into action by encouraging care homes across the United States to offer their residents regular access to personally mean-ingful music on iPods; there is anecdotal evidence that it can lead to reduced dependence on antipsychotic drugs. In Canada the use of personal playlists at home has enabled people to stay there longer, delaying admissions to institutional care. Authorities in North America are discovering that music can have an impact on the bottom line.

This approach deserves wider attention – not only because historically meaningful music appears to have an effect on flagging neural networks (which is wonderful enough), but because it cannot be delivered without personal engagement. Help is needed to produce a unique playlist for those who cannot compile their own and to work the technology. Caregivers have to get to know their clients much more intimately – and children their parents – if they are to discover their life-music and see the full effect, because a pleasant CD on a loop is not going to work. As with the cognitive and reminiscence therapies also beginning to prove their worth, the social interaction is valuable in itself.

'Human intervention,' says Henry Simmons, chief executive of Alzheimer Scotland, 'is the chemotherapy for dementia.'

As your own experience teaches us, music is the ultimate in person-centred care. A treatment that doesn't even feel like one, it affects how people are able to think, feel and act at every stage of the dementia process.

The past embedded in amber. Music, the one thing dementia cannot destroy.

26

Elephants and grandchildren

CBS commentator Andy Rooney

Your two granddaughters are chips off the old block. Margaret's daughter Ellie has inherited your famously equable temperament and my Anna Lisa your sunny self-confidence, along with your nose. It seems especially cruel that both of them should now find themselves frozen out.

Handsome young grandsons, breezing in with a guitar to serenade you, are greeted with rapture. Siggy, my second eldest, charms you into gobbling down a meal: 'Eat this up, Grandma, or it's the loony bin for you'; the second youngest, Rossie, bursts in with, 'Well, hello Joe and what do you know?' and you're straight back with news of your return from the rodeo. But girls with short skirts, low-cut tops and fashionably straggly hair are a different proposition. It's as if, now that you no longer have a clue who the grandchildren are, you judge them crudely on what they seem to be. Even in her own house you talk to Anna Lisa as if she has just wandered in from the street.

'What do you think you're doing?' you demand as she leans forward to choose a Quality Street.

'Just taking a chocolate, Grandma.'

'Well, don't. They're not for visitors.'

Even though she has learned forbearance, Anna Lisa flushes. I see her smile wobbling.

A few minutes later you accuse her of stealing from the kitchen cupboard.

'Mum, she's your granddaughter,' I say, starting to feel tetchy myself.

'Is she?' you say, interested. 'How long has that been?'

'All her life. Since she was born. You used to sing her to sleep with "I'm in Love With You, Honey" and "Little Bird".'

'Really?' you reply, as if the most astonishing idea has just been presented to you. Which is undoubtedly the case.

On days when she has volunteered to look after you in your own house, you welcome her without warmth. Her self-possession is tottering under your unfriendly gaze. She makes a point of wearing her hair scraped back and the most shapeless sweatshirt she can dig out, but she might as well hide in a burqa for all the difference it makes now to your air of disapproval. Where, you demand to know, are the boys?

I see her becoming more and more nervous and unsure around you, unable to predict when you might turn on her. She takes her place on Grandma Duty with as much grace as she can muster, but confesses she has started to dread it. She tries to remind herself that this is the same grandmother who used to roll her up in a duvet when she was ill and ply her with fruit pastilles and that week's *Dandy*, the same one who taught her the loudest way to crunch a mint. She looks into your steely brown eyes and tries to remember them smiling at her. But it's hard going.

Before she leaves for a postgraduate year in Atlanta, she pops in to say goodbye. You are in a chair by the window and she perches nervously nearby. It's all going smoothly enough until you spy her feet. Black, strappy, Roman sandals. Danger.

'How dare you walk into my house with feet like that!' you rage. 'It's time you went straight home.'

It's been said that elephants and grandchildren never forget. So what will your granddaughter remember of you? I know her biggest fear is the same as mine: that this is what she will remember for ever.

*

Her brothers, whom you welcome with flirtatious delight, see much more of the grandmother they remember. Rossie helped you up to bed one night, singing to you all the way, and was enchanted when you joined in with what he calls 'a sort of weary hum'. You even managed some advice for him, instructing him sagely not to throw himself at just any woman out there. During the best of these moments he feels as close to you as at any time since you used to pick him up from nursery school with a cheese roll to eat in the car.

In school and university vacations the boys all take their turn to keep you company, but no-one rushes to your house these days rejoicing at the thought of what awaits them. Even when they are exercising their most persuasive charms you can be tricky to engage and their song repertoire dries up too quickly. Much as they want to honour what you have been to them, they are mainly doing this to relieve me. Back home I am so permanently tight with exhaustion and low on patience that I suspect the kids sometimes find it harder than they let on.

But I am grateful for their help, because the rota is driving me round the bend. No time to stop, never a chance to clear my mind. I am losing my grasp of a swaying stack of priorities: the children, the husband, the broadcasting, the mother whose needs dominate my week, the sisters who are left with more to do if I don't play my part, the grieving brother I too rarely see, the friends who never hear from me.

There is plenty of sociological research to reassure me that feeling like this is normal. One study finds 'a high level of psychological distress and deterioration in psychological wellbeing' among informal caregivers of people with dementia, which intensifies as the condition progresses: academic speak for being screamingly, nerve-janglingly, sleep-defyingly stressed-out all the time. Although what do I know about it really? I live and mostly sleep elsewhere, sustain a job and escape when I need to. Among fulltime caregivers research shows that only 27% get even as much as a week's break a year.

Tommy Whitelaw understands as well as anyone. He gave up his job organising merchandise sales for touring rock bands to devote himself to round-the-clock care of his mother Joan at home in Glasgow and then walked around Scotland collecting testimonies from others in the same position. Their letters, which he handed to the Scottish government to raise awareness of dementia's toll on carers, are one long scream of distress.

A caregiver in Perth likens the experience to 'Alice tumbling suddenly down the rabbit hole and clutching at things as she falls in the dark'. That this is not a description of dementia itself, as it easily could be, but of dealing with it, shows how close carers themselves feel at times to mental collapse. 'I get days I feel I cannot go on like this,' writes another from South Ayrshire; 'The pressure is almost unbearable' (Dundee); 'You have no life really' (Glasgow); 'I am an exhausted nervous wreck of a person' (Highlands).

I assume this is what is meant by 'deterioration in psychological wellbeing'. It is the deep and desperate loneliness of the long-distance carer.

By Christmas Eve, our first since losing Dale, I am worn out, although with all five children around we manage such an efficient divide-and-rule strategy at dinner that you don't notice Anna daring to reminisce about your father and she is too well occupied to contest your claim of having personally saved the world from destruction during the war. You lead us in a chorus of 'Silent Night', clear and strong, and the evening passes off without incident. But the effort of including you in everything, fighting for every last social possibility and constantly guarding your tongue is wearying.

I wake up in your house in the cadaverous dawn light of Boxing Day morning, trying to calm my bell-scrambled brain and thinking I have had enough of all this. It's probably just post-Christmas tristesse, but today I feel I cannot face trying to coax you out of bed, explain everything umpteen times, respond chirpily to nonsense and divert every reference to Anna before it reaches her. I stumble downstairs to make a cup of coffee and sit in your kitchen in a blur of self-pity.

Out in the garden the branches of the pine tree are filigreed with snow and every stray stalk poking out of the ground is flush with diamonds. Through the window I watch yellowhammers and blue tits chasing each other around a tiny tree hung with nuts; a robin stands guard on the edge of the frozen-over stone trough. I remember my father's constant delight in this scene on his way through to the kettle. I think of his sharp brain in a body that stopped working for him when he so furiously wanted to stay longer and of you upstairs, imprisoned by a different kind of frailty, raging in your own way against the dying of the light.

A few days before Christmas I heard someone speaking to you with that well-meaning heartiness a nurse adopts to a patient. I looked to see if you had noticed and fractionally raised an eyebrow. You shot me a conspiratorial look back:

you had noticed all right. I winked. You winked back. You know when you are being patronised.

We are on the same side, I told myself then, you and I and Margaret and Topsy, standing together against the lowering of the lid on a box marked Dementia. As long as you refuse to get in and curl up inside, then we won't let you either, whatever the cost.

So I told myself. But in bed at the end of Boxing Day, my own bed this time while a sister takes custody of the midnight bell, I lie awake wondering how long we can manage this. Can it really be right to keep you at home as your disease advances into the later stages, when the three of us feel so incompetent and so terribly heartbroken so much of the time?

'Do you realise what you girls have done with your mother?' my husband says to comfort me. 'You've kept her part of the family and anchored to her children and grand-children. You've kept her tethered to reality, even if the rope is lengthening. You've kept her tongue active, even if it's used to lash Anna.'

A fine collection of metaphors, I tell him.

'I'm serious,' he says. 'Any other way and we would have lost her a long time ago.'

*

I almost do lose you in the bath.

I am busy trying to heave you over the side when I realise you have not an iota of power in your legs. There is nobody to help me. I don't know what to do. Just as I am wondering how mere skin and bones can possibly be this difficult to support, your head suddenly drops to one side and you are sagging in my arms, breathing oddly. Moments later you have stopped breathing altogether.

I know, no doubt about it, that I have killed you. The bath was too hot. I have raised you too fast. There should have been two of us doing this. You are dead in my arms.

Sweat pours down my back. I ease your floppy body on to the bathroom floor. You lie there white and still. I gaze down at you, trying feverishly to remember the recovery position, just in case you are not quite dead.

'Hey,' protests a small voice, 'this floor's a bit hard.'

You open an eye.

'Suppose,' you say next, reviving by the second, 'we make a break for that window-seat?'

Somehow I manage to haul you across the floor and on to the seat. You look at me, grinning broadly. Incredibly, you are enjoying yourself.

'I made up my mind to be brave,' you sigh, propped at a rakish angle on the window-seat and looking happier than you have all day.

I should have known. You were always most yourself in the middle of an emergency.

On another evening your legs give way on the stairs up to bed. I half haul, half push you as far as the landing, where you collapse panting.

'Are you all right?' I am panicking again.

You look up from the floor, where you are reclining with one arm around the banister, blink once and find a way of turning this misadventure into a laugh.

'A fellow who lived out in Yoker,' you remark conversationally.

'Hit his wife, as she slept, with a poker,' I oblige. 'But that doesn't solve the problem of how we're going to get you into the bedroom.'

'I could try going backwards,' you volunteer, and begin a shuffling movement on your bottom, the effort of which so knocks you out that you lie flat on the carpet, unable to move or speak, for several minutes after. But your eyes, when you open them at last, are shining, your face is pink with excitement. The lassitude that has gripped you all evening is gone.

'Come on, Sally. We can do this last bit,' you say, rolling on to your side and flinging an arm on to the bed while I yank at your shoulders. You leading me – how I've missed it. Somehow we make it on to the bed.

You are still flushed with vim and achievement when I bend to kiss you goodnight.

'That's the thing about you, Mum. When the chips are down, you rise to the occasion, don't you?'

'Well, you have to,' you say happily.

Later (after searching the web for a special offer on Stannah stairlifts) I sit musing over how much of what you used to relish is missing from your life: everyday drama, excitement, variety, danger, risk, goals to challenge yourself with, opportunities to be brave and put your shoulder against the closing door, the chance to walk into the wind and rejoice in the whirl of snow. Instead, you get meaningless dramas on a television screen to which you cannot relate, life in a succession of chairs, people vying to put your slippers on and pathetic, tottery walks on which your legs can barely support you.

But how to give you what you miss? Dear goodness, I can't overheat your bath and drop you on the stairs every night.

27

All this ought to be written down

Irina in Chekhov's *The Three Sisters*

Lurching from one alarm to the next, ragged with responsibility, constantly on the hunt for help. Might there be a better place to look after you than at home?

Like families everywhere we are in a bind here. With so little support from outside, home becomes more and more difficult as this illness takes hold. But the residential option is not easy either. Dementia cries out for personally focused care, but even the best care homes in the land cannot aspire to that 24 hours a day. There is no obvious path ahead.

Many residential homes do provide excellent care. Countless families are grateful for a service they cannot provide themselves and a place where their loved one is demonstrably safe, cherished, occupied and at least relatively happy. Unfortunately other care homes are downright bad, and there are plenty of those as well.

Sube Banerjee's work has shown him the full spectrum.

'Why is it,' he asks, 'that for the same unit cost, Care Home A can be a place where you really do want your mum to go, where it may be a bit battered around the edges but they're all having a nice time, they're smiling, they're happy, behaviours are managed and the staff are careful and honest and speak to people like human beings?

'And they're being paid the same amount as Care Home B, where you'd never let anyone near. It might be a bright shiny new place but you just know they're sitting around in a circle with nothing happening, being given large doses of antipsychotics. There are things other than money that determine good quality, and they are the leadership and the culture of the place.'

All the same he is blunt about the economics: 'We've privatised this industry and fragmented it. You could assure quality when local authorities were involved. You could have a career progression where people could be promoted to be in charge of the home and go and do other things. That's largely gone now. There's this vast consolidation, where people are seeking profit out of a business it's difficult to find profit in.'

Watching a committed care-home manager making the most of limited resources to make life as good as it can be for residents with complicated needs, an activities coordinator dancing and singing her heart out to a roomful of wandering attentions, or a care worker taking time to stroke an arm in the middle of a busy medications round, is deeply impressive. This kind of care may never be wholly personal, but it is decent and loving, and that's what matters.

But we also need to take note of experiences like Irene MacKay's.

Remember Irene, Mum? She works in a lively bookshop up the road from the café where you and Dad used to meet the Club for coffee. I talked to her one day about how difficult your life was becoming at home.

'Don't let her go,' she cried, startling me with the ferocity of her response. 'Keep her with you. If I had the chance again, I would never, ever let my mother go.'

She started to tell me what had happened, but there was a queue of customers behind me at her till.

'I'll send you my file,' she said. 'I've written everything down.'

It arrived by email a few days later.

On being discharged from hospital after a fall and assessed as no longer fit to live at home, her mother had gone into a home with beautiful gardens, elegantly designed rooms and a culture, as became clear too late, of shoddy indifference. After a while she had written to the manager:

> *I am not someone who constantly complains. I would*
> *rather give praise when it is due, but I am watching*
> *my mother fail under my eyes every time I visit. It is*
> *breaking my heart to see how quickly she is failing.*

The old lady fared worse and worse. In a report afterwards Irene wrote:

She had two serious falls, which were not reported. The first time it was her face and she had a large black eye, and in the second she fell out of bed and was put back in the middle of the night suffering from a double fracture of the pelvis.

Irene demanded three times that her mother be moved to different buildings within the complex, but nothing improved for long. She died in the middle of the night, four weeks after being put under a new house manager who was finally trying to improve standards.

But Irene witnessed more than the neglect of her mother in that bright place with its manicured lawns. There was an old man in the care home, whose treatment she has never forgotten:

> I personally witnessed them ignoring a male patient in a wheelchair for more than thirty minutes while he repeatedly asked for help to get to the bathroom. I heard a nurse saying several times, 'We're busy. We'll be with you soon.'
>
> After a while the gentleman started to cry and sat there sobbing for about five minutes, until a nurse finally appeared. Then in a loud, disgusted voice she announced to the other staff, 'Oh no. Old Jimmy has soiled himself again.'

It is a picture I am not able get out of my head any more than Irene could: an old man I never met, suffering in a place where the rest of us cannot hear the weeping.

Irene is right to believe that all this ought to be written down and then shouted to the world. Not, emphatically, because it is the experience of everyone in residential care, but because it remains the experience of some – and they are among the most fragile souls on earth.

*

The most interesting thinkers are proposing a different model of dementia care. They envisage a stronger system of community support that would enable people to stay at home longer, so that the best care-home providers could concentrate on offering specialist attention to those with more advanced conditions.

'Care homes are simply not affordable to live in for years,' says Professor June Andrews. 'Nor are even the best of them much fun. What we need is to make them much, much better for the last eighteen months or so of a person's life, when professional help for dementia is genuinely required, and before that keep people at home.'

Keeping people at home will require big changes in a society that has become over-reliant on institutional care. But if we get it right – if we can find ways to offer professional guidance, information, joined-up services, respite, trouble-shooting, design ideas, health checks, non-pill therapies and social opportunities, the absence of all of which drives families trying to cope on their own quickly to the edge – then perhaps one day there will not be so many like mine who don't know which way to turn. Scotland now offers a year of post-diagnostic support from a trained link worker, which is a start, but if care homes are no longer to fill up with people who don't absolutely need to be there, a much more extensive system of community-based intervention will have to be put in place.

The rewards are huge. Get this one right and every person with dementia will have the chance to live the fullest life for the longest time in the place where they are most secure, and to end their life with the professional care they deserve in an institution radically recreated for the twenty-first century.

It is an ideal. Of course it is. But according to the World Health Organisation community support is a goal which every country, whatever its starting point and resources, is going to have to shuffle towards somehow. As dementia numbers grow, there is no other way. The need to save money on residential bills will drive the move in countries like ours, if shame alone does not.

*

For our part we have decided to keep you at home. Your sister Harriet did not flourish in residential care, although others do. It would be dishonest to pretend that Irene's account has not also coloured my feelings about letting you go.

But we have no idea where this route will take us. Your dementia is getting worse and the way ahead feels lonely. Increasingly we understand there is no course of action that will send us to sleep at night knowing for sure that we are doing the right thing. If ever there was any complacency about our determination to keep you with us, dearest mother, it evaporated a long time ago.

28

I'm disconnected

Mamie Magnusson

It is our last appointment at the Memory Clinic, although this comes as news to me. You and I have returned for our annual appointment with the psychiatrist.

Waiting to be called, we watch the passing scene behind the reception desk, where a large lady in black is discussing her diet with the receptionist.

'I weighed my salad last night. I had it to the exact gram I was allowed and then my son came in and pinched a piece of chicken. Can you believe it? I was that mad. I had it all weighed. That and the rocket.'

The lady looks over at us for confirmation of the incredibility of the situation and you beam back sympathetically. I try to imagine what your mind might be doing with the image of a rocket sharing a pair of scales in space with a chicken fillet.

The doctor beckons us in, the same one as before. You take the proffered seat in front of her desk and I sit nearby, willing you, as if I were some anxious mother at a school interview, to acquit yourself well.

'How are you keeping, Mamie?' she asks.

There is a long, long pause. You gaze at her vacantly. She looks to me for a clue.

'The doctor's just wondering how you're doing?' I repeat unhelpfully. There is nothing wrong with your ears.

'No worse than usual,' you say at last.

The doctor looks at you keenly and then turns towards me.

'Your mother has slowed down,' she says, with an air of imparting something I might not have noticed. She turns back. 'Last time I saw you, a year ago, you were speaking more like a journalist. You were quite quick.'

You gaze back mutely.

'What sort of practical things can your mother still do?' the doctor asks me. 'Cook a meal? Do some housework?'

She must be kidding.

'Nothing,' I say, with a guilty glance at you. 'Nothing that I can think of at all. Mind you, domestic tasks were never her forte. She can still sing beautifully.'

You start to tell her something, but it is a muddle of words from which no sense emerges and you lapse into silence. There is a funny constriction in my throat.

'You have some understanding, Mamie,' the doctor informs you. 'There is still insight there. Your brain is picking things up, but you can't come up with any answers, can you?'

You nod. 'I'm . . . disconnected,' you muse, muddying the psychiatric waters by choosing, as you so often do, exactly the right word. Alois Alzheimer himself could not have put it better.

I notice how sharp and thin your shoulders are, pointing out of your big cream sweater like a coat hanger. You give the doctor your widest smile across the desk as she pronounces her verdict.

'Your mother has come down very quickly over the last year. There's a general deterioration physically, mentally and functionally. Last year her conversation was faster. She was using bigger sentences, having quite big conversations. I'm now seeing a reluctance to start and then –' (I glance at you, and she takes the hint) – 'and then when you want to say something, it's not coming out, is it, Mamie?'

You appear to agree. Taking this as the end of the interview you smile broadly, lean across the desk and stretch out your hand for the doctor to shake.

'It's nice to be able to come in here and speak to you,' you assure her. 'It's a home from home.'

The doctor looks briefly astonished at this tribute to her office, then glances at me warmly.

'She's still got a lovely smile, hasn't she?'

Oh, yes, a lovely smile.

I help you to your feet. I've just noticed that I am crying.

As the doctor ushers us out, she says in a friendly way that you will not be required to come back for any more assessments, as there is nothing that can be done.

I have no clue what we will do from here and what will become of you. We are wandering out into a bare landscape where not even the Memory Clinic provides refuge and in which we no longer have so much as a nominal specialist attached to your case or anyone to call on with the know-how to share the journey with us. More than ever I am oppressed by the magnitude of the hole in the medical and care system. There are charities offering a chance to talk to other carers, little bits of support here and there, well intentioned leaflets and lots of websites, but there is no service pulling the medical and care side together in a way that is personal to you and to those of us responsible for you. This is the challenge that any new model of community support will have to address.

One observer calls it 'the empty centre' of dementia care, this wild and windy steppe we are stumbling across now. Thousand upon thousand of others are somewhere out here too, feeling blindly for supports on the way.

'It's amazing,' I am told, 'how broken in how many ways the system can be.'

That's exactly how it feels as the door of the consulting room closes and you and I set off slowly back down the corridor of the clinic to pick up our coats. Everything feels quite, quite broken.

You are quick to sense it. Hanging on to my arm, you pat my hand.

'Well done, Sal. We're a good team,' you whisper reassuringly, as we head out to tackle whatever dementia may throw at us next.

29

I am, because we are

Theologian John Swinton

'Who is it that can tell me who I am?' asks King Lear in a whisper that carries right to the balcony of Glasgow's plush Theatre Royal and straight to the part of me that these days dissolves at the sight of a duckling, never mind the voice of Derek Jacobi breaking so softly that around three thousand people stop breathing all at once.

It is March 2011, and Shakespeare's tragedy has never before spoken to me so directly. How could I not have noticed what a searing study of dementia this play is? In ruined, deluded Lear, one minute incoherent in rather familiar ways and the next astonishingly acute, I see you. I hear from him your own heartbreaking attempts to school your will and control your mind, as you feel both slipping away:

> *O! let me not be mad, not mad, sweet heaven;*
> *Keep me in temper; I would not be mad!*

But it is when he asks his famous question, 'Who is it that can tell me who I am?', that my heart beats faster. For the first time I am riveted not by the existential angst this question comes to signify later in the play but by the direction of Lear's appeal. In all the times I have read the play or seen it performed, I have never noticed that the question's real focus – or so it seems blindingly clear tonight – is on those listening. Who is it among the rest of you, Lear seems to say, can tell me who I am?

King Lear is our play for today, a devastating exploration of the human condition for a twenty-first century struggling as never before with the implications of long life. As he starts to lose his sense of self, the old king is pleading for someone to help define it for him. The words are directed at us. He is speaking to me.

The Zulus have a proverb: 'A person becomes a person through other people.' The Maoris, too, are said to consider both identity and memory to reside in the group rather than the individual. What if they are on to something? Might there be a clue here to a new understanding of community, this social ideal that can mean everything and nothing? What if our elderly, indeed our mentally frail of all ages, could depend on other people to hold their identity for them and tell them who they are? What if that were not just an optional social extra but the very essence of how we are made?

What, in other words, my darling mother, if *you* are what community is for?

*

The idea that any person's sense of who they are is at least in part socially constructed and that those around them have a crucial role in validating and sustaining that self has more up-to-date exponents than Shakespeare. Neuropsychologist Professor Steven Sabat, of Georgetown University in Washington DC, has concluded that anyone's 'self' has three different aspects, one of which is entirely dependent on others.

Sabat's Self 1 is where each of us experiences the world as 'me'. This part of our selfhood exists as long as we are conscious, although (as you and Lear would be the first to acknowledge) it is certainly possible for us not to recognise it.

Self 2 comprises our mental and physical attributes and attitudes – in my case blue eyes, freckles, penchant for chocolate, fear of spiders, guilty addiction to *The Archers*, love for you and so on – all the things that help me to orientate myself to a particular understanding of who I am in the world. If I were to develop dementia, Self 2 would also take in its neuropathology and symptoms.

Self 3, according to Sabat, is our social persona. This depends on our relationships with others. For instance, I am a mother, daughter, sister, wife, aunt, niece, TV presenter, colleague to fellow journalists, client of my agent, writer for my publisher, employer of care staff. This aspect of my selfhood, in all its dimensions, is uniquely vulnerable to how others see me. If they value me, I am valued. But the reverse is equally true. So, if I have dementia and others focus exclusively on the troubling symptoms accruing to Self 2, my social persona will change and diminish. On the other hand, if their attention stays focused on the remaining attributes – in your case it might be your singing, your sense of humour, your delight in babies, your skill with the mouth organ, your love of limericks and beamer of a smile – then it's possible for anyone's third self to keep flourishing. Self 3 belongs to others.

None of this need be interpreted as exclusively about age or dementia. It's about the value we place on a person and their gifts, and our communal responsibility to uphold that person. It places the protection of identity at the heart of a truly modern understanding of society. Viewed this way it is not dementia alone that robs a person of who they are, but all the rest of us too. It is not forgetting that does for people, but being forgotten.

Daft old Lear, abandoned by the powerful and betrayed by his family, is embraced at last only by a band of fellow outcasts. I left the Theatre Royal uneasily aware that four hundred years after Shakespeare first presented his tragedy, our own Elizabethan society cannot afford to feel all that superior.

*

So, Mum, imagine a community defined by an understanding of the social nature of selfhood. It would unfold, would it not, from individuals out rather than institutions down. Crucially, it would behave as if the basic rights and freedoms guaranteed by human rights legislation in the UK apply to everyone, which at the moment they don't.

This is something the Older People's Commissioner for Wales is quick to point out when we meet.

'It is clear to me that too many older people, in practice, do not have human rights,' Sarah Rochira says, fixing me with a flinty, bespectacled eye. 'If they did, I wouldn't meet people whose loved ones were under threat of eviction from their care home because they spoke out about their poor care, whose loved ones were left to sit for hours in their own excrement, or, in the worst of cases, suffered neglect leading to pressure sores so deep that the bone can be seen.'

No wonder Rochira has made waves in Wales. In her role as independent champion for older people she is forthright about its being 'almost impossible' under the law of Wales and England to bring breaches of their human rights to court, even in respect of the right to life.

'What sort of message does that send out?' she demands. 'A message that dehumanises and strips away from those we care for – and care about – their dignity, their respect, their voice and in some cases their life.'

The Scottish Human Rights Commission keeps an eye on the implementation in Scotland of the same legislation, but they too are grappling with the gap between well-meaning statute and reality on the ground.

A new understanding of community would insist that human rights begin, not end, with those in constant danger of being written off as less than human in the first place. It would encompass a health and social care system based on the right to be free of degrading treatment, the right to be treated as an equal and the right to be regarded as a citizen with a say, to whatever extent is possible, in the decisions that affect one's life. It would measure progress by its success in bolstering the most frail identities in its midst, and moral stature by how it protects the most vulnerable minds.

No need to raise your eyebrows, Mum. Change starts with imagining the best. Change starts with Shakespeare.

30

And each day dies with sleep

Gerard Manley Hopkins, 'No worst, there is none'

You have gone down with pneumonia. No more hospitals, we swore after your hip operation, and here is the first test. We decide to nurse you at home.

On being pressed, the GP gives you a 70/30 chance of recovery in hospital. A spell there attached to a drip for intravenous antibiotics would sort your chest, but he agrees it would leave you vulnerable to other infections and risk your mind. This is just the kind of case where Cheryl Etches in Wolverhampton dreams of an acute nurse arriving pronto to sort a drip in the bedroom, but we are still in the old world here. At home with only oral antibiotics the GP thinks your chances might be reduced to 50/50.

'We can work with 50/50,' I tell him.

'I'll do everything I can to help you, then.'

He organises the delivery of an electrically operated hospital bed, visits from the district nurse and the immediate services of a private physiotherapist to get the phlegm moving. This lady proceeds, as you loudly complain, to assault you, giving us an alarming snapshot of the horror that would have awaited you in hospital when a stranger arrived to start pummelling the bottom of your left lung. Even in your own bedroom we cannot persuade you that a visitor is hitting you to make you feel better. It takes Topsy's cradling your head in her arms and encouraging you to sing 'By the Light of the Silvery Moon' to calm you enough for the gentle beating to continue.

'By the light' (pummely-pum, pummely-pum) 'of the silvery moon' (pummely, pummely, pummely-pum). If the physio is still some way from bringing love's dreams by the end of the first session, she can at least report that your lung is expanding and contracting again.

Actually the 'no hospital' decision was easy: we knew we could offer better all-round care at home. But what about the treatment? Pneumonia used to be called the old man's friend, because it brought a relatively swift and pain-less end to a life already in hopeless decline. What were we doing giving you a powerful course of antibiotics and inten-sive physiotherapy, instead of letting you drift away?

True, we did wonder if it was the right thing to do. But only fleetingly. When it came to the moment that we found ourselves on the brink, peering into the chasm of ultimate loss, we found we could not bear to do otherwise.

What mattered was the light that still flashed from your eyes, even when so ill, the humour you could still muster, the songs you could remember, the smile you could conjure, the way when I said, 'Goodnight, my darling mother. I love you,' a small hoarse whisper returned from the pillow, 'You, too,' and when I leaned in to kiss your cheek, you turned it so that you could slip a kiss on mine first and another on my hand while you were at it. Your love flamed out to meet ours, as it always had when we needed you most. What mattered was that life still burned within you, fierce and lovely, and we could not let you go.

However, we know it could be different, perhaps even should be different, next time. Drug development is out of kilter. We have medicine to stop the lungs filling but not the brain eroding. We have drugs and vaccines to counteract or slow down almost every disease that nature has organised to bring life to a close, but none to mend the mind. So thousands of old people lie in thousands of beds, waiting for a death we do our best to deny them for as long as possible. Better, perhaps, to face thinking about a time when the treatment might be allowed to stop.

So we give you the pills as prescribed, stronger and stronger ones until the infection is beaten. Your cheeks gradually lose their hectic flush, although they still look as if they have been sucked in with a straw. We bring you downstairs and life returns to its old stuttery rhythms. But your mental functioning has taken another dive. There is a scorching emptiness in your eyes. Your speech has sunk to a new low. The illness has plunged you to a worse level of dementia and infirmity and we see at once that you will not climb back.

Have we really been right to coax you back to a life like this?

'She was happier when she was just lying up there slipping away, wasn't she?' Margaret says, voicing what each of us is thinking.

And yet when is the moment to say 'No more'? I catch your face lighting up when one of us bursts through the door, feel your hand on my hair as I'm fastening your shoes, look at your beauty, cheekbones still delicate, hair strong and curly. I ask, 'Who's loved?' the way I used to interrogate the children. They would always chorus, every one of them, 'Me!' But you look me in the eye and reply emphatically, 'You!'

You are our mother still. Who am I to say your life is not worth living?

*

As the soft, green days of spring slip by, the lanes sweet with wild garlic and the hedgerows laced with hawthorn, your sense of dislocation grows. At night you refuse point-blank to be put to bed by anyone except a daughter.

I try to explain that Margaret and Topsy and I become terribly tired if we are up with you in the night with work to go to next day and we have to have somebody to help us.

'But somebody isn't anybody,' you wail, and I know what you mean: somebody isn't one of us. Then you say, with tears in your eyes, 'I'm very scared.'

'Are you, Mum?' I whisper. 'What of?'

'Of the unspoken . . .' You try again. 'Of not knowing what's going on.'

Leaving the house to go anywhere disorientates and upsets you. The last time you visited mine you had to be carried in from the car by my eldest, Jamie – carefully and lovingly, the way you used to carry him. You sat among us with your eyes closed, exhausted. It was only when I located a tinny version of 'I'm Forever Blowing Bubbles' on my laptop that you began to come round and a thin harmony escaped you.

But when the others were out of the room, you turned to me and said, with tearful anguish, 'I just feel so, so lost.' You had no idea where you were or who anyone was. We carried you back to the car, knowing you would never come again.

You are crying often these days. I remember little Joan in the Glasgow hospital, who could not be consoled, and Janet in London, who sobbed for her daughter and screamed her torment at the nurses. We have caught them up at last.

Another day you and I passed the time by watching an old video of Jamie's christening day. What a fuss we all made of that first baby. You, as always, dominate the screen, life and soul of the party, quick to snatch up your mouth organ while Dad looks on benignly from the couch, pipe in hand. I am entranced by this evocation of how life was and how you were, but you seem not to make a connection between yourself and the people on the screen. You shift restlessly.

'Are you bored, Mum?' I say.

'Not bored,' you reply, with one of the discriminating darts of analysis that always cut me to the core. 'But I've lost everything I could do myself.'

Such a heartbreaking ability you still have to articulate what dementia is doing to you. It is what I find most painful. Knowing you know.

'I'm sorry, Mum. Does this video make you sad?'

A watery smile. 'Everything makes me sad these days.'

And when you are not sad, you are often angry. Even with markedly fewer words after the pneumonia, you still manage to fling enough together to be rude to Anna. When she takes out a bottle of milk from the freezer and asks me innocently, 'Do you think it will be okay to defrost this in a basin of boiling water?' you interject tartly, 'Why don't you go and boil yourself in a basin of water, Anna?'

I wheel you smartly out of the kitchen.

'Why must you always put Anna down?' I ask, mildly enough, helping you back into your chair in the living room. 'We need milk. That's all she was seeing to.'

'It's because I can't do it,' you snarl. The anger comes from the same place as the sadness. Anna can do what you can't. You *know*.

But while it is easy enough to understand the outbursts of rage and to love you through them, it is wearying to cope with them. The milder eruptions occur when you sense another's attention straying. You feel out of it when we become momentarily absorbed in a newspaper story, or a telephone call, or even a conversation with someone else in the room that you cannot follow or a joke you cannot share. 'Hey, how about saying something to make *me* laugh?' you interrupt. Your demand for attention is becoming every day more tyrannical.

Sometimes your anger is prompted by suddenly finding yourself where you have no wish to be, having forgotten that you had expressly desired to be there only minutes before: in your bedroom, being helped towards the car, halfway into your coat, on the toilet. You lash out in fury at the hapless helper who has tried to carry out the original wish. The toilet in particular provokes turbulent emotions. You will ask to go, or at least agree with alacrity when it is suggested, but invariably sit there sobbing.

'Stop all this. I can't stand it,' you round on me one day. 'It's time to stop the game.'

Maybe that is exactly what life feels like when you are disconnected from the reasons for going to the toilet, or for eating, or for putting your clothes on or going to bed or getting exercise. Life becomes a tediously repetitive game in which people sit you down and stand you up, manoeuvre you on to a toilet seat, tug your arms in and out of sweaters and curl your fingers around spoons and forks. You stretch out your hands for someone else to dress you and to lead you where you do not want to go.

The attempt to inveigle you into bed is a titanic struggle. No matter how tired you have professed yourself to be or how late the hour, you sense you are being tricked into it, hustled out of the way before the fun starts.

It is a measure of my current desperation that I now offer late-night recitals on the electric piano which Topsy, who really can play the thing, has moved into your bedroom from her own place. The last time I made it through a piece of music from beginning to end was 'Für Elise' at the age of fifteen. Now I am amazed and gratifed to find that my halting stab at a Sonata in C, played at a more funereal pace than Mozart could have dreamed his semiquavers capable of, will calm you. Sometimes you even join in from the pillow, holding the note patiently until I locate some approximation on the keyboard.

'That's nice,' you say, closing your eyes in what looks improbably like bliss, as deaf to the limitations of my musical accomplishments as you always were.

*

I should also remind myself, Mum, that without entirely meaning to you can still be hilarious company.

On Easter Day there is a clatter at your front door. In hurtle a gang of my children, home for the holiday week-end and keen to spend some time with me. You look vaguely at your three eldest grandchildren sprawled around the room and mutter to me *sotto voce*, 'When did you start taking such an interest in these people?'

'Mum, I'm their mother.'

'Are you really?' you say. 'Well, don't tell anyone.'

When the kids have gone, I take you to sit at the kitchen table while I make the tea. 'Do you mind if I say something to the bread-bin?' you remark conversationally.

'Not at all, Mum. Go right ahead.'

You look at it pensively, while I wait with bated breath for your address to the bread-bin.

'There's a lot goes on inside there, isn't there?' is what you come out with at last.

'Well, not last time I looked,' I say, rallying. 'Just a couple of loaves of bread.' A thought strikes. 'Is this you telling me, by any chance, that you don't want bread for your tea?'

'I suppose so.'

'Or that you do?'

'Possibly.'

You laugh, and I laugh, and I have no idea whether you want bread for your tea or not. What I do know is that there is nowhere on earth I would rather be right now than giggling with you, darling mother, over a burgeoning relationship with the kitchen accessories.

At other times, though, the humour is more knowing and not nearly so funny. You are capable of coming out with a line so quick, so deft and so terrifyingly apposite that it stabs like a scalpel.

'This is a great all-round dish,' I tell you cheerfully one morning, spooning porridge and mashed banana into your mouth. 'It's got oats for energy. It's got fruit for vitamins. And it's got milk for, er, something else.'

'And it's got Mamie,' you whip back. 'Nobody knows what she's for, either.'

*

By the end of August we can no longer tempt you outside. You like the idea of going somewhere, anywhere, and constantly express the desire to be 'getting home now', but we cannot persuade you beyond the front door. It is all too frightening.

Anna, the person who most longs to sit with you, who would wait on you all day if you would let her, is banished to another room. Most of the time she is alone with the television, bearing no grudges.

'I just feel so sorry for Mamie,' she repeats over and over. Thus the twins sit out the twilight of their lives in separate rooms, islands apart.

What is threatening to defeat us daughters is not so much your behaviour as our emotions. Others, namely the stalwart women who look after you as a part-time job, seem often to manage you better than we do. We have kept a major role in what is now a 24-hour rota not just because the financial reserves are finite but because it is clear you want us. Yet each of us is haunted by a mounting sense of failure.

Margaret travels hundreds of miles to be with you regularly. She tells me that when you roared at her the other day that she had never once lifted a finger to help you, she roared right back: in the middle of a long day it can be the most ludicrous accusations that hit a nerve. Even Topsy, more inclined to store hurt and inspect it afterwards, is feeling fractious. My own temper, as you know better than anyone, has always hung on a rather shoogly peg.

The hours crawl past. If I switch on the television, you gaze at me meaningfully and then ask some question that really means: *Please restore your attention to me.* I try *Sky News.* 'Are you watching this thing?' *Dad's Army.* 'Who are these people?' *Mr Bean.* 'What am I supposed to do now?' What next? Can I bear to sing 'The White Cliffs of Dover' one more time?

Aha, *Songs of Praise* is on. Encouragingly you start to hum along to 'All good gifts around you / Are sent from heaven above'. Then, suddenly furious, you start shouting the words through clenched teeth, still in tune but loud and angry. 'Then thank the Lord, oh thank the Lord,' you bellow in a frenzy of sarcasm.

'What's wrong?' I inquire as neutrally as I can.

'YOU can thank the Lord, if you want to,' you shout. 'But don't expect me to.'

Snapping the television off, I yell back, 'Why are you doing this? You're my mother and I love you. Have you any idea how hard I try?'

'You're not my mother,' you reply calmly, which takes the wind out of my sails.

'No, you're MY mother,' I huff, with a sense of being drawn into something ridiculous.

'I'm NOT your mother,' you retort. 'We're not related at all.'

Well, I asked for it.

The only experience to which I can compare this is having a baby with colic: not really understanding what this inconsolable infant needs, unable to make a blind bit of difference to its misery and counting every long minute until another pair of arms can take over. The difference here is that when I ease you into your chair and cover you with a blanket and weep hot tears of weariness all over you, a hand sneaks out and strokes my head and pats my hair into waves. I look up, red-eyed, to find you gazing at me fondly: 'You have a beautiful face,' you say, as most definitely only a mother could.

Perhaps, we three sisters tell ourselves, we need to hand over the reins to people who are not so emotionally involved, who don't find tears flooding into their eyes every time you lash out or look lost. Perhaps we must contrive to become breezy visitors rather than ragged carers.

But even as I write this, my heart rebels.

'All that hurts me is when the people I love leave me,' you told me only yesterday.

And just the other night, seeing as I need a change of detective once in a while, we were watching *Midsomer Murders*. I was busy encouraging you to chuckle over some outlandish murder scene when you suddenly grabbed hold of my arm and squeezed it hard.

'If anyone ever does anything to *you*,' you said fiercely, 'I'll . . .'

No particular sanction for my murder came to mind, but the tigerish protectiveness was so real, welling up from such abiding stores of maternal affection, that something shifted inside me. I knew in that moment, beyond all self-doubt, that I am still a part of you, still precious and – this I must acknowledge, too – still needed.

We head upstairs to bed. You keep pulling my face to the pillow for more kisses.

'Your cheek is so seft,' you say. 'Oops, I meant soft.'

'Seft, sooft, sift, suft,' I chorus, knowing it will make you laugh. 'Not to mention seeft.' We giggle.

'I like the word "sift", though, don't you? Makes me think of white sand.'

You nod drowsily. Happy, as sleep begins to steal over you, to be with one of your daughters; any one will do. Happy to be thinking about words.

Words. The delight in playing with them. The fun of analysing them. The challenge of choosing them. The wonder of seeing how they work together to make a beautiful sentence. Which of our calm, competent, reassuring carers can share that with you, Mum? Which of them will exclaim over an egregious split infinitive drifting out of the television a second before you do? (You make little sense of the dialogue, but you still notice those.) Which of them can truly understand what words have always meant to you and how much it is costing you, day by day by day by day, to lose them?

31

Unless soul clap its hands and sing

W. B. Yeats, 'Sailing to Byzantium'

Another autumn, and I'm back on Mull, striding along the new path through the Ardmore forest, breathing in gulps of sharp, clean air and thinking about what it feels like to lose the sense of who you are.

The other night, as you prepared to glide up to bed in the hated stairlift that makes you feel like a decrepit patient instead of a girl who knows a thing or two about banisters, you said suddenly, 'I have this terrible feeling of not being here at all.'

'What's the feeling like? Can you tell me?'

'Only,' you sighed bleakly, 'that it's terrible.'

As I make for the ruined township that you and I and Anna Lisa looked for in vain all those years ago, I am trying to imagine the feeling. It must be exactly the opposite, I suddenly realise, of what I am experiencing on this fresh Mull morning: the exhilarating sense of a self I recognise and a mind I can enjoy.

This is a mind that makes plans for the day and ruminates on yesterday and then springs back to wonder whether you have woken up yet, miles across the sea, and whether my youngest has by some organisational miracle made it to school on time. This is a mind that can speculate on where this path is heading next, while simultaneously sweeping over the wasteland of bleached logs left behind after the clearance of the forest to note how the few dead trunks left pointing to the sky enhance the desolation. It can spot the first ruined stump of a house in the grass, and then another, and another, and then take a few seconds to rummage around in its memories and come up with a couple of lines from T.S. Eliot that it last met in the undergraduate library of Edinburgh University:

> What are the roots that clutch, what branches grow
> Out of this stony rubbish?

My roots, my mind replies, talking to itself as minds do.

It notices a high, lonely cry in the distance and wishes my father were here to identify the bird. It wonders how much of the hillside over there would have provided grazing for my great-great-grandfather's cattle. It is struck by the incongruity of the mobile-phone mast at the top of the nearest peak, from which a drystane dyke still marks the ancient boundary of the forgotten township below. My mind wishes very much to discuss this with you.

The trees in the forest have been thinned since I was here last. There are clearly marked paths now and the township from which our people were driven is easy to find. The ruins among which your grandmother Annie McEachern ran and played and tended the family cow stand exposed to the sky again. There is a burn running down the middle. The fallen walls of seven or eight houses lie snug in the slopes on either side.

I catch the first whiff of salt, carried on a gust of wind. A little further and there is the sea, with the snout of Ardnamurchan on the other side and the light grey shadow of Barra, or is it South Uist, just visible through the clouds far away to the north-west. The path curls downwards again and the smell of the sea grows stronger. Another twist and I am on the shore just beyond Ardmore Point, on a secluded pebble-strewn cove dotted with pools and slippy with seaweed. Two oystercatchers are foraging in the sand with their orange pencil beaks. They rise with a cry – that same high, piping note I had struggled to identify – and flit away.

I kneel down and trail a finger across an eddying rock pool, closing my eyes to breathe in the tang of salt and savour what you have lost – the taste of being oneself.

*

But what exactly has gone? And how much of you does it leave behind?

Faced with so much that is dear and familiar becoming

unattractive and alien, people sometimes say, 'She's not herself any longer. It's not my mother any more.' My problem is that I want to believe the opposite. I desperately want to believe that you are still yourself.

Cogito ergo sum, opined the seventeenth-century philosopher René Descartes: I think therefore I am. So, if we don't think very well, do we struggle to 'be' anyone at all? Is your very 'being' departing to wherever it is your memories are going, to nowhere, to nothingness, to some graveyard of the neurons, a place where you can no longer sense its presence and those on the outside may struggle even harder to detect it? In coining the word *dementia* was Philippe Pinel right, after all, to sense that it is possible to be 'outside' one's mind?

Or do we possess a selfhood that is somehow separate from our thinking processes, that exists regardless of whether we feel it is giving us the slip? A Self 1, perhaps, to borrow from Steven Sabat again, which is neither the physical self defined by its attributes nor the social self sustained by the community, but some inviolable part of ourselves that remains intact while the others shift and change?

To put the question another way, is the brain all there is to us, a fantastically clever machine that creates a mind, which in turn creates an illusory sense of an independent self, which then collapses when the brain itself starts to die? Or is there such a thing as a separate selfhood, a secret core of self which I imagine as a glossy pearl, existing separately and staying safe from the most violent assaults on the body and of the body?

In other words, are you always going to be, in some deep, hidden place, you, still in essence the person I have loved for a lifetime, or must I face the possibility that there exists no such pearl and that at the whim of faulty brain connections you are becoming someone else? Or perhaps not even 'someone' at all, as has been argued by those who point out that everything which distinguishes us from animals resides in the front cortex of the brain, the part involved in consciousness, emotion and memory, the part which Alzheimer's lays to waste. According to this theory, you are actually becoming nobody.

Only the most blinkered neuroscientist or philosopher would claim to have truly penetrated the mystery of mind and self. Science seems to have concluded nothing more definite than that a sense of self is constructed from a variety of brain systems working together, and that the very complexity of the interaction makes this construct robust enough to adapt to quite massive losses. Contemporary philosophers, such as Julian Baggini in *The Ego Trick*, tend to infer from this that the self, as a construction of the mind, may be renovated and reconstructed but can ultimately be brought down if the foundations are undermined.

But then along come the theologians with another angle. 'What makes any of us the same person we were when we were eight years old, when all the cells in our bodies have been transformed into something different?' asks Dr John Swinton, professor in practical theology and pastoral care at Aberdeen University. What makes any of us who we are, when even those with the best of memories have forgotten most of what has happened in their lifetime?

Swinton argues: 'Our memories don't make us what we are; we are what God remembers us to be.' This is a conclusion that raises more questions than it answers, although it may provide security for those who feel their grasp on faith slipping away with their sense of themselves.

The distinguished quantum physicist and former Cambridge professor Dr John Polkinghorne, Fellow of the Royal Society and now an Anglican priest, offers another perspective by identifying our essential 'me-ness' (my word) as the soul, a concept which sits comfortably in his conversation alongside quarks and hadrons.

'I don't think the soul is a detachable, spiritual bit – I think it's the real me,' he says. 'The real me is certainly not just a matter of my body, because that's changing all the time. Through wear and tear, eating and drinking, the atoms change. But the pattern in which the atoms are formed, there, I think, is what the soul is.'

According to Polkinghorne's notion, the 'real me' simultaneously holds within it the relationships that have formed it and also requires those relationships, and others, to help man its defences. It seems we are back to community again. Call this the soul, the psyche, the spirit or any number of selves, it looks as if it cannot escape other people. Which means, beloved mother, that in getting you to sing, making you laugh, talking to you, holding you, stroking you and trying, however incompetently, to entertain you, we really are cherishing the real you.

The real you. I see I have made up my mind. The pearl it is. You are Mamie, the only one there has been or ever will be. You are you.

I imagine you back home in bed this autumn morning, doubtless refusing to leave it and probably saying something rude to Anna in the process. I don't care. You are still you. I hereby throw caution to the winds and dare to believe that you will still be you when you have no words left to be rude to anyone. You will be you when the last of the fight has left you. You will be you when you no longer know who I am. You will be you even if I can recognise nothing of what you are and connect it with nothing of what you used to be. You will be you, I really do believe, until the last breath leaves your body.

As usual it is the poets who understand best. To the great William Butler Yeats I turn for the hope that, though 'fastened to a dying animal' our self, our soul, our quiddity, this pearl of great price, may still continue to be itself.

> *An aged man is but a paltry thing,*
> *A tattered coat upon a stick, unless*
> *Soul clap its hands and sing, and louder sing*
> *For every tatter in its mortal dress.*

Yeats may not provide much in the way of answers for the hungering intellect, but in 'Sailing to Byzantium' he has worked through his own longings to a way of understanding that deeply satisfies the greedy heart.

32

Fling wide the gates

John Stainer, *The Crucifixion*

And here is the best thing, the very best thing, of all.

The first time it happens in my presence I watch, open-mouthed, as Anna enters the room on your express summons and is not rejected. She takes your hand and you don't snatch it away. She casts around for shared memories and is not instantly ridiculed.

For years Anna has copped the most bitter expressions of your ravaged personality, the silliest abuse, the most sweeping sarcasm. Today, out of the blue, you have welcomed her.

'Do you remember, Mamie, we used to play the game "I packed my bag and went to London and what did I put in it?"' she ventures. 'And we had to reel off a whole list of things?'

You smile. This is going well. I even take the chance to slip out of the room. When I return you are still holding hands, your grey-white heads bent close together, wavy hair against straight.

'Look, I've got my sister Anna,' you beam as I come in.

You are resplendent in pink pyjamas and fleece today, stand-ard dress now that you never go out. Anna is in dark trousers and jumper with a fashionable black gilet. Your face is plumper than hers at the moment, the effect of steroids.

Anna is in full flood.

'And remember Archie used to impersonate a man who sang around the back courts. What was his name again? And there was that old minister, Tom Dick was his name, who talked . . . like . . . this, very slow and deliberate. You used to imitate him and I was terrified he would hear you. And do you remember in the church choir there was a lady called Miss Granger and she used to sing off-tune? And there was a man in the choir – wasn't he called Ernie Cheek? He was English and we thought it was such a funny name. And for a while there were no men in the choir, remember, and they made you and me help out by singing the tenor part. And we used to sing anthems on a Sunday. Here, Mamie, see if you remember this . . .'

And Anna, repulsed for so long, silenced for so many years, suddenly lets fly in a voice as strong and true as yours with a line from Stainer's *Crucifixion*: 'God so loved the world, God so loved the world that he gave his only begotten son . . .'

Oh, help. I hold my breath. 'I'd give my only begotten son to make you stop that racket' can only be a millisecond away. I look down and busy myself with the newspaper in case you enlist me as an audience for the put-down. I realise my heart is beating too fast. And then, then it is going to burst, because you don't say anything of the kind. You start humming the harmony, and I don't know when I have felt such elation.

'Fling wide the gates,' soars Anna, beating a hand on the arm of the chair as if she is conducting. You copy her, waving your own hand in time to the music, too.

There have been more accomplished performances of Stainer's oratorio, but never one like this.

Nothing lasts for ever, though, or in your case for more than a minute. Anna is still flinging wide the gates when you interrupt to announce grandly, 'You're free to go.'

'Am I dismissed, then?' She is smiling.

'You are certainly not dismissed,' you reply sternly.

I chortle into my newspaper. Actually agreeing with Anna would be a step too far.

Since then Anna has inched back into your life. In a way I think it's a sign of battle weariness on your part, but a small price to pay for peace on the sister front. Many afternoons, when nothing else can calm your agitation, a duet of sorts on the mouth organ will save the day. Anna plays better than you now, a turn-up for the books you seem mercifully not to have registered.

In fact, you have become so demanding of Anna that she has lately been known to invent some very important job in the next room.

'Be careful what you wish for,' we say. And she laughs, happily.

*

I wish I could report more solid progress with my own less attractive side.

I particularly despise in myself the speed with which my sympathy curdles when you screw your face up to cry. I really am ashamed of this. The tears turn on and off very fast, like a young child's, but even so they are communicating wordless unhappiness and emotions beyond your control. I am aghast at how quickly my temper frays when nothing I say or do seems to help.

Once when you were crying again about wanting home I snapped back, 'This *is* your home. Please stop crying.'

You looked at me steadily. Just for a moment the old determination flickered in your eyes as you sought, visibly, to master your will. Why can I not master my own to suppress these irritable responses that only belittle you and leave me sick with guilt?

> *And you'll be amazed at how time and practice can*
> *cut those times down until you find yourself*
> *apologising before you leave the room, or even*
> *– Heaven forfend and saints forbid! – some day in*
> *the far distant future you might actually desist*
> *from saying whatever it is you're going to have to*
> *apologise for the next minute.*
>
> *But that will happen gradually, with age and*
> *maturity.*

If only, Mum. If only.

'I will *not* cry again,' you said, twisting my heart. 'I will not.'
So I did instead.

*

And yet, and yet. I can bring you solace, too, I and my
sisters and sometimes Anna. I know I can. And it's what
keeps me in there, battling for your mind, looking out for
your pearl when I spend so much time feeling a failure.

I am thinking about this as I prepare you for bed at the
beginning of another night. You have been upset all evening.
'Where's my mother?' you were sobbing, over and over. 'I
don't know where my mother is.'

'I tell you what,' I said. 'Let's go up to bed and when
you're in there, all cosy and snug, you can think about your
mother as you go to sleep. How about that?'

'It'll make me sad.'

'No, it won't, because we'll sing together. We'll sing
"Dream Angus" and you won't feel like crying any more.'

I have no idea whether your mother, whom you described
as the sweetest person on earth, ever soothed you to sleep
this way, but you used to sing the lullaby to me, and this
night I am singing it for you.

> Will ye no hush your weepin'-o,
> All the wee lambs are sleepin'-o.
> Birdies are nestlin', nestlin' thegither,
> Dream Angus is hirplin' ower the heather.

And as I sing, I think about the weeping to come. And I think about how hard it is to bear, this horrific disease, for you and for all of us. And I think about losing Siggy and whether all those decades ago you were showing us that love is the giving out and the shoring up exactly at the times when our will is most badly in need of renovation and our heart is in shreds.

I thought I was singing the lullaby to you, but of course you are singing it to me now. You rub your smooth fingers into the hollows of my neck and curl a strand of hair around my ear.

> *Dreams to sell, fine dreams to sell,*
> *Angus is here wi' dreams to sell-o,*
> *Hush ye my baby and sleep without fear,*
> *Dream Angus has brought you a dream, my dear.*

I smile at you and know that, yes, you are still you, that you are always you, and that you have things to teach me yet.

'Thank you for upholding me,' you whisper. Though you had trouble with the word 'hand' earlier this evening, you can still find that one.

I wish I could uphold you better, but perhaps, after all, it is enough.

33

Think vascular

Psychiatrist Sube Banerjee

Researchers at the National Institute on Ageing in Baltimore have discovered that if we sharply reduce our intake of calories twice a week we can boost the growth of neurons and counteract the impact of diseases like Alzheimer's. By 'we' I think they mean mice.

There was a time when I might have raced to try it. Now I can't be bothered. This disease is killing you and I still don't know why.

For old times' sake I file 'Fasting can help protect against brain diseases' beside 'Oily fish can beat dementia', 'Vitamin B clue to dementia', 'Exercise the answer to Alzheimer's' and 'Drinking coffee reduces risk of dementia'. They are on top of 'Brain games delay dementia (but ultimately speed decline)' and 'Tests suggest dementia linked to pesticide use'.

I have been at the cuttings game so long now that another study, 'Regular dose of aspirin cuts Alzheimer's risk' has already been contradicted by 'Findings suggest that aspirin use in Alzheimer's might pose an increased risk of intracerebral haemorrages and has no effect on cognition'.

At the top is last week's chimera, 'Curries prevent dementia', and I smile at the thought of Sube Banerjee reading it, my robust guide through the snares of fallacy.

'The truth is,' he told me in his office down Memory Lane, 'we just don't have the answers. If it were easy to know, we would know by now.

'The reality is that this is an incredibly complex disease. Even the simple model that suggests we've got four illnesses – Alzheimer's, vascular, Lewy body and fronto-temporal – is unlikely to be the whole story. Dementia is probably a disorder like cancer. There may turn out to be 40,000 different interactions between particular sets of genes and particular environments, thousands anyway, because if there were just tens of them, we would have found them long before now.'

As for the newspaper stories, he had just one piece of advice of his own: 'Think vascular. Everything that's good for your heart is good for your head. No, I don't think eating oily fish and vegetables will stop you getting dementia, but it will certainly do you no harm and may make your vasculature a bit better and maybe that will give you extra time, who knows, until it becomes clear that you've got the problem.'

Who knows, indeed? What does anybody really understand about the condition that another five people have developed in the time it took to read that last paragraph? People are desperate for answers – just look at this eclectic sheaf of hopefulness before me – but what I have learned is that there is nobody in the world who knows why you or the other millions have developed this illness, or how to cure it, or what anyone else can do to avoid it. Not yet at least.

Yes, there have been genuine scientific breakthroughs, and there will be more, but for now this, perhaps, is the real dementia story.

34

Hush your weeping

'Dream Angus', Traditional Scottish lullaby

There have been times, usually amid the dark confusions of the night, when you have failed to recognise one or other of us, staring blankly with eyes wide.

But there is a deeper kind of unknowing. Others who have walked this way speak of it with tears. I have been waiting in vague trepidation for the moment you will fail not just to place me, but to know who I am.

And now it seems the time has come. On Christmas Eve I bounce into your house in a short, scarlet dress. Too much festive bonhomie? Too much make-up? Too little dress? I have no idea what triggers your response tonight, but it floors me.

In these last weeks of 2011 your mental state has deteriorated. Knowing you would be bewildered by a noisy Christmas Eve celebration, my sisters and I have planned a short, cosy time with you around the fire, just the four of us, singing a few carols before leaving you with a carer and heading off for the traditional meal at my house.

'*Gleðileg Jól*, Mum. Happy Christmas. It's me.'

I catch your look of panic right away. You glance across at Margaret, sitting on the other side of the fire. She has been with you all day.

'Who is this?' you ask her sharply.

'It's Sal,' Margaret says, sounding over-hearty, nervous for me, 'your daughter Sally.'

I make to perch on the arm of your chair and lean over to kiss you.

'Get off my chair.' You have turned on me your most basilisk stare. It is bad enough that your eyes hold neither recognition nor warmth, but I am shaken to see they are also dark with hostility.

'Mum, it's me.'

'I don't know you!' you shout. It really is a shout.

I stare at you, trying to gather my wits. I tell myself that I have been out of your company for two or three days, that dementia is up and down, that you will probably know me tomorrow. But it is no good. There is another voice that won't be silenced. My mother doesn't love me, it says. Tears and mascara flow, making me look even more like some wild, painted stranger. Margaret urges me to go home and they will join me later.

When I bend to kiss you goodbye, you hiss, 'Get your hands off me.'

Driving home, I force myself to look steadily at the situation. In order to bear this, I have to believe that you are not yourself, that there is a fundamental disjunction between the mother who believed she would love me while breath remained in her body and the mother who looked at me this evening with such intensity of loathing. So what am I saying – that you are you, except when it suits me to believe that you are not? You are you, unless I need at any given time to convince myself that the disease has turned you into a monster? You are you, except when too long an assault on the brain finally makes a stone of the heart?

Late, late in the night, when our festivities are over, the guests gone and the stockings filled for offspring old enough to be filling one for their parents, I scrabble through the drawers of my desk for comfort. I am looking for a letter you sent me long ago so that I can read again the words 'My dearest Sal'. I want to touch the bond strengthened in bereavement that neither of us thought could be broken:

> *I don't think I've ever told you what a wonderful*
> *support you were to me in those terrible days – and*
> *months – and years. You were always standing there,*
> *with your hand on my shoulder. I can't imagine what*
> *it would have been like without you.*

I read the letter through, trying to remind myself of what the deepest places of your heart look like.

I have a sudden impulse to rush around the house waking up those five grown-up children of mine, all gathered under one roof for Christmas, to impress on them the most important thing they can ever know about their own mother. At three in the morning it is an urge they can be thankful I resist. But I want them to know that what is in my own heart for them at this moment is me, the essence of me, the shiny pearl, 'the heart of my mystery', as Hamlet put it. I don't care if I am imagining such a pearl. I want them to believe in it and to keep it for me. Does this make any kind of sense, Mum? I am asking them to believe that if this disease should one day hunt me down (and for all I know it is skulking under the lamp-post already), if it should ever cause me to stare into their eyes with the icy dislike I saw in yours, it comes from a diseased brain and not from the place I will call my soul, which is theirs for ever.

And thinking about what I feel for them, I understand you. This is the moment, clutching a thin blue sheet of Basildon Bond notepaper in a cold house in the early hours of Christmas morning, that I realise it is the same for you. Whether or not I ever see another sign of it, you love me. Of course you do. Brain experts may shake their heads but I don't care. This is heart-sense. I have your own pearl safe in my possession. You are you.

On the afternoon of Christmas Day I return to your house, prepared for anything. I am told you have been agitated all afternoon, tearful, easily annoyed and upset. Never mind. I am ready. I stand outside the room and check my armour nervously. Jeans and scrubbed face . . . check. Breezy but calm demeanour . . . check. Quiet smile, no hint of an assumed familiarity that might spook you . . . check.

I open the door.

You are sitting in exactly the same place in front of the fire as yesterday. You look up, catch sight of me and smile. It is a weak, wan affair, but there is no mistaking its meaning. You recognise me.

Approaching carefully, as if you were a frightened deer in danger of bolting, I slide lightly on to the arm of your chair. You tolerate it. Softly, slowly, I reach out to stroke your hair. You lean back and close your eyes. You feel for my hand. Oh no, I am crying again, all that armour useless because I never thought to protect myself against this.

Later I sit curled at your feet and look into your eyes.

'You quite like me today, don't you?'

You gaze down at me, eyes clear and warm. 'I love you.'

Outside the wind howls and rain pelts the dark window. We sit together listening to it, catching the moment as it flies.

You know me, you know me not. It really does not matter. I know you.

*

You have a cough, a chest infection threatening. We have told the doctor we are reluctant to give antibiotics, as long as we can be sure you are comfortable. This time it feels wrong to pump you with drugs in order to prolong the life you are now enduring. He says he will support us.

'Feels wrong.' What is that supposed to mean? Only that last time your life appeared more endurable than it is now. Your body – so it seems to us as we try uncertainly to do the right thing – is looking for a way out. On such whims are life and death decisions taken. We ply you with pain relief and leave the infection to take its course.

You have been in bed for the past two days, all strength in your legs gone. Dropping in to see you on my way to work, I stroke this dear forehead now finely mapped with mauve veins. 'It's a lovely day tomorrow,' I sing hopefully. I feel your chest expanding as you take a breath to join in. Eyes tight shut, you manage a tremulous harmony.

Topsy looks after you overnight and next day we change your incontinence pad together. You protest vigorously at being rolled on to your side, unable to understand why we are invading you in this way and incapable of being soothed into compliance. Afterwards you are exhausted, indignant and tearful.

I settle myself in a chair beside your bed and let the babble drift over me. 'It looks good that that's . . . What it . . . How do I keep alive . . . But let's be . . . I won't be able to . . . Is it right . . . Please.'

At that 'please' I rouse myself.

'Please what? What can I do for you, Mum?'

Your face contorts and you begin to cry. 'Folk will think I'm a child.'

'But you're not, are you?'

'No.'

346 WHERE MEMORIES GO

From time to time you reach out to touch me and stroke my arm. You are all too aware that you have lost the capacity for independent action, that your body is giving up on you and life has been turned hideously upside down.

'You shouldn't be doing this,' you say. 'You shouldn't have to.'

'Of course I should,' I say.

Of course I should.

In the middle of this New Year crisis, winds of 90 mph rip across central Scotland, tearing off roofs, overturning lorries and rampaging through electricity lines. A power cut plunges the house into darkness for several days, stranding your hospital bed in a sitting position which it takes us hours to dismantle and cutting off your electric air-flow mattress. But you are still warm and snug. A portable gas heater throws out a cheery orange glow into the Dickensian gloom and a camping lamp emits a small comforting hiss. We flit around with hot water bottles and candles, feeling like Florence Nightingale.

A couple of days later the doctor sounds your chest and pronounces it clear. You have beaten an incipient chest infection all by yourself and I am jubilantly proud of you. Well done, Mum. You have refused to turn your head to the wall and tiptoe away. You were never one to give up.

But a new emotion follows, one that takes hold as soon as the doctor leaves and the surge of relief has passed. I realise how heavily I had invested in the belief that there would always be a way of allowing you to leave before the worst ravages of dementia set in.

I recognise the emotion as dread.

*

Within every website about Alzheimer's there is a section explaining the last stage of all. By then the plaques and tangles will have destroyed the motor functions controlled by the cerebellum ('little brain' in Latin) low down the back of the head and started to affect the brain stem itself, so that in the end the body will forget the biological functions necessary to sustain its own existence. This stage signals the loss of everything. Even when avid for information, I have tended to pass over this bit with averted eyes and thumping heart.

As always with dementia the bare facts obscure a multitude of nuances and a number of different – and in many cases rather gentle – ways in which death may approach. This final stage is not necessarily to be feared as I have feared it. But you are arriving at its threshold now and there is little yet that is gentle about the mounting agony of your mind.

> **Rave:** verb [intrans.] Talk wildly or incoherently, as
> if one were delirious or insane. [Origin Middle
> English: probably from Old Northern French *raver*,
> related obscurely to (Middle) Low German *reven*,
> be senseless, rave.]

You have been doing it all day.

'Ouch.'

'What's sore?'

'The lid of the castle.'

None of it is funny any more, not even slightly.

Mum, would you please stop crying. I can't stand this. I don't know how to help you.

Sounds emerge in the shape of words run together in a mumble of consonants. I can't make out more than the odd few in a hundred. 'Topsy, Topsy . . . I said . . . see them . . . always I can . . . always . . . there are some very good ones . . . catch Betty coming . . . please . . . PLEASE.'

It's like an old 78 record with a piece of fluff on it: snatches of sense emerge but little is connected. I think of those plaques and tangles reaching yet another vital pathway. I imagine a great bonfire of the synapses shooting sparks of memory into the velvet night. Siggy is among them. At 1.30 a.m. one night you jangle your bell wildly. 'The boy,' you sob. 'The boy. Dead. Killed just like that. No warning. No warning.'

Sometimes your weeping has a perfunctory air, but not this night. You are sobbing in great, shoulder-shaking gulps, breaking your heart.

> **Keening:** An eerie wailing sound: *the keening of the cold night wind.* [Origin mid-19th cent.: from Irish *caoinim* 'I wail'.]

A high-pitched scream bursts from you when we move you from bed to chair or, worse, have to change a soiled pad. Your keening rises and falls like a terrible lament.

It seems to be a wail of alarm rather than pain, a primitive scream of desolation at being carried into the unknown, your limbs flexed by others.

Margaret and I have helped you downstairs so that you can smell woodsmoke again and watch the flame curling among the logs. Moving you into the wheelchair and then the stairlift and then the wheelchair again and then the armchair by the fire has been as heart-tearing as it always is. No matter that you keep saying you want out, no matter how carefully we try to prepare you, still the unearthly cry goes up. It is wildly distressing to hear.

Once in the armchair you revive just long enough to manage a passable air on the mouth organ, until your hand drops, the mouth organ falls forgotten and your face is distorted into a grimace of soundless misery.

'Why are you crying, Mum? Can you tell us?' asks Margaret gently. 'Are you sad?'

'Yes, I'm sad.'

'Do you know why?'

You say nothing. What could there possibly be to say to a question like that?

> **Hallucinate:** Verb [intrans.] Experience a seemingly real perception of something not actually

present. [Origin mid-17th cent.: from Latin *halluci-nat-* 'gone astray in thought', from the verb *hallucinari*, from the Greek *alussein* 'be uneasy or distraught']

You glare at the cupboard as if it is has spoken out of turn, mutter indignantly at the chest of drawers, issue threats to the sofa, gaze with narrowed eyes at the wall, from which we have already removed an unsettling mirror, and pick restlessly at the yellow duvet. When the furniture leaves you in peace, you talk incessantly to thin air.

You have cried and rambled for hours today. You try to say a word, then your eyes flutter closed with effort and frustration, then you weep. At one point you suddenly fix your eyes on the piano and stare at it: 'The king's there. The king. He's there. At that table.'

'Where, Mum? Here?' I say, touching the piano. 'What does the king look like?'

But you can't elaborate.

I flip my laptop open for some surreptitious browsing.

'Hallucinations are caused by changes within the brain that result from Alzheimer's, usually in the later stages of the disease. The person may see the face of a former friend in a curtain or insects crawling on their hand. In other cases, they may hear people talking to them and may even talk to an imagined person. Hallucinations can be frightening.'

How much more, my darling mother, are you going to have to bear?

*

Watching you suffer makes us ask, all over again, if others could be doing this better. Is there a place where you might be protected more effectively from the desperate desolation and mental anguish of dementia's final assault? Has it been a kind of pride to think we know best and that love is always enough?

There is nobody to ask. There has never been anybody with us on the journey to ask. Nobody to advise, 'Stick at it, girls,' or, 'Now is the time to stop.'

Then a sign appears from far away, streaking into the middle of our doubts like a comet. Someone has unearthed a bundle of cuttings that escaped our father's vigilant filing. Here, written in February 1968, is a column in which you are commenting on revelations of cruelty to the elderly in a Scottish hospital. One sentence catches our eye:

> How many old folk would gladly exchange the
> super-clean sheets and specialised care – and even
> a few years of life – just to be among their own
> folk.

As is obvious from the sentimental tone of the article, you didn't have a clue about fullblown dementia. Your mother came to live with us in old age and even as young children we knew we had to keep an eye on her and lock the doors, but Grandma sat quietly in a chair all day, docile and uncomplaining, idly engaged in the passing scene and eating whatever she was given; she died of a heart attack in her bed, giving no trouble there either. Old age can be like that for some, even for those with a degree of cognitive impairment or a milder form of dementia. It was how I once imagined you would pass your own final years, dozing in a chair by my window between mouth organ medleys, after being gently steered away from the banisters and discouraged from hitching a bungee rope to the roof.

All the same, these words of yours do help to quell the doubts. Being cherished among your own folk to the very end is what you considered right. 'Specialised care', insofar as it exists, would not be your priority.

The carers who are helping us nurse you agree. They try to reassure us from their own experience that there is no better care somewhere else, no magic medication we have missed. Most importantly of all, they say, there is no place in the world where at this stage of the disease you can be better loved to death than here.

35

This is what it means to love

Reverend Giles Fraser

You have never given us the slightest sign of wanting to be off. Not now. Not ever. While my doughty mother-in-law is forever informing us that it's time she was on her way, you have said nothing of the kind.

An official sheet of paper on the bedroom bookcase, now emptied of books in favour of bottles, syringes, plastic gloves, wet wipes, a thick care diary and all the other accoutrements of illness, reads: DO NOT ATTEMPT CARDIOPULMONARY RESUSCITATION. A box is ticked: 'The likely outcome of successful CPR would not be of overall benefit to the patient.' It has been signed by the GP.

I imagine you reading this, raising an eyebrow and murmuring, 'Well, I'll be the judge of that.'

Our judgements are probably, if I'm honest, all too heavily influenced by the trauma of seeing you suffer. Do not resuscitate, we accede airily on your behalf. Yet none of us dares to admit that if you were in a position to be consulted there is a chance that you might, with your great lust for life, disagree sharply.

If you had known what was coming, might you have guided us differently? Might you have directed that 'life-sustaining measures serving only to prolong dying be withheld or discontinued' – a typical living will directive – or, alternatively, that however awful your life might appear from the outside we should do our best to enable it to continue?

Dearest mother, I wish we had talked about this long ago, although I suspect you would have laughed it off and left it up to us. You knew life has a habit of resisting construction to personal design. You would have trusted us to love you and do our best.

But what about the question that comes hot on the heels of the last one? If I too were to develop the condition, staring ahead and knowing all that I now know, what would I do?

*

The veteran British broadcaster and novelist Melvyn Bragg has no doubts about the action he will take. When he reaches the age of eighty he will tell a close friend to alert him to any signs of the dementia that struck down his mother. If any are noted, he will tell his children of his plans, spend three months sorting out his affairs and then arrange to terminate his life.

'Legal or illegal, I will do it.'

Individuals have to decide on their own threshold of suffering, but is it, I ask myself, necessarily a good thing for their families to be spared the opportunity of sharing it? The kind of self-sacrificial loving required here is not something to wish for or, heaven knows, to romanticise, but it is precious. I can say that now. For all the horrors we are experiencing as the end draws near, I don't begrudge a moment of what we have given you over the years and you have given us.

The turbulent Anglican priest, Dr Giles Fraser, who resigned as Canon of St Paul's Cathedral over his support for the Occupy London protest on its doorstep, expressed the same thought in a column for the *Guardian*. With typical pugnacity he declared that if being a 'burden' was the point at issue, he most certainly wanted to be one, just as he wanted his loved ones to be a burden on him. 'It's called looking after each other,' he wrote.

> No, we are not brains in vats. We are not solitary self-defining intellectual identities who form temporary alliances with each other for short-term mutual advantage. My existence is fundamentally bound up with yours. Of course, I will clean you up. Of course, I will hold your hand in the long hours of the night. Shut up about being a burden. I love you. This is what it means to love you. Surely, there is something extraordinarily beautiful about all of this.

Well, it doesn't feel all that beautiful much of the time, but I know what he means. I think of where we have been with you – Margaret and Topsy and I – and the sore privilege it has been to accompany you into the deepest, darkest places and sometimes to be able to turn on the lights. There is a beauty in that. But here is where I most agree with Giles Fraser: to do this for you, to be this for you, has been to learn how to love. And what, really – and this is something I do want my children to know – is the point of life if not that?

What, in any case, should I say in my advance healthcare directive? 'Do something drastic, kids, assuming it's legal by then, when I can no longer read a book. That, I assure you, will be the end of any meaningful life for me'?

But will it? Even if I get to that point but still enjoy a podcast? Even if I have lost interest in stories altogether but still find pleasure in the flit of a bird or the dusky leaf of a tree? Even if I still smile at a joke or nuzzle the softest nook of a neck the way I always have?

Who knows, who can ever know, what it will be like and when it may be judged to be the time to say 'Enough'?

36

Gang gaily

Robert Louis Stevenson, 'The Counterblast'

It is raining. The daffodils are cowering and even the tough little primroses clinging to the bank of the burn are drooping today. The smudged remains of Sunday's Easter egg-rolling are being washed from the road. I walk fast. There is a pulse of anxiety behind every step. I cannot be away for long because you are dying.

No more decisions. No more suffering that we can discern. We have all gathered to be around you, Anna and Margaret and Topsy and Jon and I, to sing you to ever longer sleeps and keep one hand in ours. You can no longer manage even the tiniest drip of water. You are still opening your eyes from time to time, still trying to speak, but your lips are moving soundlessly because now, at last, there are no more words.

There is a small, fierce triumph in all this. Dementia has not destroyed you. It may have all but killed you, but it has not won.

'That cruel bloody disease has had its comeuppance,' Topsy says fiercely, curling her fingers round your right hand, warm beneath the blankets. 'It never beat her. It never took her over completely.'

She is right. At the core of the nightmare your life became, there is a glow of selfhood that really has remained inviolate, as I had dared to hope. It is a place the darkness did not make it into – or, if it did, was repelled before it mastered you. Even during the ranting, raving horrors just passed, you kept returning to us.

It gives us a strange thrill that in the democracy of dying you have become just like everyone else again. Whatever brings people to this place in their lives' journeys – the sudden sickness or unexpected injury, the lingering decline – they come to it just as you have and lie just as you do now, immobile, sweetly breathing the allotted number of breaths that are left.

*

I will not pretend, Mum, that these last weeks have not been the hardest of all. Or that the 'terrors of the tattered mind', as the poet Lorn Macintyre describes them, which continued to advance on you with the shadow of evening, have not proved the most difficult to witness of all your struggles. Through February and March, those months when the countryside outside your bedroom dripped and sagged and the light took too long to return, you suffered. To look into your eyes and see your face contorted with anguish, with no means to ease your distress beyond pouring ever greater quantities of bowel-binding, knockout medication down your throat, was to enter hell itself.

But memory is sometimes merciful. Like one of those airport signs ordering 'No Re-Entry', mine flatly refuses access to the worst of the places it has so lately been.

I see you on your bed, covers off, looking unbearably fragile as you are rolled on your side and gently washed. Such a little thing of skin and bone. I recoil still at the hunted, stricken look on your face – that part of the scene will doubtless flout the no-entry signs till the end of my memory days – but am riveted by the continuing elegance of your bone structure, the softness of your cheeks. I marvel at the way your face is developing a new luminosity as everything else darkens.

I see you turning to me in the middle of a long, incomprehensible, furry-tongued ramble to say, clear as water from the hills, 'Let me give you a kiss.' I lean over and put my cheek to your lips.

I see how in those weeks you wanted, with increasing intensity, your daughters with you. You were fond of the band of carers who attended you on this last stage of the journey with humbling dedication, but as words drifted away you made superhuman efforts to communicate your need for your own folk. On one dreich and dreary Saturday morning in February I arrived in your room to be almost eaten with kisses.

'Stay,' you pleaded, closing your eyes in your effort to form a sentence that would make me and our gentle weekend helper, Kelly, understand. 'The familiar . . .' you managed at last. Your point, if we needed further confirmation, was just as you said in that old article: you belong with your family.

'I know I'm daft with things,' you remarked later that afternoon. You are in bed, wearing pyjamas patterned with owls and stars. Who designs these things? Your hair is off your forehead in a great wave, flat with stroking and frizzed up at the sides. I tidy it down with a hairbrush. It's getting long. The mattress hums and shifts. Rain beats at the window.

'No, you're not daft,' I protest weakly, before adding, 'well, you are a bit.'

You reward my honesty with an electric smile, one of your most radiant, showing all your teeth, lighting up your eyes.

It's not that I don't remember how you were suffering, or have forgotten so quickly the lurch of nausea as I arrived of a morning to read in the carers' notebook that you had been shouting at them to get you out of here, or the contraction in my heart as one of them, our wonderfully competent Morag, told me how you had tried to wrestle her off as she attempted to change your pad.

'Why do you have to fight me, Mamie?' she had said. 'We'll get on much better if we can do this together.'

You just looked at her and said, 'I've got to keep fighting. Fight is all I've got left.'

I know all that. I know it. But I also know that when expression and recognition and communication are so fatally impaired, it is easy to imagine that feeling is also broken, and yet what has come to us most powerfully in these weeks is the understanding, painful at times and joyous at others, that yours is absolutely not broken. What I see are outstretched arms when I peek around the door one evening and an endearment that floors me.

'Hello darling,' you cry, visibly relieved at the sight of me.

The deepest instincts remain, even if the names are interchangeable. 'Don't leave me, Margaret,' you tell me. 'I love you.'

What I see is a continued heroic ability to summon words to express what you are going through.

'I've reached a stage where everything is nothing,' you said just the other evening, gazing at me, willing me to understand.

We were holding hands. You kept reaching out for me, putting my hand to your lips, leaning towards me for hugs.

'I don't know what's wrong with me,' you said. I grabbed a Post-it note and scribbled down the scattered phrases. 'I love you . . . I don't know what I've been doing to myself . . . it's just horrible . . . I've got a sickness all round my head and arms.'

I thought then about your high score for language in the Memory Clinic and how you were still deploying it to try and make us understand. 'I'm just daft . . . I think I've maybe taken something that I didn't know it.' And worst of all to hear, the bleak cry: 'I just felt the whole world was going.'

I see one or other of us singing and playing the piano for you in the evenings, when the sadness of your plight is upon you and nothing will make it better. The music makes you cry even more and we falter. Should we stop? Or is it reaching emotions you cannot express except through tears? At times like this the old songs seem only to bring a searing sense of loss. Lovely music like Mozart's Sonata in C (my rendition of which, as you may have noticed, has improved with practice) makes you weep harder then ever.

But within a few bars of the Mozart you are joining in, la-la-la-ing tearfully to the melody, acknowledging a yearning beauty to which I am sure you are still vividly alive.

So many of the scenes from the last few weeks contain music. I see the pair of us singing 'I like coffee, I like tea' one afternoon, me grumbling 'I always forget which coffee beans are which.' And here you are, flashing me a smile, so quick, so fleet of understanding, that I almost miss it.

Another day you welcome me with a sleepier grin. When I say, 'Do you want me to leave you in peace?' you bat back softly, 'Pieces,' which is pretty sharp.

As that day's companion slips out of the room and closes the door I whisper, 'Just you and me now, Mum.'

You mutter something I can't make out. 'What's that?'

You say it again: 'And us and we.'

You and me and us and we. It must be a song. 'Can you remember how it goes?' I say, not expecting much.

Hoarsely, barely audible, you sing a line: 'For you and

me, for us and we.' I rush to look up the lyrics on the internet, but can't find anything. I am desperate to find this for you.

'Can you give me the next line, Mum?' I have to lean right into your face, almost brushing your lips, to hear it, but it's there.

'All the clouds have rolled away . . . something like that.'

And there it is. I find the words on the laptop at once. 'Got it! It's a hap-hap-happy day,' I shout in triumph. You nod delightedly. I can offer you a Judy Garland version and another by Arthur Askey, so you get both, and I sing along, karaoke-style, jiggling from side to side with the music.

> It's a hap-hap-happy day
> Toodle-oodle-oodle-oodle-oodle-lay.
> For you and me, for us and we
> All the clouds have rolled away.

You lie quietly listening, watching me and enjoying it. Or possibly wishing I would shut up and let you get back to sleep. Either way you are right here with me.

Anyone seeing you for the first time reclining here on your high bank of pillows with your eyes almost closed, pale and motionless, in the last stage of a terminal disease that has thoroughly overrun your brain and started to close down everything else, would surely imagine there was nothing more to this inert form than hollows and shadows and bones poking through polished skin. 'A breathing cadaver' is how I once heard this stage mercilessly described. They would never have guessed that you were inside. You, the woman with a head crammed with songs. You, the mother who has remained a mother. You, the lover of words who has continued to conjure them from somewhere until almost the very end.

'Hey, Little Hen' I play next, dancing about to hold your attention, tapping the time on my laptop, clapping my hands. You lie with an eye half open and an affectionate smile playing around your lips. I see, Mum, that you are humouring me.

I lay my head across your lap and you move an arm to my face. You push the waves on my hair back, the way you did when I was a child. Then your hand finds mine and you rub a thumb across my fingers.

That evening you even rouse yourself to rudeness. Perhaps the music has revived this, too. When Maggie, a delightful new addition to the team, comes in for the night-shift and rolls you into my arms to change your pad, you grimace at me and say something. I lean in to hear. There is a knowing, wicked smile on your face.

'When can I kick her in the face?' you whisper.

*

And here is an extraordinary thing. The precious essence of yourself has continued to shine out in these very last weeks. If anything, it has seemed to shine brighter as you have faded, politely refusing all food and finding it increasingly hard to swallow your blackberry juice. Despite finding words almost impossible to enunciate, you have been more 'here' than ever, more tremulously yourself than we could have dared hope. I remember the golden days with my father before the final plunge and wonder if these are yours, the last flaring of life before it is snuffed.

One day I arrive to find that, for the first time in ages, you have been moved into your chair. It has been turned to face out of the window, which is open a little, allowing the birdsong of early spring to bubble in. You are gazing out at the great pine, behind which a pale sun is making half-hearted efforts to break through the mist. In your red flannel pyjamas you look gaunt and fragile, your cheeks hollow with that sucked-in look again, now that the steroids have been stopped. But you are alert. I see it at once. Your eyes are bright and clear.

One of my boys calls from university and I put him on loudspeaker. 'How are you, son?' you ask, like any grandmother. This is astounding. He sings you 'Cowboy Joe' down the phone and you join in. A duet.

'Do you hear the birds out there?' I say.

You grin. 'The *b-doys*.' It's the word one of us used as a baby, trying to say 'birds'. It was Siggy, I think. A memory. Take that, plaques and tangles.

After a while you point to the sofa and say, 'Go over there and we'll have a hooch-aye.' A hooch-aye? A ceilidh? Good grief, Mum, yesterday you were nearly dead. You stopped breathing at one point. What now?

I sit down across from you and become your audience. You offer me a ragged 'White Cliffs of Dover', the words a little strange but the tune spot on. I listen in continuing amazement. Your eyes are closed, you are tiring, but you are singing to me. You are performing.

Then, gradually, it becomes too much. You begin to mutter incoherently, kicking your legs restively. It is enough.

After a sleep in bed you wake distraught.

'Magnus,' you call. 'Mag.'

Tears roll down your cheeks. 'I don't know what has happened,' you cry.

You sob and sob and sob, wiping your eyes and your nose with a tissue and twisting it in your hands. With renewed consciousness has come awareness. With the return of life has come memory.

*

'I need a doctor,' you found the lucidity to wail when you woke up a few mornings ago. 'Nobody is listening to me.'

It is hard to write this. With all my fancy philosophising about letting the end of life come naturally, I hadn't realised how dreadfully ill you were feeling. Scribbling your words admiringly on Post-it notes, I never even wondered what you might have meant by 'a sickness all round my head and arms'.

Mum, I'm sorry. How is it possible to keep getting things so wrong?

The GP came at once. He confirmed that your lungs were filling up once more and that you were indeed very ill.

Soon I was sticking a tiny patch on to your shoulder. Such an insignificant little thing it looked, the size of a postage stamp, but the flow of opiate put an immediate stop to the pain you had tried so hard to communicate. It marked, too, the swift end of the resurrection days.

*

These last few days have been a pool of peacefulness. Topsy holds you often in her arms and sings you the songs you used to sing to her. You fall asleep against her chest, like a child. Once she asked if anything was sore, and you responded, 'My heart.' You might have meant your chest, but I can only hope not. Better that the last thing anyone can remember you saying should have been a wry one-liner.

A team of NHS palliative nurses has taken over your care, lifting the responsibility from us at last. They have switched the delivery of morphine to a syringe driver and return as often as we need them, quick, efficient, sympathetic.

I rush in from my rainy Easter walk and look down at your sleeping face, the skin stretched tight over these high cheekbones, your hair stroked back, your mouth that can no longer laugh. Somehow you manage to be beautiful still. And your nose never changes, with its characterful bends and bumps, and the cheeky snub at the end with those flared nostrils. A little tear hovers in the corner of your right eye.

You have fought all the way, just as you said. You can stop now.

With the school holidays upon us you could not have chosen a better time. It means Margaret has been able to bring all her children north. My four boys are home for Easter, too, and Anna Lisa has insisted on flying back from university in the United States. Jon is with us, back at the centre of the family to lead and steady us. We will be able to see you out in force.

*

There is something good about a death in the family – a dying achieved in the middle of chattering grandchildren, Margaret's dog knocking about with a lampshade round its neck to keep it from licking an injured paw, a huge jigsaw of Henry VIII half finished in one corner, phones ringing, laptops tapping and the smell of chicken casserole wafting up from below.

We spend the last evening but one sprawled all over your room in gales of laughter as Margaret reads out a stash of old letters. You lie there as we reminisce, small and still, impervious to everything. Later, as we guard your night, I find a position on the sofa where I can fix my gaze on a patch of blue duvet, watching it rise by an infinitesimal degree and then fall softly as a feather. Your breathing is butterfly light; your face carved in bone, with deep, deep eye-sockets, all the softness gone from your cheeks; your hands limp in ours, their curl and clench gone.

Dawn arrives with the distant whistle of birds and light leaking through the curtains. Topsy leans over to stroke your head and soothe a murmur of agitation. She sings quietly in your ear. Song still has the power to calm you. You hear us and you know us, and the old lullabies and hymns and ballads still work their magic on your mind.

All day you labour, your breathing no longer light and fluttery, but deeper and faster. It sounds sore. You may be comatose but it looks such hard work. We are like husbands at a birth, helpless and beginning to feel traumatised. In the great symmetric arc of life, you are labouring to bring forth death.

In the early hours of the morning your breathing changes to a little snuffly thing, a whimper, like the shudder at the end of a sob. Topsy strokes your face, running her finger down your cheekbone, singing softly. I imagine you thinking wryly that your number must be well and truly up if we've started on 'The Lord's My Shepherd'.

It is light outside. Margaret opens a window and suddenly we can hear the dawn conversations in the trees, an animated chorus of bubbles and trills and whistles. An oystercatcher startles us by screaming past the window, miles as we are from the coast. I think of the rockpools in the cove at Ardmore and your people in their houses on the hill.

Outside, the sycamore tree has burst into leaves that were not here yesterday. The cherry blossom has started to flower. There are drips along the telegraph line behind the garden, a necklace of dew. In the distance four high-rise flats stand sentinel on the horizon, white in the early morning light.

I become fixated on the collar of your pyjama jacket, which is standing up against your neck and fluttering softly with each breath. Your life in a flap of fabric. I move it aside to kiss you in the hollow of your neck, the small place where everything is still soft, even your hair there, and fill my nostrils with the smell of you. Your hair smells lovely, too, a fine advertisement for not washing it for weeks. On your forehead the veins stand out blue like the tributaries of a river.

The nurses arrive soon after 9 a.m. Oh, the joy of seeing them. They say the hard work of breathing is not hurting you, but they increase the pain-relief all the same, just to be sure. The whimpering stops and your breathing slows. The two experienced nursing sisters, exuding calm and kindness and as much concern for us as for you, say it won't be long. Nurses like these, and the system which provides it to us, are the bright, shiny side of the battered NHS coin.

Jon and Topsy and Margaret and I settle back around you to watch and to wait. One or two of the grandchildren slip in. Anna is holding your hand, here with you at the end as she was at the very beginning.

*

The slim R.L. Stevenson anthology is a 1918 edition in a faded dark green cover with lingering traces of golden lettering. I find it in your bedside drawer. On the flyleaf is a dedication in black fountain pen, the hand bold and strong with a hint of impatience:

> To my young friend Mamie –
> With all her life before her –
> *To a steigh brae a stubborn back!*
> *And up the rude,*
> *Unbieldy track*
> *O' life, gang gayly!*

Your old editor James Borthwick was sloppier with his spelling than he would have allowed you to be. He had in mind a stanza from one of the poems inside, 'The Counterblast', which celebrates those who climb life's wind-tossed tracks with a merry heart.

> *The evil wi' the guid they tak:*
> *They ca' a gray thing gray, no black;*
> *To a steigh brae, a stubborn back*
> *Addressin' daily;*
> *An' up the rude, unbieldy track*
> *O' life, gang gaily.*

He had signed it:

From James Borthwick
This Book of his Youth
15th May 1947

How well he understood you. This, his own well-thumbed
volume, was his gift when you left the *Sunday Post*. Gang
gaily, he urged as you set out on a new adventure at the age
of twenty-one. Go gaily, however exposed and difficult the
path may be.

And that is exactly what you did, my blithe and merry
mother, until the road became too unbieldy even for you.

*

You take a breath, a tiny, shivery gulp of a thing. Then the
flap of flowery pyjama against your neck is still.

My daughter is gazing at you. In this instant she understands why death is called a passing away. You pass. No
doubt about that. Yet in the very next instant, the very next
second, back you come, surging in to fill the empty space
she has been keeping for you all this time.

'I saw her striding down the road in her long macintosh,'
Anna Lisa writes to me later. 'I saw her entertaining the
Sunday lunch crowd by playing her teeth with a pencil,
singing at Hogmanay in her long woollen black and white
skirt, waiting to collect me at the train station with arms
open and that very silly cap on with the ear-flaps. There she
was, whizzing round the garden on a micro-scooter,

teaching us songs in the car, telling me to keep my hair out of my face, bending over double when she laughed, bringing me gargantuan white socks when I got wet, telling me that story she made up about Pimple Pie in the dark. Oh, and smiling. Smiling the most beautiful smile I have ever seen. She just came back, almost as I watched. I can't describe it properly, but she just came back to me in that moment and she's never left.'

I slip to the window and open it wide. I'm not sure why, except that this is what people used to do in the days before anyone told them not to be silly, that souls don't fly away. Your soul, that wonderful essence of you that dementia could not destroy, has always liked to fly.

> *Open the curtains*
> *on a storm of light,*
> *know the best was never*
> *ahead or behind.*[*]

You knew that all along, didn't you? You knew there was always light streaming in somewhere and happiness to be caught on the wing.

Sunshine storms into your room now, along with a clamorous symphony of birdsong. The rest of us look at each other. It is time to do what you would have done and have a cup of tea.

[*] Andrew Greig, 'A Resurrection of a Kind' in *As Though We Were Flying*.

37

Lost to the world

Friedrich Rückert

A few months later I was in the Benjamin Franklin Hall in Philadelphia, listening to a young black American soprano perform Mahler's *Ich bin der Welt abhanden gekommen* ('I am lost to the world'). A few blocks away I had just been visiting the excavated foundations of the house in which America's first president lived from 1790. As I listened to the music I was thinking of the nine black slaves George Washington had kept there, carefully rotating them out of the state and back again to get round a Philadelphia law which entitled them to be freed after six months' residency.

I was thinking, too, about the Declaration of Independence, signed right across the road from this hall, and how slave-owners like Washington and Franklin had managed to proclaim there without irony their belief that all men are created equal with an unalienable right to liberty. Franklin did later free his slaves and Washington stipulated the emancipation of his own in his will, but the contradiction to which the founding fathers of the United States of

America put their pens in 1776 highlights how selective even the most enlightened of us can be about human rights and human dignity.

As the music dipped and soared, I found myself thinking about an old man in a wheelchair in a twenty-first-century care home, and the casual cruelty of those who had held him in their power. How fatally easy it has ever been, through ignorance and the failure of empathy, to convince ourselves that some of our fellows are not as we are, that they do not feel as others feel.

The song, in German, was about a mind lost to others and a world which

> *Has heard nothing from me for so long*
> *That it may very well believe that I am dead.*

A world that acts as if it believes that some of its people are less than alive is a world I recognise. The only protection against it – the ultimate guarantee of civilisation for any society in any century – is that every mind, every person, is regarded as equally precious.

In our century this involves not just eloquent declarations of principle but political priority, institutional leadership, organisational practice, the application of human rights law to every citizen and a communal recognition (dictated by self-interest, if nothing else) that whatever is done for the weakest today is also done for the strong and whole of mind whose decline into invisibility lies in the future.

A nation discovers its truest dignity when it cherishes the dignity of those from whom it has not heard for a very long time. That much I have learned, beloved mother, from your living and your dying.

And all this time I thought I was the one talking to you.

What Happened Next

The most compelling social change is the kind that wells up from below when the people speak.

When *Where Memories Go* was published at the beginning of 2014, I hoped it would encourage some of that. I knew how many other families were in the middle of experiences similar to mine. I knew exactly what they were itching to say to the healthcare professionals and decision-makers. I knew that many who had ostensibly put the experience behind them years ago had never felt able to talk about it, and wished they could. I also knew that, with a bit more enlightened understanding all round, people just starting to live with dementia could look forward to some unexpectedly fulfilling times along the way and they needed to hear it.

In short, I had come to believe ever more strongly that if the loneliness and the ignorance and the stigma and the poorly construed notions of care were ever to be undermined and overthrown, more of us needed to speak.

And here's the thing. People did speak. They are still speaking. I have been staggered by the response.

From the moment Radio 4's *Book of the Week* serialisation hit the airwaves and extracts began appearing in newspapers, people talked. A spate of letters, emails, articles, tweets, blogs and social media posts became a deluge. All over the country people reached for keyboards and pens and smartphones to express what many said they had never attempted to describe before. It was as if the articulation of my experience had given thousands a kind of permission to voice their own, permission to say at last, 'Listen to me. I was in that place too and it still hurts. I am there now and I don't know where to turn. LISTEN TO ME.'

Speaking to audiences across the land from Shetland to Guernsey, Stratford to Tobermory, Glasgow and Edinburgh and Bristol and Bath to Scarborough, Pitlochry, Nairn, Keswick, Melrose, Wigtown, Hexham, Cheltenham and a host of other localities, great and small, I have heard the same message in person, over and over again. Every story different; every story the same. When I was invited to Iceland, my other homeland, to launch the book's Icelandic translation and present a public lecture in Reykjavík, I learned that dementia is wreaking its unique brand of havoc among families there too, forcing this tiny nation, like every other, to look for new, more sustainable models of care. I was ushered from television studio to radio microphone, from newspaper to magazine interview, and within a week the book's Icelandic edition, *Handan Minninga*, had become the country's number one bestseller.

Truly, the floodgates have opened.

Some of the pain I hear about still catches my throat. A woman wrote from Norfolk of a mother who had been a passionate gardener with the lifelong gift of making everything she grew flourish: 'Seeing my mother rip to shreds a bunch of sweet peas I had given her is a memory that will stay with me for ever.' The snapping of those fragrant, hopeful blooms, the raging ache that the mother could not articulate and the daughter could not assuage, have stayed with me as a heart-piercing symbol of how this illness hurts everyone.

From Cambridge came the story of a school English teacher, loved by classes for her non-judgemental warmth, and the 'ten years of hell' the family endured until her death in 2010, a family who 'still weep inconsolably for all we missed out on.' Another daughter penned a card from the middle of the battlefield: 'My sisters and I have found the whole experience bewildering, frustrating and lonely. We like to think of ourselves as pretty competent individuals but have been floored by the illness, the system, the options, the decisions – and the heartbreak.'

Laughter comes too. Letters tell of smart, knowing comments that dart out of nowhere, confounding the notion that people with advanced dementia are 'gone'. They describe the fun that can be relished in the moment, the teasing banter, the sense of humour that continues to thrive in the wasteland. They tell stories, too, about the revived spirits that come with sharing musical favourites. 'It always lifts my heart when she joins in and keeps me right with the lyrics. It's one of the things the two of us can still enjoy together and for a wee while I have my mum back,' wrote a daughter from Livingston. Those letters are about so many things we can learn to value. A man in his nineties ardently described 'a new way of loving'.

Indeed I have been bowled over more than once by the uncomplaining sassiness of those older spouses, women and men who have figured out in the course of 80 years or more that laughing is generally better than crying. 'Fortunately my generation are tough old cookies,' writes a lady from Norwich, adding, 'As another friend said, "It comes to something, Christine, when the high point of the week is whether your husband has been to the toilet."'

Anger sizzles in the correspondence, too, firing off in every direction. Anger at dementia itself and its wearying catalogue of losses; anger about the lack of understanding of the condition and its effects; anger about hospital horrors; anger at being abandoned to cope alone at home; anger, often accompanied by guilt, at themselves for failing to do anything as well as they wanted to or as they believed love dictated. In a development that would have amused my mother, I learn that others have found comfort in my own ill-disciplined temper and the realisation that they are no worse than anyone else – or at least no worse than me. 'I read your book and was able to let all that guilt of mine go for the first time in years,' said one.

Listening to voices like these, and indeed to the articulate people diagnosed ever earlier who are increasingly

making their own views heard, is what will lead the revolution in dementia care. These are the people who know how
much more there is to someone than the cognitive deficits
by which others are prone to judge – especially, perhaps, the
psychologists and neurologists trained to assess in precisely
those ways.

Countless readers have begged me to find a way of
making this book compulsory reading for those in a professional caring position or training for one, from, as one put
it, 'the highest government minister in the land to the
humblest care assistant.' I mention this not to make immod-
est claims for the work itself but because understanding
dementia from the inside really is the key to making the
right practical and policy decisions for the people who live
with it. Dementia training, both within residential settings
and for homecare workers, is in too many places hopelessly
inadequate and sometimes non-existent. How can you
possibly look after someone with dementia and help to
realise his or her remaining potential without having a clue
about what it might be like to *be* this person?

'I'm currently studying an Open University module on
Dementia Care,' wrote one student. 'Reading your book I
have been transformed and inspired far more than by any
amount of academic studying.'

It has been humbling to hear from care organisations
who are already using *Where Memories Go* to help their
staff understand better, from a doctor who insists that her
trainee GPs read it, from a health board which has placed it

on the reading list for occupational therapists, and from many individuals who say it has altered the way they work. I was touched to hear from a healthcare assistant on a demanding medical ward for the elderly, who explained that she had long clung to the comforting notion that people in the later stages of dementia had nothing left of themselves that could be nurtured. Now, she wrote, her eyes had been opened to a realm of new possibilities. 'By reading your book,' she concluded, 'I believe you have enabled me to improve the care I can provide.'

I have met or heard from other health and social care workers like her, and I have been blown away by their determination to learn as much as they can about dementia so that they can offer their very best to the people they look after, whatever the organisational obstacles. None of them will ever get rich doing this job, but they themselves *are* the riches of the caring system. What they bring to those we love and, even more vitally, to those who have nobody else to love them, is a precious service. Our society should treasure them.

I have heard, too, from a number of GPs trying valiantly to nurture the individuals in their care within a medical and social culture that leaves patients with nowhere to go and has done nothing to meet the overwhelming need for remedies beyond the prescription pad. These doctors feel their hands are empty.

I suspect some of them would sympathise with Dr Bill Thomas, who founded the revolutionary Eden Alternative in the United States for the care of older people, when he complains that he can write a prescription for a $1,000 a month anti-depressant but not for, say, a personal music intervention. 'Why are we able to medicate these people,' he asks, 'but not respond to the deep needs they have?' Echoing the frustration of many in his profession, he laments, 'We haven't done anything, medically speaking, to touch the heart and soul of a patient.'

These are deep waters for the medical profession, with implications far beyond dementia. But they ought to be waters worth dipping a toe into in the case of an illness so profuse and variable in its symptoms, so lavish with its losses and so profoundly a matter of heart and soul. It takes novel ways of looking at a person in the round to see not only what dementia is stealing but how much it has left intact for now.

Every day of those last years of her life, my mother proved how much was left. I wish I had learned earlier to view the onset of dementia as a shifting in the way she experienced the world, rather than a blot on the way I did. If only I could have realised sooner that the really knotty problem I had to wrestle with, all the way along, was not her way of thinking, but mine.

It is almost three years since her death and I am still learning. For a long time, for instance, I thought I was at fault for encouraging her to make a fool of herself at the funeral where her tribute turned into a groundhog speech. Yet today I have a new question for myself. From whose perspective exactly did that occasion go wrong? Someone asked me about this recently at a book reading, and it was only as I tried to answer that it came to me, in a gust of understanding, that my mother did not make a fool of herself at all. She just delivered a speech (very competently) twice, because her memory wasn't working very well. And because she was within a community in her old friend's church who mostly knew her and largely understood, a congregation who were willing her on, applauding her and making her feel good about herself, it was actually a perfect example of how someone can be supported to function happily in the world with dementia and why it can be worth taking a risk on that person's behalf. How many years it has taken me to realise that there was nothing to be ashamed of that day and nobody at all to pity; that the only problem in the church was me.

My mother was able to revel in her public self again that day because a community held her in its arms. Imagine the difference if communities in general – churches, shops, offices, buses, hospitals, banks, theatres, schools – were well enough educated in what it means to have dementia (and, crucially, what it doesn't mean) to do the same for the mentally frail in their midst. No pressure then to hide away. No silly shame at a loved one's social solecisms. No stigma to bring out the coward in us all.

What if *you* are what community is for, I mused to my mother. What I have been most grateful for in the past year has been discovering that the conclusions I stumbled towards as I sought to understand her experience and make her life continue to count, do chime with others', too. In sensing the role of the community in helping to bolster a person's identity, I know now that I was on to something. In grasping at in-the-moment happiness, I was on to something. And in believing that to the very end my mother had much to give, I was probably on to the most important thing of all.

*

The development of the *thinking* around dementia is what interests me most as I cast an eye over what has changed or moved since *Where Memories Go* was first published. Attention is turning to how much people can still do, especially in the earlier stages of the illness, as opposed to what they cannot. Which is good, as long as it doesn't lead to a revisionist airbrushing of the suffering dementia causes and the deep desolations it may bring as time goes on.

One of the most innovative thinkers in this area is the American geriatrician Dr Al Power, who argues for a profound shift of focus from medical intervention to the enhancement of wellbeing, and from what doesn't work to what does.

Even in people who live with severe cognitive disability, there are millions of neurons working perfectly well. And their brains continue to work to compensate for the broken connections, just as a person with a stroke learns to compensate for a paralysed limb. Even a heavily affected brain continues to adjust to adversity – problem solving, creating new maps and new narratives, or calling on novel nerve pathways to process and respond to information presented to it. In other words, what is commonly seen as confused or challenging behaviour is, in actuality, compensatory or adaptive behaviour by an individual who continues to express agency and purpose in his own unique way.*

There has been fresh thinking in this country, too, about the ways in which people diagnosed ever earlier and with many years of reasonable functionality ahead, can be supported to enjoy a fulfilled life. Reports such as 'A Good Life with Dementia' have examined how family and community might foster a continued sense of identity, how someone can be helped to live in the present rather than being continually egged on to retrieve lost memory, and how to carry off the difficult trick of balancing natural protectiveness with the universal human need to exercise spontaneity, risk and choice.

* G. Allen Power, *Dementia Beyond Disease: Enhancing Well-Being*, Health Professions Press, 2014

Along with this has come a realisation that in lobbying hard for more research, better services and a keener seriousness in addressing what is without doubt a monumental social need, campaigning groups have painted dementia on such an unremittingly black canvas that the populace is plain terrified. Now there are signs of a more balanced approach.

The danger, though, is that we end up only balancing our terrors. Even as we are urged to be less afraid of dementia itself, to regard the distress it occasions as behaviour with a cause that can be ameliorated, if understood, and to focus on engaging those parts of the brain that are still working well, our fear of a health and care system that is in a poor position to do any of that – that seems in some respects to have the barest idea where to begin – is arguably stronger than ever.

On the other hand, the lobbying has to some extent paid off. On the scientific front, politicians have nerved themselves to act. At a London summit at the end of 2013 the UK Prime Minister David Cameron won plaudits for persuading G8 leaders to pledge increased funding for research. Dementia, he said, was 'one of the greatest enemies of humanity'. To keep up the momentum he appointed a World Dementia Innovation Envoy, who has made it his business to agitate for a global effort on the scale of the campaign against HIV/Aids. Most eye-catching was Cameron's ambition to identify a cure, or at least a disease-modifying therapy, by 2025. Even the most sceptical observers pinched themselves at the unwonted sight of world leaders showering not only their attention but their largesse on the Cinderella disease that for more than 20 years had been kept firmly away from the ball.

The sceptics have a point, though. The new investment has to be seen in the context not only of dementia's historically low resourcing, but of the mounting pressure on medical research of every kind – including in the United States, where federal funding through the National Institutes of Health, the world's largest source of medical research money, has been dramatically scaled back.

Over lunch in Manhattan, just up the road from his office in the prestigious Cornell Weill Medical College, Professor Flint Beal pronounces gloomily that it is 'becoming very difficult to research anything at all' because of lack of money. Still, he is cautiously optimistic about the slow, patient discoveries that are cumulatively adding to the dementia picture. An international authority on neurodegenerative disorders, he believes there will be meaningful progress within five to ten years, although he confirms that the most promising drug developments are still being stymied by a stubborn failure to work as well on human beings as on mice.

Big breakthroughs remain elusive. Yes, newspapers have continued to feature hopeful-sounding progress, from a blood test that can detect Alzheimer's in an earlier form to the more eccentric finding that those of a cynical bent are twice as likely to develop it. The vigilant reader will spot a wary quote from a dispassionate commentator towards the end of most of the news stories, expressing polite reluctance to get unduly excited in the absence of wider replication/ more evidence/clinical proof/ human trials/actual drugs.

The key focus of scientists remains the relationship between amyloid plaques and tau tangles, one which appears only marginally better understood today than when I gazed at the mesmerising golden threads through the microscope at St Andrews University and first wondered where memories go. The hope remains that understanding this interaction better, and especially how tau spreads, will lead to ways of interfering with that relationship and limiting the damage.

But there is a further reason for scepticism, one that may matter more than how much money there is to probe the secrets of the brain and whether ambitious deadlines can be met. As Al Power writes in *Dementia Beyond Disease*:

> The more we focus on tangled neurons, amyloid plaques and tau proteins, the less we are able to see the *person* surrounding them... We pin all of our hopes on the next pill, putting millions of lives on hold while we wait for that discovery that may or may not be coming next week, next year, or maybe not at all.

This brings us to the key question still crying out for an answer. How are we going to support the growing numbers of people actually living with those defiantly mysterious plaques and tangles: those people who have heeded their government's call to get an early diagnosis only to be left, too often, alone with their fears; those living on their own at home, ever more isolated, whose numbers are set to rise steeply; those stuck in the 'empty centre' of dementia care, with multiplying needs but many years of potential that could yet be harvested; those in the later stages with profound physical and mental infirmities, who are individuals still and should be soothed and supported through the final stage to a dignified death?

The fact is, there is a plethora of ways of helping people with dementia to feel better, day to day, that have nothing to do with drugs at all. Why, then, are investigations so narrowly focussed on medical science? Where is the funding to research (and to produce a rigorous methodology to measure) the effects of music? Where is the drive to research other ways of making people with dementia feel better, more secure and more like themselves, and to measure the economic effects?

Hearteningly, there is a growing determination today at all sorts of statutory levels to improve the way people are looked after. In the last year I have been invited to attend high-level meetings, chair discussion panels and listen to earnest pledges at NHS conferences. There is a great desire to do better and a raft of more enlightened policies being developed at government level, especially, it is commonly agreed, in Scotland. But the distance still to be travelled, not just from mediocrity to excellence but from dreadfully bad to just about passable, remains huge. In all parts of the

UK there is still a frustrating disconnection between commendable policy frameworks, charters of rights and promoting excellence plans – and the actual experience of some of the most vulnerable and incapacitated of our citizens.

In June 2014 Scotland's Mental Welfare Commission dampened any complacency north of the border with the revelation that people were still not getting 'acceptable care' in NHS dementia units a full seven years after exactly the same shortcomings had been denounced in 2007.

'There was too little pleasurable or purposeful activity going on,' the commission's Dr Gary Morrison commented after publication of the report. 'Too little person-centred care, too little access to the outside world, to fresh air. And there was too much medication.'

The previous month an equally shocking review of two hospitals in Wales, ordered after the neglect of an 82-year-old patient, highlighted 'a sense of hopelessness' in the care of frail and elderly patients and cited 'a lack of suitably qualified, educated and motivated staff'. It described patients being told to soil themselves and an ignorance of dementia needs. One patient had told the review team: 'I am in hell.'

In October 2014 the Care Quality Commission, England's independent health and social care regulator, lambasted the variable quality of care in more than 90 per cent of care homes and hospitals. 'It is likely that someone living with dementia will experience poor care at some point while living in a care home or being treated in hospital,' the CQC report declared bluntly. 'This unacceptable situation cannot continue.'

Except that it does.

At the centre of all this 'variable' care, there lies, broken and trampled underfoot, the human right to dignity, respect and, in the worst cases, life itself. Those rights are also being casually smashed, day in, day out, by the inappropriate and in some cases unlawful administration of antipsychotic medication in those hospitals and care homes where staff have not been educated in how to respond to the challenging behaviour associated with advanced dementia. This is an area where, again, knowing the illness from the inside, grasping the extent to which people can be helped to feel better if the reasons for the way they behave is understood, and giving doctors access to a more imaginative range of non-pharmaceutical tools in the prescription box would have an enormous impact on patients and staff alike. Just imagine if the doctor were instead to prescribe an iPod loaded with musical memories.

So much of what needs to be done is about knowing the person. Indeed, if we do want care homes and hospitals to know everyone in their care as an individual with a rich life history, someone with likes and dislikes and foibles and maddeningly frustrated desires that can't be expressed, we have to begin the process of getting to know him or her much earlier.

And here is what would help, while making a difference

to care at every other level as well: a skilled professional to coordinate the services around every person with dementia, whether at home or living elsewhere, bringing consistency of insight and understanding from the beginning. Everybody I have heard from believes this would have transformed their family's experience. It would certainly have made the world of difference to mine.

'People are crying out for a person to relate to,' says old age psychiatrist Dr Nori Graham, former chair of Alzheimer's Disease International and the Alzheimer Society. 'This doesn't require more money – it requires organisation. The people we want are all there already, working in the NHS in different teams with different managers. We just need to find a way of getting them to work around the individual as a multi-disciplinary force.'

She is now medical director of the independent healthcare company Red and Yellow Care, launched in London in March 2014 by the visionary Dr Bahbak Miremadi, a young psychiatrist who became so disillusioned at not being able to offer integrated dementia care within the NHS that he set out to test exactly this multi-disciplinary model. Currently the service is only for those who can pay. The hope is that if a bespoke care package can be shown to be good for both the individual and the bottom line, the government will start to buy in.

In Scotland, where a dedicated link worker is already on offer for a year after diagnosis, a 'dementia practice co-ordinator' to support people through the next period is now being tested in five pilot sites. The idea again is that all the staff with whom a person with dementia comes into touch should act in concert. Carers coming into the home to help with practical tasks, for instance, might be guided by advice from the psychiatrist or the occupational therapist. Alzheimer Scotland, who developed the model for the Scottish government, is also proposing a similarly coordinated service to see people through the final stage. After all, in which other terminal illness would you be offered next to no help at all until the local palliative team finally knocks on your door with only days to go?

New kinds of residential care are also being tried. Across the Atlantic Al Power shows me two 'Green House' homes in Rochester, the town in upstate New York where he is the university's clinical associate professor of medicine. They are homes for just ten residents in their own community, houses that look just like every other in the street but with skilled staff and access to clinical services – the opposite of the high-volume, economy-of-scale model common in the rest of the USA. Following him through a garden of home-grown vegetables, I find myself in an open-plan kitchen/ living room in which a caregiver is keeping an eye on residents as she cooks lunch, a nurse in jeans is feeding the pet dog and an elderly lady who loves flowers potters in and out of the garden. Health and safety rules insist that numbers are placed on the bedroom doors opening off the communal living space, but these are secreted right at the bottom. 'No rules about *where* we put them on the door,' grins Dr Power. This is no institution. It's a family home.

Many in Britain also hail the small-scale community model as the way ahead. Henry Simmons of Alzheimer Scotland hopes that residential homes will one day be as embedded in local, multi-generational life as the neighbourhood school. Al Power – doctor, musician and now passionate communicator of better ways of caring for the whole person – says the Green House homes taught him what is possible.

'They have shown me the right environment to enhance wellbeing,' he says. 'They continue to show me how much joy there can be.'

*

I know about joy, too. I have witnessed it time and again in the people reached by Playlist for Life (www.playlistforlife.org.uk), the charity I founded in 2013 as a result of looking after my mother.

I have described in these pages how fascinated I became by the way she responded to the songs she had known all her life and how I began to wonder whether the musical phenomenon that improved her state of mind and was helping us, her family, to stay connected might have wider relevance. I looked at the available research (patchy but promising) and sought the advice of Dan Cohen, a former social worker who was delivering personalised music on iPods in American nursing homes, in which he had then seen the prescription of antipsychotic drugs plummet by up to 50 per cent. Federal-funded, state-wide programmes in Wisconsin and North Carolina are now underway.

With his encouragement I took a deep breath and founded Playlist for Life to spread the word in the UK.

I rather think it was not a deep enough breath. Journalism is the perfect career for someone with the staying power of a moth, but being good at flitting from story to story is not such a great foundation for running a charity. I have had a lot to learn. However making the playlist case has never been a problem: since the types of memory and abilities connected to music tend to resist the depredations of dementia for longer than any other, music is an obvious side-door into people's speech, their strengths and their identity.

Playlist for Life urges families to offer relatives their own personal music at home and advises people in the early stages of dementia (and everyone else, come to that) to start selecting a playlist of meaningful favourites while they can. We prompt residential homes to incorporate individual playlists into care packages rather than always reaching for the easy pill. We encourage hospitals to think of ways of integrating music into their care for the whole person and homecare workers (in a utopia for which I am not, to be honest, holding my breath) to help compile a playlist between whisking around with the vacuum cleaner and preparing their clients a tasty lunch.

It is a stupendously simple idea: a lifetime of memory and feeling and rootedness evoked in song, symphony or TV theme tune, captured on a tiny device and available at any time of the day or night.

Which is not to say it is easy to implement in a harassed institutional setting. Personal music belongs in, and can help to drive, a flexible system which treats people as complex human beings with needs that cannot be fully met by a drug round on a trolley three times a day. Our institutions have a long way to go in this regard. But give people regular access to the uniquely meaningful music that has provided the soundtrack of their lives and there is every chance that the music will cheer them up, calm them down, transport them to somewhere familiar and help keep them connected to a self they recognise and the people they love.

This is not a panacea that removes with a flourish of drums and the sob of violins the wildly distressing reality of some dementia experiences, but it does often help. My goodness, it helps. Stories shared on www.playlistforlife.org.uk/your-space/your-stories and on Playlist for Life's Facebook page are a testament to its potency. People write of 'infectious joy', of its being 'like switching on a light bulb', of 'the wonder' of seeing language restored in song.

Of course those who have not enjoyed this kind of success with music are less likely to have written to tell us, and much research needs to be done into where and how and when and in what circumstances and with whom this can work best. But that a playlist of our life can revive and refresh a sore and wandering spirit is not in doubt. Just ask Venetia Troop, who described a much loved grandmother responding on her deathbed with 'small movements with her fingers, her eyes flicker[ing] and head turned towards the music... she passed away that night.' Or Leanne Bettis, who posted a video of her father-in-law on Facebook. 'Ken cannot dress himself and his spatial awareness is very bad, but just look what happens when he is listening to music.' She and Ken are seen, hand in hand, dancing joyfully to Chubby Checker's 'Let's Twist Again'. Leanne notes jubilantly: 'He comes alive.'

I have seen it myself, have watched open-mouthed (and usually in tears) as people in the most advanced stages of dementia have returned to a sense of themselves with finger-waving, foot-tapping, eye-flashing joy. In this respect at least, my mother would have been delighted to discover what a lovely day tomorrow has proved to be.

*

As for me, I have found it easier to evangelise about playlists than to master my own grief. It has taken a while to be able to conjure this dear figure back into my memory hale and merry and singing with the lightest of hearts, rather than white and stricken and afraid. The guilt I advise others to let go of still sweeps over me in waves. How could I have said that, not said this, been too tired to do that? How could I? The sharpest returning images are always the ones that shame me.

And then I realise that guilt is a symptom not of neglect but of love, real love, the kind that is only too painfully aware of its scratchy imperfections. My mother understood. 'Thank you for upholding me,' she said.

Some people never receive that validation and never hear those words. They need to hear it from the rest of us. That is what this book aspires to do.

It is why we have to keep talking.

Sally Magnusson
January 2015

A selection of readers' comments

This is but a short selection of the hundreds of messages received by Sally since the first publication of *Where Memories Go*. If you'd like to share your dementia story, you can join our Facebook page at facebook.com/wherememoriesgo or send an email to wherememoriesgo@gmail.com.

'The experiences described in the book so closely matched the experience my family had with our beloved mother, who also died with dementia, aged 81, in 2008. Mum had always loved music, of all sorts: we soon realised that a CD, or a song, would lift her spirits and bring her back to us in no time at all. She grew up in Mull, and had been part of the Gaelic Choir tradition taking part in the Mods, so anything like that was great; but she also loved Glenn Miller, a memory of when she first met our father shortly after the war. Music is a great gift – and Playlist for Life is a fabulous venture.'

Susan

'So much of what I read in this amazing account of dementia reminded me of my own mum's story as she too battled the disease. My mum was a little Welsh lady and poetry and music would just flow from her. People never understood why she was unable to recall really important events in her life, and yet she could finish off a whole poem or a song if I said just one line. Thank you for giving me an understanding of how this all works and for also giving me the reassurance that what I did to enhance mum's life right up to the end was indeed the right thing to do. Your story has been therapy for our story.'

Nicky

'Having previously managed care homes, some of which provided specialist care for people with dementia, I would suggest that *Where Memories Go* should be compulsory reading for all who work with people with dementia, be they doctors, social workers or care workers. It could revolutionise care.'

Richard

'Thank you for highlighting your (and your family's) experience with a loved one with dementia. I am a care worker and continually see the struggles that families go through to ensure that their loved one is safe and happy and cared for. I believe everyone in the healthcare sector needs to read this moving and emotive story. The love and compassion you have shown over the years pours out from the page and into me. I will be encouraging others to read your tale. Thank you.'

Emma

'I'm a mental health nurse by trade, although I've had to retire for health reasons. I miss it every day. Reading about the huge part music can play with dementia sufferers really inspired me, and what a joy to realise a connection can still be made when others fail.'

Michelle

'Reading your book has inspired me to try and keep both my gran and my mother (they both have dementia) entertained with music, and just in the last two weeks I've got them both tapping their feet, and my mother especially swinging her arms at the lovely sound of Mario Lanza.'

Karen

'Thank you, Sally, for being willing to stick your head above the parapet and criticise the system where it goes wrong, as well as applaud those who do a good job in offering support to vulnerable people and their families. I will commend this book (and already have done so) to everyone I know.'

Derek

'Sally, I had the privilege of hearing your mum speak at a West Sound Burns Supper about 20 years ago and remember her as an exceptional speaker – extremely articulate and highly amusing. My dad began to show the first signs of dementia when he was only 59 and passed away in 2010 when he was 78, so I completely understand when you say that you hate dementia. The sense of helplessness is beyond words. However I also felt that it reminded me of how amazing the human brain is when it works properly, the difference good nursing care can make and the huge responsibility we have to support those who care for people with dementia and their families.'

Elaine

'I think this book explains dementia on such a human level that anyone can understand it and relate to it. I am about to start a new job as a Dementia and Delirium Clinical Nurse Specialist and will definitely be recommending *Where Memories Go*.'

Anne

Acknowledgements

W arm thanks to the many people who have helped along the way.

A number of university professors were particularly generous with their time and expertise. In particular: June Andrews at Stirling University, Sube Banerjee now at Brighton and Sussex Medical School, Ian Deary and John Starr at Edinburgh University and Frank Gunn-Moore at St Andrews. Thanks also to Rev Professor John Swinton of Aberdeen University for permission to borrow from his lecture 'Theology and Dementia', delivered at the Bethesda Institute's 2012 Theology and Disability conference in Toronto, now available on YouTube. Sarah Rochira, the Older People's Commissioner for Wales, went out of her way to answer my questions. Manjit Nijjar from Wolver-hampton shared her experience of looking after someone with dementia within the Asian community.

In the United States I am indebted to Connie Tomaino at Beth Abraham Health Services and Dan Cohen of Music and Memory.

Henry Simmons, chief executive of Alzheimer Scotland, cast an expert eye over the manuscript, as did at various stages of composition June Andrews, Frank Gunn-Moore and John Starr. I am grateful to them all. Any errors or infelicities that remain are mine.

At New Cross Hospital I was made welcome by David Loughton, chief executive of the Royal Wolverhampton NHS Trust, chief nursing officer Cheryl Etches, matron Karen Bowley and a volunteer, John Homer, whose testimony from his own family experience about how dementia care had changed for the better there was particularly persuasive. Dr Daryl Leung also offered support.

Tommy Whitelaw made available the letters he had received from hundreds of carers and Irene MacKay generously allowed me to share her personal file. Ninety-one-year-old Robert Forsyth gave me an excellent interview and continues to remind everyone what a good old age can be.

I am especially grateful to ninety-three-year-old Else Blangsted, an award-winning former motion picture sound editor in Los Angeles, who flatly refused to let me give up, and for the enthusiastic encouragement of Lizzie Pickering, author and historian Alistair Moffat, Princeton-based academic Will Storrar, writer Will Schwalbe, novelist Nigel Williams and holiday hosts *extraordinaire* Gillie and Nigel Goodwin.

The team at Two Roads managed to bring to the publication rigour, sensitivity and enthusiasm all at once. Special thanks to Lisa Highton who believed in this book all the way, to Tara Gladden for her editing skills, to Dr Nick de Somogy for his impeccable proofreading and to the excellent Rosie Gailer and Federico Andornino. Their patience with shifting deadlines and desperate excuses never flagged. Thanks also to my agent Pat Lomax, who encouraged me from the start.

The poets Andrew Greig and Lorn Macintyre were quick to offer personal permission to quote from their work: Andrew Greig, 'A Resurrection of a Kind', *As Though We Were Flying* (Bloodaxe Books, 2011); and Lorn Macintyre, 'Dementia', *A Snowball in Summer* (Argyll Publishing, 2009). Thank you for that – and for the poems. Emily Ezust allowed me to quote her translation from the German of '*Ich bin der Welt abhanden gekommen*' by Friedrich Rückert.

Dementia can be a lonely experience for everyone involved, but that makes every bit of help all the more treasured. I would like to pay tribute to Carolyns 1 and 2, Dione, Jacqui, Kelly, Maggie, Marion, Morag and Pat – the carers who, at one point or another and for varying spells, became part of my mother's life and helped to make it worth living. Nor should I leave out the minister and congregation of Baldernock Church, who kept her singing, an exemplary GP practice and some wonderful neighbours.

Since the book was first published in hardback in early 2014 I have spent much of my time speaking at book festivals and other events. I am enormously grateful to all the people who have come to listen, ask questions, share stories and stand uncomplainingly in book-signing queues while I blether on to the people in front. It was a particular joy to return to Rutherglen and find myself surrounded by folk who remembered Mamie Baird, usually with a funny anecdote about her to tell. I was somewhat disconcerted to be introduced to a relative of the blameless Ernie Cheek, he of the English accent in the church choir – but fortunately the lady was thrilled. I confess I was relieved not to bump into any relatives of poor Miss Granger, about whom I have cheerfully repeated the libellous accusation that she sang off-tune.

In 'What Happened Next' I mention a few of the many people who wrote to me after publication. Here I would like to thank everyone who put pen to paper or finger to keyboard to tell me their thoughts. Those responses meant more than I can say. Deciding to write such an intimate book was difficult, and those letters helped me to feel I had made the right decision.

For the writing of that extra chapter I sought out Dr Nori Graham in England and the long-suffering Henry Simmons in Scotland, as well as Professors Flint Beal and Al Power in the United States (to whom I owe two fine meals). Thanks to all of them.

I have recorded in the preface the debt I owe my siblings and our aunt Anna. I also want to add here my gratitude to and pride in my children, Jamie, Siggy, Anna Lisa, Rossie and Magnus, and their cousins, Robbie, Calum, Ellie and Louis. They never once failed their grandma.

Final thanks to Norman, who kept me strong when life was at its most testing and who by some miracle is still speaking to me at the end of the tortuous process of writing about it. My mother was right about him.

Permissions

Text

Grateful acknowledgement is made to the following for permission to reprint previously published material:

'It's A Hap-Hap-Happy Day' by Winston Sharples, © Winston Sharples Estate. Reprinted by permission of Sony/ATV Music Publishing.

'It's A Lovely Day Tomorrow' by Irving Berlin, © Irving Berlin Music Corp. Reprinted by permission of Williamson Music Co. and Universal Music Group.

Pictures
Front page 1 (from left to right, clockwise)
Twins Mamie (left) and Anna sharing a pram. At the Braemar Highland Games. Wedding day. A long day at the typewriter. Anna (left) and Mamie, aged 16. Glamour girl.

Front page 2
Dressed to the nines. Mamie, Sally at 5 weeks and Magnus.

Fooling around in the newsroom. Topsy, Sally, Jon on knee, Siggy, Margaret. Young reporter.

Back page 1
With Topsy. On Palamos beach, 2009. Mamie and Magnus. Just Mamie. Giving it laldy on the mouth organ, 2009. Magnus, Anna and Mamie, Golden Wedding, 2004.

Back page 2
With Sally at the Templeton Bowling Club Fete, Rutherglen, 2010. Trademark smile and Icelandic coat, 2009. Jon, Sally, Mamie, Margaret, Topsy and Magnus at Laxamýri, 2006. Mamie, Archie, Harriet and Anna Baird.

Photographs courtesy of family collection, the *Scottish Daily Express*, Derek Prescott, Lorna Allen.

About the author

Sally Magnusson is the oldest of the five children of journalists Magnus Magnusson and Mamie Baird. A journalist and broadcaster herself, she has been a BBC news and current affairs presenter for many years. She is the recipient of the Glenfiddich Spirit of Scotland Award for Writing 2014 and was shortlisted for the Saltire Literary Book of the Year award for *Where Memories Go*. She is the author of six other works of non-fiction and three children's books.